DISCARD

"Sherrie Eldridge has done it again! She reaches deep into her soul and shares vibrant and moving insights for all of those in the adoption triad and for those involved in their lives. Eldridge leads readers down a road of truth and helps them understand the unique journey of an adopted person. If you have any connection to adoption, this book will both validate your experiences and provide you with new perspectives."

— GREGORY C. KECK, PhD, Attachment and Bonding Center of Ohio, coauthor of *Adopting the Hurt Child* and *Parenting the Hurt Child* and author of *Parenting Adopted Adolescents*

"As an adoptive dad, I'm glad to see Eldridge tackling questions my daughters will be asking. *Questions Adoptees Are Asking* provides hope and encouragement through the Scriptures for adoptees and those who love them."

— BILL MYERS, author of *McGee and Me, My Life As . . .* , and *Soul Tracker*

"Sherrie Eldridge is a leading expert on adoption issues, and she powerfully communicates from the platform and through her well-researched books. Sherrie poignantly reveals the misunderstanding, insecurity, anger, uncertainty, and ache in the soul of many adoptees. Her own remarkable story of searching for her birth mother and eventually experiencing the paradox of resolution and rejection results in a captivating foundation for *Questions Adoptees Are Asking*. This book is filled with practical help, honest emotions, and step-by-step assistance for adoptees searching for answers to their deepest questions."

— CAROL KENT, speaker; author of *When I Lay My Isaac Down* and *A New Kind of Normal*

QUESTIONS ADOPTEES ARE ASKING

about beginnings

~

about birth family

~

about searching

~

about finding peace

SHERRIE ELDRIDGE

NAVPRESS

NavPress is the publishing ministry of The Navigators, an international Christian organization and leader in personal spiritual development. NavPress is committed to helping people grow spiritually and enjoy lives of meaning and hope through personal and group resources that are biblically rooted, culturally relevant, and highly practical.

For a free catalog go to www.NavPress.com
or call 1.800.366.7788 in the United States or 1.800.839.4769 in Canada.

Revised edition of *Twenty Life-Transforming Choices Adoptees Need to Make*, 2003, NavPress.

NAVPRESS and the NAVPRESS logo are registered trademarks of NavPress. Absence of ® in connection with marks of NavPress or other parties does not indicate an absence of registration of those marks.

ISBN-13: 978-1-60006-595-8

Cover design by Arvid Wallen, Matt Wallen

Some of the anecdotal illustrations in this book are true to life and are included with the permission of the persons involved. Some names have been changed to protect people's privacy. All other illustrations are composites of real situations, and any resemblance to people living or dead is coincidental.

This publication is designed to provide accurate and authoritative information in regard to the subject matter covered. It is sold with the understanding that the author and the publisher are not engaged in rendering legal, accounting, or other professional service. If legal advice or other expert assistance is required, the services of a competent professional person should be sought. From a Declaration of Principles jointly adopted by a Committee of the American Bar Association and a Committee of Publishers.

Unless otherwise identified, all Scripture quotations in this publication are taken from the HOLY BIBLE: NEW INTERNATIONAL VERSION® (NIV®). Copyright © 1973, 1978, 1984 by International Bible Society. Used by permission of Zondervan Publishing House. All rights reserved. Other versions used include: the *New American Standard Bible* (NASB),© The Lockman Foundation 1960, 1962, 1963, 1968, 1971, 1972, 1973, 1975, 1977, 1995; *The Message* (MSG). Eugene H. Peterson, copyright © 1993, 1994, 1995, 1996, 2000, 2001, 2002. used by permission of NavPress Publishing Group; *The Living Bible* (TLB), copyright © 1971, used by permission of Tyndale House Publishers, Inc., Wheaton, IL 60189, all rights reserved; and the *Amplified Bible* (AMP), © The Lockman Foundation 1954, 1958, 1962, 1964, 1965, 1987.

Library of Congress Cataloging-in-Publication Data

Eldridge, Sherrie.
  Questions adoptees are asking / Sherrie Eldridge. -- Rev. ed.
    p. cm.
  Rev. ed. of: Twenty life-transforming choices adoptees need to make, 2003.
  Includes bibliographical references.
  ISBN 978-1-60006-595-8
  1. Adoptees--Psychology. 2. Adoption--Psychological aspects. I. Eldridge, Sherrie. Twenty life-transforming choices adoptees need to make. II. Title.
  HV875.E383 2009
  362.82'98--dc22

                          2008042154

Printed in the United States of America

1 2 3 4 5 6 7 8 9 10 / 13 12 11 10 9

To my late birth uncle Dave Clark, who, like the Good Shepherd, left the ninety-nine and came to find me, the lost sheep of the Clark family.

The Beautiful Braid of Adoption

Long ago in eternity past, God determined that there would be a beautiful braid made of shining ribbons—a braid woven in the secret places, a braid called "adoption."

Each ribbon would be a different color. One was the deepest of purples. Another, the richest of greens and the third, the most vibrant of reds.

Each ribbon had a purpose, each a vital contribution, and each a unique position with the other ribbons.

The green represented the birth family and their deep, often-forgotten contribution to the adoptee's life. The purple represented the adoptive family, chosen to nurture that God-given gift passed on from the birth family. The red was the adoptee—a unique weaving together of nature and nurture into one marvelous human being, with awesome potential.

The challenge for the adoptee would be to learn how to integrate, or braid the green, purple, and red ribbons. This would be no small task.

However, the more the adoptee knew about both biological and adoptive families, whether positive or painful, the greater the potential for integration and maturity.

All the days ordained for me were written
in your book before one of them came to be.

Psalm 139:16b

CONTENTS

ACKNOWLEDGMENTS

This book is due to the incredible contributions of:

- Bob Eldridge, my husband, for being ever faithful and loving.
- Traci Mullins, editor and treasured friend, for always believing in me.
- Carol Kent, for seeing the open door before I could.
- Amy Slivka, for paving the way for acquisition by NavPress.
- Steve Eames, former acquisitions editor at NavPress, for initially catching the vision for the project.
- Contributing adoptees and friends, for sharing your hearts so that others know they are not alone:

Shirley A. Reynolds, Joy Budensiek, Sheila Rounds, Kim Norman, Laurie, Maggie Backiewicz, Sharon McGowan, Joe Soll, Scott Stephens, Penny Callan Partridge, Paula Oliver, Pamela Hasegawa, Phyllis-Anne Munro, Kimberly Steiner, Sandra Garrett, Ron Hilliard, Richard Gilbert, Connie Dawson, Renee Mills, Greg Berger, Michelle Van Keulen, Deborah Anne Rainey, Richard Curtis, Frieda Moore, Cheri Freeman, Sharon Partridge, Susan Coons, the late Dirck Brown, Lois Rabey, Carol Peterson, Bob Blanchard, Dawn Saphir, Michelle Chance, Stephanie Ericksen, Derek Jeske, Rebecca Ricardo, Teresa Armor, Janet Carnright, Kasey Hamner, Jody Moreen, Melinda Faust, Erika Hill, Paige Wilson, Kenny Tucker, Robbin Puckett, Amy Abramson, Judith Roberts, Carolyn Halliburton, Karen Stinger, Emmary Nicholson, Sue Drese, Patricia DePew, Rick Ennis, Viorel Badescu, Deb Wood, Cheri Manternach, Lori Ann Pewsey, Jodi Strathman, Issie, Vicky Rockwell, and countless others.

PART ONE

THE SEARCH WITHIN OUR HEARTS

A safe but sometimes chilly way of recalling the past is to force open a crammed drawer. If you are searching for anything in particular and you don't find it, something may fall out at the back that is often more interesting.

— JAMES MATTHEW BARRIE

Errors, like straws, upon the surface flow; he who would search for pearls must dive below.

— JOHN DRYDEN

CHAPTER ONE

WHY WAS I ABANDONED
BY MY FIRST FAMILY?

S ometimes, it really hurts to be an adoptee. Sometimes, it doesn't. Sometimes, we are hurting and don't know it's from adoption. That's the way it was for me for many years.

Adoption was no big deal to me in my growing-up years. It was just part of my life, my history. It was kind of like a door with a peephole: The only times I peeked through it were when somebody asked my nationality or when I had to fill in a medical form. Otherwise, it was completely shut.

When I was pregnant with my first child, it changed. I wanted to open the adoption door. When I read the little brochures in the obstetrician's office about how the baby was developing within me, when I began to see my tummy bulge, and when I had midnight cravings for sausage pizza, thoughts turned to my birth mother. *What was it like for her when she was carrying me? Did she think about me? Did she care about my development? Did she crave pizza too?*

After experiencing the miracle of the births of my two daughters when I was twenty-one and twenty-three, my desire to go through that door intensified. I wondered, *How could a woman carry a baby sacrificially for nine months amid the stigma and shame of the 1940s, give birth to that baby, and not worry about it every day of her life?* I wanted to find my birth mother and tell her not to feel guilty because I had good parents and a happy upbringing.

I kept the door shut, however, because of the reactions of my husband and adoptive parents to the possibility of finding her. They thought such a move would be unwise. After all, they reasoned, she had closed that door after my birth. I took their advice, shoved myself into high gear as a mother and wife, and became "Superwoman." Super mom. Super executive wife. Super tennis player. That was the only way I could keep the questions submerged.

And so life went on. The kids grew up, went to college, and got married. The feelings and thoughts didn't reemerge until one brisk autumn afternoon when I was about forty years old. I was attending a convention, and I'd had to sign up ahead of time for the seminars I wanted to attend. When I got to the seminar of my choice, it was packed to the gills with no seating available. Disappointed, I searched for another seminar and discovered one where an attractive, animated, middle-aged woman was saying from the podium, "My life was changed forever."

"I BECAME CURIOUS WHEN HEARING ANOTHER PERSON'S ADOPTION STORY"

That got my attention.

There were seats available, so I quietly slipped in. As I settled into my chair, the speaker started using words and phrases like "birth mother" and "give up for adoption." Those words hadn't entered my head since I was a young mother. I began tapping the end of my pen on my notebook as I took a deep breath.

It wasn't long before I figured out that the speaker was a birth mother. Apparently she'd had a date with a colleague who was hosting a party at his home. When she arrived, she waited expectantly for the other guests to arrive. Minutes turned into hours as she came to the frightening realization that there wasn't going to be a party. Instead, she had been set up for something that would mar her life forever—violent rape, which resulted in pregnancy. As she neared her delivery date, she made an "agonizing decision" to give her baby up for adoption, believing she would never see her again.

For the finale of her presentation, she told a poignant story of how the infant daughter she had relinquished had recently found her, twenty-three years later. With a radiant smile, she held up a huge, close-up photo of their faces. It was amazing. Same color of hair. Same eyes. Same smile. They looked exactly alike!

When the seminar was over, I walked out into the noisy crowd, oblivious to the noise, as if a veil had fallen over me and inside that veil a new thought pounded my consciousness: *I wonder if I look like my birth mother.*

I had been caught unaware by this woman's story of reunion and redemption.

"I BECAME INTERESTED IN WHAT MY PARENTS COULD TELL ME"

A few months later I visited my eighty-three-year-old father in my hometown of St. Johns, Michigan. That evening Dad pulled out the rusty, old steel file box that was to provide all the information I needed when he was gone.

I could see it coming, like a freight train bustling down a track. I knew what he was doing; he was preparing for death and wanted me to be prepared as well.

The thought of losing him was unbearable. I hadn't allowed myself to even go there in my thoughts until then. Mom had been dead for eleven long years and because I was an only child, my father's impending death would leave me without a family. I would be an orphan once more. How I dreaded that reality.

Dad sorted through the papers with his gnarled fingers and age-spotted hands. When he came to a folded, yellowed document, he said, "I haven't seen this in a long time."

"What is it?" I asked.

"Your adoption certificate."

"My adoption certificate?" I gasped. "The *original* one? Can I see it?"

As he handed over the official-looking document, he sighed deeply, reached across the table, and grabbed my hand. "I still remember the day your grandmother brought you through the front door. You were so small! I could hold you in the palm of my hand! Your mom and I came running from the kitchen to welcome you home. We were so happy."

I choked back tears. My dad's mom had been the dedicated caseworker who had arranged for my adoption.

As I opened the document, my eyes riveted to four simple words: Mother: Marjorie Elizabeth Clark.

"Why didn't anybody ever tell me my birth mother's name?" I asked.

Dad said he thought I had known it all along. I didn't press him any further because I was afraid that the kindling interest in my birth mother might hurt him.

Memories about what my late mother had told me about my adoption came to mind. She had given scanty birth history in the growing-up years. *Your dad was an executive at GM in Flint. If you ever want to be rich, look him up. Your mother worked for your dad. The doctor who delivered you was Dr. Fillinger.*

Then I remembered sitting in Holly's restaurant in Lansing when Mom and I were shopping for my wedding. We were all under intense pressure, for I, like many adopted females with unresolved grief and loss, was pregnant and not married. We were in the midst of planning a small, shotgun wedding to Bob, the young man I adored.

As I casually ate the tossed salad with Holly's famous Thousand Island dressing, Mom shifted in her seat, looked me straight in the eyes, and said, "Your birth mother's name is Marjorie Elizabeth Clark."

The announcement rolled off me like water off a duck's back. After all, how can you think about an event long past when you are facing marriage and motherhood at the vulnerable age of twenty?

I often wonder why Mom felt so compelled to tell me prior to my marriage. Perhaps she was releasing responsibility for me and, in an indirect way, giving me "permission" to search someday.

Something changed the night Dad pulled out the adoption papers. No longer was this meaningless information. The adoption door had swung wide open and on the other side was a woman. And not just *any* woman. This woman was my *birth* mother, with a *real* name and *real* address.

"I BECAME INCREDIBLY CURIOUS AND SNEAKY"

I couldn't wait for Dad to go to bed so that I could look in the local phone book to see if she lived anywhere nearby.

After good-night kisses, I tucked the little phone book with the yellow plastic cover under my bathrobe and went to my bedroom at the back of the house. As I sat on the edge of the bed, my sweaty hands turned page after page. *Clark.* Was there anyone by that name in Ovid? No. In Fowler? No. Well, how about St. Johns? No, there was no one.

I tossed and turned all night. The moon peeking through the well-worn, green curtains made just enough light for me to stare at the plaster swirls in the ceiling. I remembered sleepless nights during childhood when I did the same thing. I must have dozed off just before dawn.

I awakened to the sound and smell of fresh coffee brewing in the kitchen. Dad was already up, barefooted and dressed in a slightly soiled white terry cloth robe tied loosely around his waist. How I loved that knotty pine kitchen with the yellow Formica counters and Mom's framed needlepoint designs . . . especially the one of the ladybug. This had been my home, my haven, since I was adopted at ten days of age.

As always I gave Dad a good-morning hug and kiss. We ate our usual bowl of Wheaties as he gave me fatherly instructions to be careful driving back to Indiana. And then it was time to say good-bye. How I hated to say good-bye, for I never knew when it would be the last time.

As I pulled out of his gravel driveway, Dad, still in his bathrobe, stood waving at the doorway of the screened-in porch. My heart welled up within me.

I headed up Oakland Street, the tree-lined street that had had so much prestige only a few decades ago. I drove as if heading for Indiana, but when I was out of Dad's sight, I turned toward the county courthouse. Surely they would have more information about my birth mother.

"I WAS TREATED LIKE A CHILD WHEN I BEGAN MY SEARCH FOR BIRTH INFORMATION"

I felt very small as I walked the darkened hallways with the twelve-foot ceilings that led toward the county clerk's office. It seemed like an eerie tomb where the identity of my birth mother was buried.

A friendly clerk asked if she could help. I gave her a big smile, introducing myself as an adoptee, wanting information about my birth mother.

Suddenly her neck stiffened. "You will have to make written application to the probate judge for release of any information," she snapped as she handed me a form titled "Non-Identifying Information."

This was my first lesson about searching for birth information. Never mention the word "adoptee," for it almost always closes the door for further information. "Genealogical research" is the socially correct term, I later learned.

After returning home I completed and returned the paperwork and haunted the mailbox every day. A few weeks later a form letter arrived.

I am sorry to inform you that I do not find any consent for release of identifying information from either of your biological parents.

As we are prohibited from giving out identifying information without these consents, the following is the only information that can be given at this time. This data is from your original birth certificate. Date of birth, August 4, 1945, Clinton Memorial Hospital, St. Johns, Michigan, County of Clinton, Time, 5:57 a.m. Pregnancy full term. Parents married. Father, 27 and a sergeant in the U.S. Army. Mother, 21 and a housewife. No other children, living or dead. Parents voluntarily consented to this adoption.

"I WAS SHOCKED THAT A MARRIED COUPLE WOULD 'WILLINGLY GIVE UP' THEIR FIRST CHILD"

I froze.

First child? *Married* parents? *Willingly* consented? How could that be? How could a young, married couple with *no* children *willingly* give up their firstborn child? What kind of people were they anyway? It would have been different if they were sixteen and unmarried. That I could understand. But *married*, twenty-one and twenty-seven?

Then one detail caught my attention. "Time [of birth], 5:57 a.m."

Wow! *I really was born!* I wasn't an alien who was dropped down into my adoptive parents' arms. I was a *real* baby who experienced a *real* birth from a *real* mother at a *real* time of the day. For me, that tidbit of information was like a meal to a starving woman.

That did it! I had just stepped over the line. There was no turning back. I knew in my heart of hearts that I *had* to find my birth mother.

I wanted to tell everyone I knew of my intentions. It was no longer going to be a secret journey. I wanted everyone to cheer me on.

And did they?

Unfortunately, no.

Bob was afraid I would be hurt and at the least be disappointed. I got up the nerve to tell my elderly dad and he asked why I would want "to open up that can of worms." Some family members were conspicuously quiet. Some people told me I *already* had parents . . . why would I seek out another mother? And well-meaning religious people remarked, "Why do that? You already know your identity as a child of God."

That really hurts.

However, there was one person who stood by me all the way — my husband's cousin, Jan. I stayed at her house when the time came to do my actual search in Michigan.

From that point forward, I was *obsessed* with adoption! I read every book I could get my hands on, and for the next seven years I did everything conceivable to find a Marjorie Elizabeth Clark in the state of Michigan.

Nothing materialized.

At one point I went to the hospital where I was born to request birth records. Surely they would be able to at least tell me about my birth. I was not aware of any law that prohibited it. I knew enough by then to not mention the "A" word.

The administrator of records came from behind sliding glass office doors into the lobby, sat down next to me, put her hand gently on my knee, and said, "Now, dearie, do we have an adoptee here? I'm sorry, but we can't give out that kind of information to adoptees."

My face flushed. Adrenaline rushed through my veins. It was all I could do to keep from punching her! I felt like a naughty little girl who had just had her hands slapped.

"I COULDN'T BEAR THE THOUGHT OF MY DAD'S IMPENDING DEATH"

My dad's health was steadily declining. One day we got a call from the hospital saying that we should come as soon as possible. Did we want life support? the doctor asked. Dad and I had already discussed that option so I knew he would want me to tell the doctor no, without any guilt or regret.

Three of us rushed to his bedside. He was in a coma but roused when he heard our voices. Paul Jopke, his best friend for a lifetime, slipped in at one point. I tried to get Dad to gain consciousness, but Paul gently pulled me away from the bedside, wrapped his arms around me, and held me as I sobbed. He didn't say a word. He didn't need to.

Within twelve hours Dad was gone. I don't think I have ever cried as hard and long as I did in the days that followed.

I don't do loss well.

"I HIRED A SEARCH PROFESSIONAL"

Dad's death intensified my search. Finally, overwhelmed with seven years of failed attempts at finding my mother, I hired an adoption professional named Marian. As I waited for her to arrive for our break-fast appointment at a restaurant on the east side of Lansing, I put on my "I-have-it-all-together" mask, but beneath it was a terrified child. Before long, a spunky, redheaded, middle-aged woman came bound-ing through the door. She had been helping others do their searches for years, just out of the goodness of her heart and her love for adoptees.

"What do you think she'll be like?" she asked.

"Nobody has ever asked me that," I said sheepishly. "Probably a bag lady. I really don't have any positive feelings about her."

In the hours that followed I tagged behind this sleuth as she combed old city directories at the State of Michigan Library, searched death indexes at the Mormon church, and ordered birth, marriage, and death certificates at the Michigan State Department of Health.

The break came with my biological grandfather's death certificate. The name of the funeral home that took care of his remains was on the certificate. It was in Cheboygan, Michigan.

"We've hit pay dirt!" Marian exclaimed, as I tried to figure out what that meant. "Let's both go home and I'll call the funeral home to see if they have any next of kin listed on their records. I'll call you as soon as I find out something."

On the drive back to St. Johns, my thoughts turned to my parents. What would they have thought and said about all of this? I decided to stop by the cemetery where they were buried. The wind whipped around me as I walked toward their tombstone. If only I could talk to them. If I only could have one more hug. If only I could hear them say one more time how much they loved me and I could tell them one more time how much I loved them. If only I could tell them that we found her. Tears spilled down my cheeks as I returned to the car.

"I TALKED WITH MY BIRTH MOTHER"

Two hours later Marian called to say that she had found my birth mother's current name and address, which was a miracle, for she had remarried twice and moved several times. Marian asked what I wanted her to say to my birth mother. "I want to know my nationality, medical history, and who my father was," I said. At the last moment before hanging up, I choked back tears and said, "And tell her 'thank you' for giving me the gift of life."

One hour later the phone rang.

"Good news or bad?" I asked.

"Both," she said. "Your mother wants you to know that she is a mother you can be proud of. Her voice sounds just like yours! Your heritage is Irish and she knows of no major health problems in the family. However, she doesn't want to talk about your birth father and wants no further contact with you."

My heart sank, but at the same time I was grateful for the tidbits of information I did get—it was better than nothing.

Marian and I talked a few minutes longer and then her "call waiting" signal clicked in. It was my birth mother; she had changed her mind and wanted me to call, with one stipulation: that I not ask about my birth father again.

"I WAS TERRIFIED OF REJECTION"

A voice that sounded like mine said, "Hello."

"Marjorie?" I said.

"Yes," she said and we began talking about trivialities. *What do you look like? How tall are you? Do you have a dimple in your chin?*

I frantically took notes the entire time, not wanting to forget a single detail. Minutes turned into hours as she told me about her successful social and professional life as an interior designer. "Clients used to send their personal jets to pick me up for jobs."

Hmmm, I thought. I had always loved interior design. In fact, I almost studied it in college. People tell me I'm good at it. Now I knew where I got the talent. But I kept having to reassure myself, *Sherrie, she's your mother. She's not going to reject you because you are a woman without an exciting life like hers.* Still, that fear kept popping into my mind.

"I HEARD SHOCKING NEWS AND WONDERED IF MY LIFE WAS A MISTAKE"

Then, in a somber tone, she announced that she wanted no questions about my birth father. If I asked, she'd cut off contact immediately. She claimed to have been raped but didn't want me to feel bad about the news. After all, he really was a very nice man. Emotionally, I felt like I'd fallen flat on my chest on the ice. The wind was knocked out of me as I feared that my life was a mistake. It wouldn't be until years later that I would realize that rape victims don't call their perpetrators nice people.

The next week a hand-addressed envelope came in the mail. I tore into it and found two photos. My first reaction was one of disappointment. She looked so different from how I had pictured her. Along with the photos was a note:

> *Enclosed are two photos—one taken last week and one when I was nearly your age. I didn't sleep a wink last night, as I'm sure you didn't. Best wishes to your husband and thank you for the lovely visit. I am reeling from all of it. Hoping to hear from you soon.*

She received my letter and photo the same day. Later when we talked she said, "I just got your photo and you know what? When I look at your sweet face, I just know that you're mine."

They were like the words of a new mother adoring her child and I will always treasure them.

"I WAS INVITED TO HER HOME AND MY ADOPTEE FANTASIES SURFACED"

A few days later she invited Bob and me to come to her home for a reunion.

Marian, the adoption professional, recommended that I take a photograph album with photos of myself and my life from birth until the present. I got neurotic over that! I must have exchanged the photo albums three times. And of course I had to find designer paper to wrap it in—it had to be artistic, like her, so that she would like it . . . and me. Baby footprints would be the first thing she would see, then a year-by-year chronicle of my life.

Prior to leaving for the reunion, I coached Bob about what he was to do. Poor Bob! I wanted *everything* videotaped. I envisioned Bob exiting the plane first and then when everyone else was off, I would descend the flight of stairs with silk roses in my hands and run into her waiting arms as we both sobbed with joy.

On the morning of departure, being the good husband that he is,

Bob followed my orders!

"Okay," he said, camera rolling and aimed. "Start talking. How are you feeling? Are you ready for this?"

"It is September 5, 1992," I said. "Today I'm going to meet my mother for the very first time. Her name is Marjorie Elizabeth Clark and she lives in a small town in New Mexico." I quickly put my fingers over my lip as it began to quiver. "I can't believe I'm so emotional about all of this."

I was overwhelmed with the goodness of God to me that morning as I looked out from the plane's window at the blue sky and cumulus clouds. That he would let me meet my birth mother was more than I could have ever imagined. A familiar verse came to mind: "No eye has seen, no ear has heard, no mind has conceived what God has prepared for those who love him."[1]

It seemed like an eternity getting there. I didn't know if I would laugh or cry as the small plane resembling a flying banana approached the small airport in the middle of nowhere. No one was in sight when we arrived, save one lonely flight attendant who wheeled a decrepit stairway toward the plane's door. As Bob prepared to deplane, video-cam over his shoulder, I reminded him, "Be sure and get it all on film!"

"I DIDN'T KNOW IF I WOULD LAUGH OR CRY WHEN I SAW HER"

The plane emptied quickly. I gathered my belongings while I watched the last person exit. When I was positioning the pink silk roses over my arm, the attendant peeked into the cabin and said, "Ma'am? You *have* to get off the plane *now*. It's not legal to stay on."

I explained to him that this was a very special occasion and that I had to wait a few minutes before going into the airport. He said he understood, but wouldn't budge. I would have to get off the plane.

So much for my adoptee fantasy of descending the stairs like

Scarlet O'Hara in *Gone with the Wind*!

My shaking knees had trouble navigating the narrow portable stairway. As I walked across the tarmac toward the glass entrance door, my body stiffened. It was then that I heard someone cry out, "Oh my God, there she is!"

There she was — the mother I had never met, dressed in cowboy boots and a red suede jacket with fringe on the arms.

Next to her was my half sister, Susan, who was not on speaking terms with my mother until she learned of my coming.

"Look at her nose!" Susan screamed.

I tried to smile.

All the while, Bob was trying to video the event. The result was footage of the airport ceiling, for the most part.

Oops . . . another adoptee fantasy bites the dust!

We piled into the back of their SUV. Marjorie, Susan, and Susan's husband sat in the front seat and chatted as if Bob and I weren't there. Bob and I rode in silence as he held my hand.

One of my mother's best friends owned an inn and gifted the best suite to Bob and me. The view from the room was beautiful and on the table was a bouquet of purple irises, my favorite flower at that time, with a note that said "From your mother."

When we came to her condo for dinner, she had prepared home-made soup and ordered special bread for the five of us. There was a buffalo head above the fireplace, copper pans hanging from the mantel, and photos of herself on the table next to her easy chair. Nervous laughter punctuated every sentence over dinner.

Conversation then turned to their family memories. At one point my mother went to get a large portrait of herself when she was younger. I wondered if it had graced the wall of a former home. How I longed to take it home but didn't have the nerve to ask.

After getting ready for bed that night, I made some notes in my journal.

Today seemed like the longest day. Such a long trip getting here. I felt scared when I met them and somewhat disappointed that they are so different. You can tell Marjorie is very artistic by the way she dresses and decorates her house. I found out she didn't even know when my birthday was. She truly did forget about me once my birth was over. It became evident as she recounted all the hard things in her life — me being one of them. She has no compassion. It hurts. Deep inside it hurts. I wanted her to say, "I thought about you often." I am disappointed that this is not turning out to be a mountaintop experience, but a painful one. I feel the initial abandonment by her forty-seven years ago when they all talk and leave Bob and me out. I felt like a stranger. Like I don't belong.

I tossed and turned for hours as Bob snored beside me. Finally I dozed off but woke up again at 6 a.m.

"I COULD SENSE MY BIGGEST FEAR WAS COMING TRUE"

Thanks to social engagements, my mother managed to keep me at arm's length for the first half of the one-week reunion. She kept saying to me, "This is a happy time for you, but remember it's a painful time for me."

Why would this be such an unhappy time for her? I wondered. *Was I doing something wrong?*

Like many adoptees, I have "antennae" that can sense rejection a mile away. They were registering high on the Richter scale.

Bob was only able to stay until midweek because of a business trip. I looked forward to time alone with Marjorie because we would finally have our one-on-one time as mother and daughter. I envisioned us going through the photo album, photo by photo, and me listening to her saying how proud she was of me. *Oh, look, you were a cheerleader! You looked beautiful on the homecoming court. Your children are so precious.*

When the time came to give her the photo album, she opened it, ran her fingers over the tapestry cover, flicked through the pages, and said, "You sure were cute." She then proceeded to close it and push it aside.

The next day one of her wealthy friends gave a luncheon for us. A former movie star came. There was an indoor pool in the basement of the house. Women were dressed to the nines. The diamonds on their hands looked like boulders. Conversation at lunch was about facelifts and tummy tucks.

I sat silently, dressed in my simple black knit dress with roses painted on it.

I couldn't relate.

After lunch one of them asked if we had discovered any similarities. I laughed with delight as I told them that we both loved ketchup. No sooner had the words come out of my mouth than Marjorie approached the group looking at me like she had just sucked the biggest lemon in town.

"I WONDERED WHAT I WAS DOING WRONG"

That evening as we watched television and chatted, she said suddenly, "I've had it up to here," pointing her index finger to her throat in a slitting fashion. "This whole thing is going too fast and too deep for me."

My lip began to quiver as I asked what she meant.

She then reached for the TV remote and turned up the volume several notches.

I told her I was terrified that she was rejecting me and offered to go home early. She said she didn't want me to, reassured me that she would never reject me, and then added that I must be terribly sensitive to have the comments about her stress bother me.

On the day I left, I asked her on the way to the airport if she would like me to take the photograph album. She grabbed the steering wheel as hard as she could, looked straight ahead, and screamed, "You don't know how hard it is to give up a baby! I have thought of you every single day of my life."

It was the first time I had seen her cry.

"Oh, Marjorie!" I replied. "That's the best news I've ever heard! I thought you had forgotten about me."

"Now you're happy that I'm sad," she snapped.

We rode the rest of the way to the airport in silence.

After arriving I slipped a little gift—an angel figurine that had a verse about mothers attached to it—on the front seat. I knew enough about adoption to realize that for birth mothers saying good-bye is often traumatic, for it triggers that initial separation. I wanted her to be comforted.

While I waited in line to board my plane, she stood alone, looking wistfully through the big airport windows. I imagined that she might be thinking about what life might have been, had she decided to keep me. She came over to me with that same wistful look and said, "I always wanted to be tall like you."

At that moment I looked into her beautiful green eyes that were misty with tears and said, "Marjorie, I love you and I am glad you are my mother."

Then I gave her a hug and boarded the plane. My heart was still filled with hope. No, it wasn't a *perfect* reunion, but at least it was a start. We would have years to work on it.

"I WAS REJECTED AFTER OUR REUNION"

Two days later I called to thank her again for the visit. When I heard the tone of her voice, all of a sudden I had a sick feeling in my stomach. She began verbally abusing me, taking everything about me and turning it to the most negative interpretation possible. "No more contact," she ordered.

As she was spewing those hurtful words, emphasizing that she wished she would have aborted me, these words from the Bible came to mind: "Can a mother forget the baby at her breast and have no compassion on the child she has borne? Though she may forget, I [God] will not forget you! See, I have engraved you on the palms of my hands."[2]

I knew without a doubt that God was IN me, AROUND me, and BESIDE me.

I ran downstairs to Bob, sobbing. He held me close as I wept.

WHAT ABOUT YOU?

You may identify with parts of my story. Maybe you were adopted internationally and your parents were given a "Certificate of Abandonment." You're a teen now, wondering how you'll ever resolve identity questions. That hurts.

You may have been passed from foster home to foster home, like a pawn in a game of chess. No one was willing to help you through the tough issues. That hurts.

You may be experiencing an open adoption, with relationships with one or both of your birth parents. Some say it's the panacea, the answer to all the hurts, yet you lost your first parents in their parenting role. That hurts.

Your birth father may have been an anonymous sperm donor twenty years ago and suddenly you're waking up to the reality that you've got another parent out there. You've searched, but there's no information. That hurts.

You may be an older adoptee who is just "waking up" to the fact that adoption loss had and continues to have a profound impact on your life relationships. That hurts.

You may have searched and found your first family, only to be slapped in the face by rejection. You know you're not the adoptee television producers are scouting for—the happy, happy reunions. Seeing the sugary reunions on television only increases your self-doubt. That hurts.

This is serious, fellow adoptee friends. You've hurt too long. It's time to talk frankly about the repercussions of relinquishment by our first (and perhaps many more) family.

Come with me and seventy other adoptees who participated in this book project, from ages seven to seventy-seven. Whatever the circumstances surrounding your adoption, you'll be amazed with their thoughts. After reading the book, like all seventy-seven, you will hopefully conclude, *"I know I'm not alone anymore."*

There's a lot more to my story, which I will share with you later. Perhaps by now you are being caught unaware with thoughts or feelings you didn't know existed. Let me assure you that it is a *good* thing if this is happening! There are so many advantages to being caught unaware.

"What kind of advantages?" you may be asking. Well, to name a few, the advantage of having an unexpected opportunity to successfully grieve our early-life losses; to enjoy healthy relationships; to develop an unshakable sense of self-esteem; to find our unique purposes in life; to have peace about our adoption experiences; to find our true identities. I was caught unaware many times in many ways during my own healing process, but how glad I am that I was caught. Why? Because now I am alive . . . fully alive and on the cutting edge of my life's journey. What better place could one be?

HOW TO USE THIS BOOK

One chapter builds upon another. However, if a particular question piques your interest, by all means, read it first. When you have time, go back and read the other chapters, for one precept builds upon another.

At the end of every chapter will be three sections:

1. *Our Choice*

After listening to my story in this first chapter, you'll hear the voices of fellow adoptees throughout the remaining pages of this book. After examining research on the topic, we'll come to the place where we must choose what we want for our lives. The painful feelings from being separated from our families will always wage against the healthy, truth-based choices we make, but we must continue, knowing that God will increase our strength to resist the old patterns as he gives us strength to live according to truth.

2. *Questions for Support Groups or Personal Reflection*

Being in an all-adoptee support group is like a tomato being in a hot house! It's the *best* way to grow. If you don't have a support group in your area, think about starting one yourself. This book will make it easy.

If you're not ready for a support group, then you may want to use these questions for personal reflection, for journaling your thoughts, or for working with a counselor who is trained specifically in adoption-related issues.

Included in these sections will be an assignment to write a letter *to* and *from* your birth mother. Yes, to and from! What would you call her? How would you address the letter? What would you say? What do you envision her responding to you? Experts say that this is the best way for surfacing buried pain and that's our goal. We want to bring it to the surface and deal with it in a healthy way.

3. *Digging Deeper for Answers to Our Adoption Questions*

This section will give you an opportunity to see what the Bible says about the topics we discuss. For me, answers from God's Word have brought confidence for tough decisions, wisdom about searching, comfort in rejection, and discovery of my life purpose and passion.

If you are not familiar with the Bible, it's okay. You may just want to read along with the story of Moses, an adoptee who lived in biblical times. Believe it or not, he had the same struggles as many adopted people today.

Whatever your religious persuasion, I welcome you to glean what you can from this book and toss the rest. Now, let's get started with the questions.

DISCUSSION QUESTIONS FOR
SUPPORT GROUPS OR PERSONAL REFLECTION

1. Have you been exposed to the stories of other adoptees? How and when? Tell us what your reactions were. Could you relate?
2. Could you relate to Sherrie's story? Even though times and circumstances are different for adoptees, do you see any common emotional threads that parallel your experience? Describe your common threads.
3. What is the status on your birth family? Do you know them? Do you know information about them? Do you ever wonder why they placed you for adoption?
4. If you were to draw a picture of the day you were placed for adoption, what would your picture show?
   - A baby by a roadside
   - A baby in a field, in a basket
   - A child, being taken away from his parents whom he still loves
   - An older child, being transferred from foster home to foster home, like a pawn in a game of chess

- An older child in an orphanage, crippled and about to "age out" of the system
- A baby in an orphanage, sleeping in a crib with eight other babies

5. Write a letter *to* and *from* your birth mother about the topic just discussed: Why was I abandoned by my first family?

DIGGING DEEPER FOR ANSWERS
TO OUR ADOPTION QUESTIONS

1. Read Psalm 91:4. Where are we to seek safety when we feel anxious about being separated from our first family?
2. Read Psalm 139:13. What does this verse say about who created us?
3. Read Psalm 139:15. Were we ever alone?
4. Read Psalm 139:16a. Who saw our unformed body?
5. Read Psalm 139:16b. Who planned every day of our lives before we were born?
6. In light of this psalm, what conclusions do you draw about yourself?
7. When we try to figure out how to deal with the pain of separation from our first family, what should we be seeking more than anything? See John 8:32.

I think you will be pleased to discover that the book you hold in your hands is *for* you—not about you. It is a celebration of the fact that we were adopted for a purpose and that adoption is an experience that has the potential of teaching us some of life's richest and deepest lessons.

Now, let's discuss an issue many of us deal with—looking at life like victims. Our birth parents' decision had a profound impact on us and we must learn to recognize it and then we can deal with the repercussions.

CHAPTER TWO

DO THEY EVER THINK ABOUT ME?

Between our feelings and actions lies our power to be free, to take control.

— JUDITH VIORST

When I first became a grandmother and my twin grandsons were old enough to sit in the little seat on the grocery cart, I would take them by the bakery section in the supermarket and ask if they would like a goodie.

I'm sure you know what the answer was!

They looked wide-eyed at all the sweets and then said, "I want that one."

I'd say, "okay," and then they would change their minds and choose another item. Two seconds later they'd change their minds again and choose another.

It was very frustrating for this grandma who should have learned the lesson when her own children were young. However, I didn't and needed to learn it from my wise daughter, Chrissie, who is a fabulous mother.

She said, "Oh, Mom, they don't have the ability to choose yet. It is far too confusing for them—so confusing that they can't make a decision. What you have to do is narrow it down to two goodies. Ask them which of the two they want and then they'll be able to choose."

That's kind of the way it is for us adoptees sometimes. The goodies in the bakery are the choices that face us every day in life—choices that can lead us to becoming the people God created us to be. Like my grandsons, however, our ability to choose is often not well developed. Why? Is there something wrong with us? Far from it! It is simply because something happened to us before we ever had words to describe it that had a tremendous impact on our sense of personal power. That something was the loss of our birth mothers and fathers.

Because our birth parents made a choice for us that dramatically changed the course of our lives and over which we had no control, many of us have a foundational belief (often unconscious) that we don't have the right to make choices. We feel instead that we are at the mercy of others.

Cheri Freeman is an adoptee activist and owner of Brick Wall Survivors, an online support group for adoptees who have been rejected at reunion. She recalls feeling deprived of choice by the fact that when she was a child, life-altering decisions were made *for* her, to which she was unable to consent but by which she is bound as an adult. She is learning to take back her personal power by making life-transforming choices, but she first had to face the fact that losing her sense of personal power at such a profound level early in life impaired her ability to choose some of the life-giving options available to her as a free human being.

Like Cheri, and like my young grandsons in the bakery, we might be right in front of the goodies (choices), but they don't seem "choose-able" to us. They are a blur. The result? We see ourselves as victims.

WE MIGHT UNCONSCIOUSLY BELIEVE WE AREN'T WORTHY TO MAKE CHOICES

Some of you may be saying, "No way! I never have nor will I ever fall into the category you are describing. I am successful in every area of life." Stay with me. You may feel strong, but I challenge you to read the rest of this chapter.

I hear you. I, too, believed I had my act together, as did most everyone else in my world. I thought I was making good choices and was in control of my life. But when my adoption door began to creak open at midlife, I started to discover that a victim mindset can be hidden beneath a variety of lifestyles, including successful ones, depending on our personalities and the nature and nurture we have received.

Certainly, not *all* adoptees feel or act like victims—just as not all the topics discussed in this book apply to all adoptees. However, if you don't immediately identify with the word "victim," I'd encourage you to set aside any preconceived ideas about where you are in regard to this subject. Shift into neutral gear for just a few minutes and hear what the experts—our fellow adoptees—have to say about this topic.

First, what do I mean by "victim"? The word may sound like psychobabble until you read the synonyms from visualthesaurus.com: unfortunate person, survivor, weeper, crier, sufferer, prisoner, captive, castaway, outcast, mourner, have-not, lamenter, griever, desperate, abandoned, shipwreck survivor, someone for whom hope has been abandoned.

Beneath our victim perspective is the fear of being forgotten. No matter what our age at adoption, we wonder if our first parents think about us. Moses, an adoptee who lived in biblical times, shows us how this fear manifests in our lives. If you read the account of his life in Exodus, you'll see that God addressed his greatest fear at every significant turning point in his life. "I am here."[1]

I sometimes hear adoptees and professionals say in a droning tone of voice, "Adoption is a lifelong journey." They make it sound like we have to walk around for the rest of our lives with balls and chains around our ankles because of early-life trauma. I don't believe this! *Because* adoption is a lifelong journey, we have a future filled with the potential to learn invaluable lessons. But many of us *haven't been taught* that we have a *choice* in every situation in life.

This was the case with sixty-six-year-old Connie Dawson, PhD, an educator in the fields of parenting and adoption, and coauthor of *Growing Up Again: Parenting Ourselves, Parenting Our Children* and *How Much Is Enough? Everything You Need to Know to Steer Clear of Overindulgence and Raise Likeable, Responsible and Respectful Children.* She says that she's only consciously recognized herself as a victim since becoming aware of how her first experiences in life affected her earliest, and subsequent, decisions about others and herself.

Adoptee Frieda Moore, an adoption support group leader and lay counselor, says that it wasn't until her mid-thirties that she realized she had many options in life. Because profound and permanent decisions were made for her at birth, and no one taught her she had choices about how to respond, she lived according to her natural inclination, which was to always let others make choices for her.

What is the result of being a victim and letting others control us? Resentment toward those whom we think are withholding freedom from us. Author Judith Viorst says, "Some of us, in fact, will passively settle for a state of genetic victimhood, willing to define ourselves as helpless playthings of forces beyond our control."[2]

But does it always have to be this way? Do we have to remain victims for the rest of our lives? No! We *can* choose! We *can* learn how to make choices from all the goodies in the bakery. We *can* live free and empowered lives in our relationships with others and God.

Let's begin by looking at how a victim's mindset is created and take a closer look at a portrait of a victim.

WE NEED TO UNDERSTAND HOW THE VICTIM MENTALITY BEGINS

Authors Rosamund and Benjamin Zander give us a good start at understanding the origin of "victim thinking." If you're having trouble with the word "victim," think of it as passivity or living life without intentionality. They say, "Experiments in neuroscience have demonstrated that we reach an understanding of the world in roughly this sequence: first, our senses bring us selective information about what is out there; second, the brain constructs its own simulation of sensations; and only then, third, do we have our first conscious experience of our milieu. The world comes into our consciousness in the form of a map already drawn, a story already told, a hypothesis, a construction of our own making."[3]

Let's apply the Zanders' theory to our situations as adoptees. First, after birth our senses brought selective information about what was "out there." More often than not, that information was a primal sense of "She's gone. I am all alone." If we're older, it may be "They're gone. What did I do wrong?" Second, our brains constructed simulations of sensations—sensations of abject terror and panic. "What will I do? How can I survive? Maybe I'll die." Third, we had our first conscious experience of the world, which for many adoptees separated at birth from their birthmothers is inevitably, "This world is not a safe place. I am helpless." Older adoptees who have been removed from their homes because of neglect or abuse are likely to deduce the same negative messages.

Thus, many of us, either at birth or later in childhood, developed the core belief that other people and circumstances control our lives, and we have lived accordingly.

How does this flesh out in everyday life? How can we tell if we are thinking and behaving like victims?

WE NEED TO THEN EXAMINE OUR LIVES — A PORTRAIT OF A VICTIM

A victim is someone who believes he or she is at the mercy of everything and everybody. But more important, a victim is at the mercy of his or her own personal thoughts, feelings, and beliefs. There is little feeling of control; instead the primary feelings are of *being* controlled. Victims see themselves as powerless. They believe they have limited choices in life. They wreck good opportunities even when others believe in them. If I were to sum up the victim mentality in two words, I would say *no intentionality*. And what do victims want more than anything?

We who are victims want to live life with intentionality, carefully making choices. The grandsons mentioned in the opening of this chapter are now thirteen. They're on the threshold of an exciting future, and their parents and grandparents want them to live life with intentionality. We want them to learn to make healthy choices, now that their cognitive ability has matured to do so. We are coming alongside them to pour whatever wisdom we've learned into their lives.

How many of us wish we would have had someone explain to us the trauma and repercussions of losing our first families. How we wish we could have heard someone speak truth, confront reality, and then teach us how to make healthy, life-giving choices.

However, taking a look at the following characteristics of a victim, we see the opposite is true.

We Might Believe Others Are Taking Advantage of Us

Many fellow adoptees could identify with my grandsons' confusion with making choices. Dr. Richard Gilbert, BCC, DMin, is the director of the World Pastoral Care Center and author of *Finding Your Way After Your Parent Dies: Hope for Adults*. He says, "Age has only added to the frustration. As I get older, the questions about adoption seem to be more complex and perplexing."

Shirley A. Reynolds, a freelance writer, outreach volunteer, and employee of the Federal Probation Department, says that she felt confused as a child in elementary school when someone would say, "It must be awful to not know who your *real* parents are!"

Trish DePew, age thirty, wife, mother of two preschoolers, and coleader of an adoption support group says, "I get confused about enforcing my boundaries and then I feel angry because people are taking advantage of me."

Another aspect of the victim mindset is powerlessness.

We May Feel Powerless and Resentfully Let Others Make Our Choices

What do you picture when you read "powerless" and "at the mercy of others"? For me, I remember when one of my counselors asked me to visit a local hospital nursery, to pray and ask God what I had lost when my birth mother disappeared from my life at birth.

A nurse friend and I gowned up and went to the nursery she worked in. I prayed, but no flash of lightning hit. What impressed me, however, was the innocence and dependence of those babies who were going to be adopted. They were clearly *at the mercy* of circumstance and people. Later that day I penned these words:

Oh little baby, so soft and pure. How sweet and precious you are. How could anyone give you away? How could anyone act like you don't exist? There you are—so tiny and helpless, lying there in that incubator. Isolated and cut off from all human touch. Not a sound around you. Only a bottle to feed you. No nurturing, warm breast. No mother's arms. No one. There is no one for you. Oh, little baby. I feel so sorry for you. How could anyone forget about you? You are so very precious. You are so beautiful. No one to protect you. No one to care for you. No one to sing lullabies to you. No one. You have no idea of the struggles you will go through in the years ahead because of this. You have no idea that you will be terrified of abandonment and rejection and that you will prefer isolation to people. You just sleep on, as if there is not a care for you in the world. You have no idea that volcanic anger has been born in your breast toward the one who gave you away. You have no idea that the seeds of fear lie buried in your heart, ready to ripen as the years go by. You have no idea there is a God who is watching over you, who loves you deeply. You have no idea the tears he weeps as he looks at your life from beginning to end, and sees the devastation resulting from this moment in time. You have no idea. You just sleep on.

Kasey Hamner, a school psychologist in California, licensed educational psychologist, and author of *Whose Child? An Adoptee's Healing Journey from Relinquishment to Reunion and Beyond* and *Adoption Forum*, says that she feels like a victim of circumstance. The adoption agency failed her in many ways by not thoroughly investigating her adoptive home, and by not doing follow-up through the years. "That is a huge problem with the system," Kasey says. "They place babies and assume that everything will run smoothly. In my case, that was WRONG!"

We Sometimes Ask "Why Me? Why Did I Have to Be Adopted?"

Self-pity is an insidious parasite that sucks the life out of us, like an octopus with its prey. When we allow others to take away our power of choice, we feel trapped and it's easy to feel sorry for ourselves. We often throw a party and invite the three proverbial guests: me, myself, and I!

Kimberly Steiner, a twenty-seven-year-old Korean adoptee who's dealing with cultural as well as adoption issues, has moved from a sense of abandonment to acceptance. She says that when she's dealing with adoption feelings and issues, however, she secretly thinks like a victim and does the "poor me" thing.

Even though we may be having a pity party inside, we often put on a strong facade.

We May Present Ourselves as Strong and Successful

This is one of the "acceptable" ways we can unknowingly become and remain a victim. We are not off in the corner having a pity party. Heavens . . . that's the last thing we would ever do. We present a strong facade instead. We are the perfectionists of the world. The overachievers. The outwardly successful ones.

But what is the motivation behind all of this seeming success?

A counselor friend once told of an adolescent female who came into her office acting as tough as could be. Her parents had done everything to keep her from acting out in destructive ways. When my friend asked, "So, how long have you been too much to handle?" the girl's perfect mask crumbled, revealing a young woman who felt like a victim and who was in incredible emotional pain.

Here is a poem I wrote some time ago about my former (most of the time) strong facade:

An Ode to Insecurity

Please, don't let my strength fool you,
    For it's only a veneer you see
Built up from years of silence
    From those who I would their victim be.
I need for you to see the person deep down inside,
    Who beneath the veneer is trying to hide.
For years I didn't know it was adoption,
    Then I got depressed and believed I had no options.
But now I am beginning to see
    All the people who have victimized me.
I feel frustrated, shamed, and abandoned.
    Is there any way out?
Will I ever be free?
    Oh, God, please deliver me.
Where can I go?
    Where can I flee?
Will anyone ever believe me?
    When people look at my perfect life
They think it is absent of shame and strife.
    But it's only an illusion, filled with delusion
A life of desperate seclusion.

Where can I go?
Where can I flee?
Who will let me just be me?

We May Remain Silent Because of Shame

Richard Curtis, cofounder of the Adoption Triad of the Treasure Coast support group serving St. Lucie and Martin counties in Florida, says he became the "silent son." He learned quickly that keeping silent and asking no questions was the safest path to choose.

Connie Dawson says, "For years, I didn't think I could afford to have an experience of being adopted, for if I did *and* talked about it, I risked shunning, the usual family messages to 'stop right there.' Shunning is dangerous and leaves the one being shunned alone and feeling unsafe in a primal way. Once one has experienced the ultimate shunning of being sent away in early life, into the frightening and inhospitable desert, so to speak, deep-bone knowledge reminds one to be careful, for being abandoned again is always an option."

We May Reject Others Before They Can Reject Us

So how does the victim feel about himself? Does he feel that he is worthy of success, acceptance, and well-being? Far from it. The victim mindset says: "I am a loser. I am worthy only of rejection. Therefore I will set the stage for it and make it happen before others have an opportunity to reject and hurt me."

Todd, age twenty-nine, does this in his relationships with women. He says that he tests them to see if they will leave him by seeing how much they will take of his passive-aggressive behavior. But here's the clincher. He says, "The end result is always the same . . . it feels like I am unworthy and being rejected, but in actuality I give them no choice but to leave."

Beverly says that she also tests people to see if they *really* like her. But she says that they always fail, which is her sad little proof that she can't be loved. She builds up resentments about the failures of the people she loves and distances herself from them.

"Instead of waiting to be rejected, I will most likely do something outrageous in which the other person will reject me," admits Kimberly Steiner.

WE CAN HAVE TRANSFORMED MINDS AND LIVES

The aforementioned characteristics aren't an exhaustive list of a victim's mentality and behavior, but they'll give us a launching pad to begin assessing if we fall into the victim category. If we *do* identify, what is the answer? What can we do to get rid of this victim thinking that has plagued some of us since birth? How can we find liberation — the longed-for freedom to make our own life-giving choices?

First of all, many of us need help in acknowledging our reality. Joe Soll, CSW, author of *Adoption Healing: A Path to Recovery* and creator of the Annual March on Washington for Civil Rights and Healing Weekends, says, "I felt like a victim until I began to understand that losing my mother at the beginning of my life hampered my ability to have good, intimate friendships, and experience my emotions. I think all of us adoptees, *and* our mothers, were victims and remain that way until we find a way to get some help in dealing with our issues. Then we can easily remove our victim status."

And how do we get this kind of help? Probably the best way is by listening to the stories of other adoptees, getting professional counseling, joining an adoption support group, and talking in-depth with a fellow adoptee. But *self-intervention* is possible as well, according to Spencer Johnson, MD. One of his clients said, "Sometimes I start feeling like I'm not getting a fair shake. Usually it's over something small. I still don't like it very much when I feel I'm not being treated well. But as soon as I stop and see that I'm feeling like a victim, I know who my persecutor is. Myself. Soon I remember that I can either be my best

QUESTIONS ADOPTEES ARE ASKING

Our Choice

To realize the problem is us, not other people, we must choose to quit blaming and take responsibility for how we live our lives. We have never had control over other people and never will.

friend or my worst enemy. It all depends on what I choose to think and choose to do."[4]

Right now you may be distressed by the reality of what your mind has been thinking all these years. That's okay. Stay with me. We're working through this together, with many of your fellow adoptees.

DISCUSSION QUESTIONS FOR
SUPPORT GROUPS OR PERSONAL REFLECTION

1. Did any of the descriptions of the "victim" resonate with you? Would you be willing to share them with the group or a friend?
2. Share your birth and adoption stories.
3. How do you think you felt when everything that was familiar was removed from you?
4. If you were a foster child, did your parents threaten to send you back if you behaved badly?
5. Are you ever aware of a fear of being forgotten by your first family? How does this manifest in your everyday life?
6. Write a letter *to* and *from* your birth mother about the topic of this chapter: Do They Ever Think About Me?

DIGGING DEEPER FOR ANSWERS
TO OUR ADOPTION QUESTIONS

1. Look up Romans 6:16: The Bible says that we can be "slaves" to the wrong thing spiritually. What do you think this means?
2. According to Romans 6:16, being a slave to sin (refusing to let God be the love of our lives; not reading and obeying what He says in the Bible, etc.) leads to death. Do you think it is physical or spiritual death? What would spiritual death mean? Could it be our connection with God?
3. From a spiritual standpoint, if we're "dead," how can we ever have the power to make new decisions?

Just as my grandsons had someone point out only two options, it's clear that there are options available to all of us, in our relationships with others and our relationship with God. If the verses listed above don't make sense to you, that's okay. If you're seeking God, or even if you aren't, say this prayer before bed tonight: "God, if you're there, please make yourself real to me."

Why do many of us have thoughts about our first family unexpectedly pop into our minds? We'll talk about that next.

PART TWO

OUR QUESTIONS THAT REQUIRE ANSWERS

The remarkable thing we have is a choice every day regarding the attitude we will embrace for that day. We cannot change our past. . . . We cannot change the fact that people will act in a certain way. We cannot change the inevitable. The only thing we can do is play on the one string we have, and that is our attitude.

— CHARLES SWINDOLL

Instead of looking at life as a narrowing funnel, we can see it ever widening to choose the things we want to do, to take the wisdom we've learned and create something.

— LIZ CARPENTER

CHAPTER THREE

WHY DO WE THINK ABOUT OUR BIRTH PARENTS?

God whispers to us in our pleasures, speaks to our conscience, but shouts in our pains: it is His megaphone to rouse a deaf world.

— C. S. LEWIS

I have yet to meet an adoptee who can honestly claim to have never thought about his or her birth mother, especially on birthdays. If you never have, I would like to meet you!

It's no wonder. Just think about how intimately we were united with the woman who gave us birth! What a connection we had for at least nine months. An inseparable bond. As inseparable as tea is from hot water. As inseparable as a bud is from the stem of a flower. As inseparable as the ocean is from the sand. Renowned author John Bowlby says that the mother is the hub of life.[1]

Author and physician Peter Nathananielsz says that much of the way our bodies work is molded and solidified during our time in the womb and that there are critical periods during prenatal development when our cells and organs decide how they will behave for the rest of our lives.[2] Just think . . . at the very moment of conception, our entire genetic code was established that determined our sex and the color of our hair and eyes. At three weeks we had a beating heart, and at forty days detectable brain waves.

Perhaps even more fascinating is a phenomenon that goes on between a mother and her unborn child that absolutely boggled my mind when I learned about it.

WE HAD OUR FIRST CONVERSATION WITH OUR BIRTH MOTHERS

Who do you think was the first person with whom you had a conversation?

Would you believe it was your birth mother?

And where and when do you think it might have happened?

This is the mind-boggling part—in the womb!

Dr. Thomas Verny says that during the last three months of pregnancy, and especially the last two, we are mature enough physically and intellectually to send and receive fairly sophisticated messages to and from our mothers. Our mothers set the pace, provide the cues, and actually mold our responses.[3]

What messages did we get from our birth mothers? I believe it all depended on her attitude toward us. If we heard, "I love you and am so glad you're a part of me. I will do all that I can to help you develop into the person you were created to be. I can't wait to see you. I will welcome you into the world in a way more wonderful than you can possibly imagine," our response was certainly positive. We would have thrived on it. "Oh, Mommy," our little preverbal minds might have "said," "I love you so much and I can't wait to be born so that I can suckle at your breasts and be held in your arms."

On the other hand, what if we heard, "I don't want you. I don't even like you. In fact, I think of you as an 'it,' and frankly, I can't wait to get rid of you. I wish I could"?

Our little minds may have responded like this: "All alone. All alone. Hurts so bad. No one will ever take care of me. I must 'buck up' and be strong so I can survive. Be strong. Be strong. Tense up. Be on guard so I won't be tortured like this again."

This kind of message to us would be unimaginably painful. Author Judith Viorst likens it to being doused with oil and set on fire.[4]

But it's a subconscious pain. Dr. Arthur Janov says that this kind of pain is "not like a pinch where we yell 'ouch,' shake our fingers, and in a few minutes get over it. Instead, it's like being pinched so hard you cannot feel it, so that the pain goes on forever because it is continually being processed below the level of conscious awareness. It doesn't mean it is not there doing its damage — it just means that it is too much to feel."[5]

Some of us can identify with those negative conversations, and many of them are still playing in our heads even though they were communicated so many years ago. Some of us feel at a primal level that we *need* her love and welcoming attitude in order to survive.

Marvelous and miraculous things occurred while we were in the womb, being knit together cell by cell, bone by bone, and tissue by tissue. In a poignant Old Testament psalm, King David describes our Creator's intimate involvement in our conception, development, and destiny:

> *For you created my inmost being;*
> > *you knit me together in my mother's womb.*
> *I praise you because I am fearfully and wonderfully made;*
> > *your works are wonderful,*
> > *I know that full well.*
> *My frame was not hidden from you*
> > *when I was made in the secret place.*
> *When I was woven together in the depths of the earth,*
> > *your eyes saw my unformed body.*
> *All the days ordained for me*
> > *were written in your book*

before one of them came to be.

How precious to me are your thoughts, O God!
How vast is the sum of them!
Were I to count them,
they would outnumber the grains of sand.
When I awake,
I am still with you.[6]

Whatever the case, whether conversations with our birth mothers were positive or painful, prenatal experiences are encoded in our bodies, souls, and spirits, resulting in questions and thoughts that pop into our minds, often unexpectedly, throughout our lives.

WE MAY HAVE THOUGHT ABOUT OUR BIRTH MOTHERS AT AN EARLY AGE

Folks who aren't adopted are often amazed at how early some of us think about our birth mothers, especially when I tell the story about the adopted girl who asked her mom prior to her third birthday party if her "lady" was coming. The mother asked what lady she was talking about. Her daughter answered, "The lady I grew inside. It's my *birthday*, isn't it?"[7]

Cheri Freeman thought about her origins at an early age also. She told herself stories at age three or four about how her birth parents missed her and how happy they would be to finally meet her.

Joe Soll, CSW, a psychotherapist and author of *Adoption Healing: A Path to Recovery*, says that from the moment he knew he was adopted at age four, there has never been a day that he hasn't thought about his birth mom.

Frieda Moore found comfort when hurting by imagining her birth mother coming to find and rescue her, taking her home to live with her forever.

Pam Hasegawa, a fifty-nine-year-old adoptee advocate, says that when she had the lead in a play, she remembers thinking, "If she could only see me now! Would she be proud of me?"

Where did those positive attitudes come from? Could they have begun in the womb?

And what about those of us who have negative attitudes? Laurie, even as a young child, worried that her birth mother must be struggling and depressed. Others of us didn't begin to think about our birth mothers until we hit puberty and shot up to six feet tall even though both our adoptive parents were short. Shirley Reynolds says that when she became a teen, she realized that she looked much different from her adoptive family. This propelled her into a fantasy world where her mother would be dark-haired and petite, like Shirley. And of course, she would be beautiful!

Some adoptees claim to never think about their birth mothers. Sally says that she feels guilty because she doesn't think about hers, knowing that so many other adoptees do.

Sally is not alone. Many don't think about their birth mothers for various reasons, but the predominant reason is usually shame. Shame is that awful feeling, not that we have *done* something wrong, but that something is inherently wrong with *us* as individuals.

How about hearing your adoptive mother talk derogatively about the twenty-one-year-old down the street who was unmarried and pregnant, raving about how much shame she brought to her family? Connie Dawson heard this message at the tender age of ten as her mother delivered a veiled message that Connie herself was shameful and shouldn't be "bad," like her birth mother was. Or how about Sue who struggles with a haunting belief that something dreadful must lurk within her, which if found out by her adoptive parents, would cause them to bolt from her?

WE WERE DEEPLY IMPACTED BY OUR
BIRTH MOTHERS

Whether positive or negative, and whether we like it or not, our birth mothers are a forever part of us. How we choose to respond to that reality will deeply influence the course of our lives.

Author Louise Kaplan says that in the death of a parent (which I believe can be likened to adoption separation), the dialogue between parent and child continues within the child and that the child remains attached in profound ways to that dialogue throughout life.[8]

When my dad died, one of his friends said to me, "You never lose your parents. They are always a part of you." In my grief, I was rather skeptical, but since that time I have found it to be true. For instance, after every meal, Dad, in a mischievous way, picked up the unused silverware saying, "This one's clean!" We'd all laugh and say, "Yeah, Dad!" Over the years it became an endearing behavior, and in the years since his death, whenever I pick up clean silverware after a meal, I think of him and smile.

WE MAY THINK FIRST ABOUT OUR
BIRTH FATHERS

We have examined a very important part of our existence—our birth mothers. But what about our birth *fathers*? Did they have no influence? Last time I checked the books on reproduction, it takes two to make a baby.

When I was almost finished with the final draft of this book I talked with a reunited birth father who adored his daughter but who had been rejected by her. His heart was breaking as he wept while telling me that he would do anything to have a meaningful father-daughter relationship.

Do many birth fathers feel the same way? Would they want a relationship with us if they had an opportunity? Do they feel the loss of us to the same degree that birth mothers usually do? As we do?

As I've said, I believe that adoption can be likened to a big door. Over the top of the door is written "Birth Mother," for our thoughts about her usually come first. It is often *after* we have gone through the adoption door that we find the words "Birth Father" written on the other side.

Ron Hilliard, of Palm Beach Heights, Florida, focused mainly on his birth mother and blocked out thoughts of his birth father because his father didn't want to marry his mother and also urged her to have an abortion. Ron's search for his birth mother ended in a cemetery and he is now looking at the back of the adoption door and wondering who his father is—and who he is as a result. This curiosity is being fueled by the fact that Ron has a fraternal twin brother who resembles his birth mother's photos, while Ron doesn't. This makes him wonder who he *does* resemble.

Some of us see the words "birth father" first on the adoption door. Richard Curtis says that the loss of his birth father was the first loss of a male figure in his life, followed by the loss of his adoptive father when he was only five years old. As a result, Richard had no male role models and was left with what he terms a "father hunger" that he believes many adoptees experience.

Like Ron, Richard's search for his birth father ended at a tombstone. However, after finding people who knew his father prior to his death, Richard can see that many of the choices and behaviors he has made in life closely parallel his birth father's.

Crystal speaks of father hunger by calling it a "void" that colors her relationships with men and keeps her longing for a daddy even though she is forty years old. A friend recently asked her what she would do if she ever found him. To Crystal the answer was simple—"I'd quit my job, move in with him, and have him take care of me." She then added, "I am joking . . . but not really."

When our curiosity is aroused, our speculations about him increase. What kind of a person was/is he? Did he refuse any responsibility and abandon our birth mother, as in the case of Laurie? Out of deep hurt, she says she prejudged him as a jerk because he chose not to marry her mom or encourage her to keep her baby. She is actually happy that she doesn't have to know him.

To Issie, her birth father is a nonissue. A few years ago she thought briefly about trying to locate him, but her fear of rejection was too strong. In addition, she has no proof, short of DNA, of who her father is.

Then there's the nasty subject of incest. Sheila says that her birth father is her mother's stepdad. She's glad he died before she met her birth family because she doesn't know how she would react to him. She's accepted that he's a part of her, yet she can't comprehend his deplorable actions.

Dawn Saphir, twenty-seven, born in Seoul, South Korea, and adopted at six months of age by a Caucasian family, says that based on what she's learned of Korean culture at the time of her birth, she doesn't have a lot of positive feelings about who her birth father may have been.

Some of our birth fathers may be completely ignorant of the fact that we even exist.

How might our lives have been different had they been informed?

Karen says that she feels a great tenderness for the father who never knew about her. "He never had the chance to 'give me up,'" she explains. "He never had the chance to know he was a father."

Renee says that she had the amazing experience of finding her birth father recently and that the hardest part was discovering that he never even knew her birth mother was pregnant.

As I finish this section, I am reminded of my own birth father. Even as I write, he doesn't seem real, for I have never met him, nor do I have any hope of meeting him because my birth mother took his identity to her grave. I know, however, that he is a forever part of me because I am always searching for him, even on an unconscious level.

Not long ago I sat next to an attractive elderly gentleman on a plane. Guess what my first thought was? *I wonder if he could be my dad.*

I had a dad in the growing-up years who loved me dearly and whom I dearly loved. But I also have *another* dad out there somewhere who may not even know I exist. I long to know him. I long to look into his eyes and have him wrap his arms around me.

WE HAVE A GOD-GIVEN NEED TO THINK ABOUT OUR BIRTH PARENTS

If we were created by God from the very fiber of our birth parents' physical and emotional beings, don't you think our need to think about them would be innate? If we had primal conversations with our mother in the womb, wouldn't you say it is natural for us to think about her as we are growing up and growing old? And if our birth father's DNA helped determine the color of our hair and eyes, wouldn't you say that he is just as much a part of us as our mother and it is normal to want a relationship with him?

Our Choice

To give ourselves permission to think about our birth parents without reservation.

Wherever we are in the spectrum of perceptions about our birth parents, we must rest assured that our thoughts are normal and healthy. They are part of the fiber of our being. Part of the package of being adopted. It's all about our identity . . . our dual identity.

So what must we do for ourselves? What healthy choice must we make to move closer toward who we were created to be by a loving God?

Giving ourselves permission to let natural thoughts surface reminds me of when I am getting sick. I feel nausea and the urge to toss my cookies. I hate that more than anything, so I concentrate on something else so that I won't. But when I finally let myself think about the possibility, up comes my lunch, followed by an incredible feeling of relief. A similar sensation often results when we allow ourselves to freely think about our birth parents. The urge to do so is really unstoppable.

Penny Callan Partridge, beloved poet of the adoption world who has been active in the adoption reform community since 1973, writes:

Pandora in Later Life

And what if I had not?
I would be dead by now.
Dead of my anger.
Dead of my goodness.
Dead of my anger
at my stinking goodness.
Imagine yourself
in a room with a box.
And you don't know
what's in it.
And you don't know
why you shouldn't.
When you closed your eyes,
you would see that box.
When you opened your eyes,
you would see that box.
That box was my life.
My life was in the box.
When I opened the box,
I was letting out my life.
Oh you get blamed
because of other people's
closed boxes. But even
with all of the openings
and closings my life

has been since then,
I have
not
ever
once
even
a single
second
regretted it.[9]

Perhaps all these thoughts are new to you. You want to begin your process of making positive, life-transforming choices but don't know how. The following section will help. (You'll find such a section at the end of every chapter.)

DISCUSSION QUESTIONS FOR SUPPORT GROUPS OR PERSONAL REFLECTION

1. Imagine a door with a sign above saying "Adoption." Are you curious about the door? Where are you in the scene? A casual observer? Moving closer to the door?
2. Write a letter *to* and *from* your birth mother and father. Do you think they ever think about you? Write about this topic. Be sure to date your letters, even though they'll never be sent. You'll be able to look back and see your growth.
3. Where is God in your perception of adoption? Do you believe what the Bible says about him creating you in your birth mother's womb?

Now that we've given ourselves permission to let thoughts about our birth parents rise to the surface, we may begin to have mixed feelings about our adoption experiences. We'll discuss that next.

DIGGING DEEPER FOR ANSWERS
TO OUR ADOPTION QUESTIONS

1. Look up Isaiah 49:15-16. Who will never forget you?
2. If God himself was in our birth mother's womb, creating us, wouldn't we have a "father hunger" that goes deeper than the human level? Wouldn't we miss his presence? Moses, the adoptee who lived in biblical times, at the end of life looked back and saw three sets of arms that held him throughout life—his birth parents', his adoptive mother's, and the everlasting arms of God the Father.[10]
3. In addition to the conversation in the womb with our birth mothers, who else was with us and what do you think he might have been saying to us? Whose voice would be the strongest? Whose voice will we believe?

Oftentimes, many of us have what we called "mixed feelings" surrounding our adoption experiences. Let's discuss that next.

CHAPTER FOUR

WHY DO WE FEEL LIKE SOMETHING'S NOT RIGHT INSIDE?

Like both sides of a coin, the emotions present seem to be opposite, yet they both exist side by side.

— RON HILLIARD

Have you ever run your fingernails over a blackboard? I have, and my gut reaction is to cringe, curl up my fingers, and wince until the physical and aural discomfort I've just experienced has passed.

Did you know that there is a similar finger-over-the-blackboard *psychological* sensation that occurs when incoming information doesn't line up with our built-in belief systems? Clinicians call it "cognitive dissonance," but laypeople like us simply call it "mixed feelings." It's important that we understand this psychological phenomenon because it has a strong impact on our lives . . . most of us, anyway.

WHERE DO OUR MIXED FEELINGS ORIGINATE?

Every baby born into this world innately expects that his or her mother will provide care, nurture, and love. That's the way we're wired in the womb, adopted or not. However, that privilege of being cared for by the one who gave us birth didn't occur for most of us who were adopted. It might have for a short time before we were relinquished, but eventually the separation came.

We expected and needed to drink from her breasts, lie on her warm body, and hear the sound of her familiar voice. But instead we were placed into the arms of strangers. Loving strangers, in most cases; nevertheless they *were* strangers to us at the time.

This experience frequently produces the mixed feelings. Incoming information — "I am being held by someone who doesn't sound, smell, or look like my birth mommy" — doesn't line up with "I love the feel, sound, and smell of my birth mommy. In her arms I feel so safe."

Our basic belief system is being violated. Maybe that is why many of us often feel an unexplainable sense of chaos and like something inside just isn't right.

Cheri Freeman knows that adoption brings joy to many people, and even to her. Yet she has a deep sadness that she is trying to overcome, stemming from the fact that a mother who gives you life is supposed to *love* you and *keep* you, not discard you.

Adoptive parents often say about adoption day: "It was the happiest day of our lives!" While most of us are happy to be adopted, our own hearts tell us that adoption day was the most painful day of our lives, for the person with whom we shared deep intimacy suddenly disappeared from our world.

Ron Hilliard says that almost everyone showered him with the positive aspects of being adopted. "You are loved," they would say. Yet in his heart he didn't *experience* being loved. "I felt unloved, given away, and unwanted," he says.

Frieda Moore says she "felt like an intruder—unloved, unwanted, and not worth loving," even though her parents lavished her with unconditional love.

I am confident that Moses, an adoptee who lived in biblical times, experienced the same mixed feelings. He was born to an Israelite family, who along with the rest of the Israelite nation was in slavery under the wicked pharaoh of Egypt. God had called the Israelites to multiply and be fruitful, and even though they were suffering in abject slavery they flourished. This disturbed Pharaoh, for he worried they might rise up and take over his kingdom.

The more God's people multiplied, the meaner Pharaoh got. Finally he sent an edict throughout the Israelite huts that all male babies must be killed at birth by the midwives.

Just imagine how Jochebed and Amram, Moses' parents, felt when Jochebed became pregnant during this time. This probably affected their other two children, Aaron and Miriam, as well. Of course you couldn't find out the sex of a baby during those times, but I can just see Jochebed fearing the worst when she heard Pharaoh's soldiers riding through the village, repeating the edict.

Jochebed *did* have a boy, but the midwives valued life and loved God and didn't kill him or other male babies at their births. This sent Pharaoh into a rage and he gave a second edict: All male babies must be drowned in the Nile River at birth.

Jochebed probably kept the curtains on her windows shut so that the soldiers riding by couldn't see her baby. I can imagine her holding Moses close in fear that a loud cry would bring a fast death. They didn't have pacifiers then, but if he didn't need nursing, perhaps she put the tip of her little finger in his mouth for him to suck on. Anything to keep him quiet.

One day when Jochebed was nursing, an idea came to her. She would make a watertight basket coated with tar and pitch that was just big enough to hold her son. There would be a lid that would cover him and protect him from the sun and insects.

She knew that Pharoah's daughter Hatshepsut came to the Nile to bathe daily. Jochebed believed that she would hear Moses' cry or see him in the basket and have pity on him and let him live.

Jochebed rehearsed this plan with her daughter, Miriam, for she was going to be a key player in the plan to save the baby. "You hide behind a tree, and when Pharaoh's daughter discovers and opens the basket, she will look for a wet nurse. That's when you are to approach her and say that you know of someone who would be willing."

What an incredible faith Jochebed had in an impossible situation! She believed firmly that God would take care of this little life that he had given her.

Jochebed was able to keep the baby's cries muffled for a few weeks. But when the cries got louder, she knew it was time to implement her plan. As she carried her beloved son down to the Nile, hot tears streamed down her cheeks as she sang his last lullaby.

When she let go of the basket, she quickly hid behind some brush. The baby sent out heart-wrenching wails and every scream felt like a knife piercing Jochebed's heart. Every time she heard a cry, her breasts engorged with milk, which reminded her in a vivid way of the separation from her baby. She buried her face in her hands, weeping.

I have often wondered how Moses reacted emotionally to being in a dark, stuffy basket. A totally foreign place. A place where all human connections were broken. The record simply says, "He was crying."[1] The root of that word means "to weep, bewail, mourn, sob, weep continually, weep longer, wept bitterly."[2]

Jochebed's plan for her baby was carried out to the last detail. She was asked to be the wet nurse for Hatshepsut until the time of weaning, which during those times was about four years of age. Thus, in an incredible turn of events, Jochebed once again held the child she cherished. It seemed overwhelming to grasp the fact that the daughter of the one who wanted her baby annihilated was the one who snatched him from the jaws of death. I can imagine Moses' mother joyously telling him during those four years how he was miraculously saved and returned to her, but don't you wonder if every time he heard the story, he may have felt an unexplainable anxiety?

The years flew by quickly until it was time for Moses to be weaned. Before they knew it, the dreaded day had arrived. Can't you imagine Jochebed and Amram on the evening before the adoption? She may have gathered his favorite toys and clothes and put them in a knapsack while Amram may have been in the other room silently rehearsing a child-friendly explanation of the adoption. All the while he was praying to God. *Where should I begin? How can a four-year-old child possibly understand that we are going to stop being his parents and give him to someone else?*

When the grieving family walked together to Pharaoh's palace, Hatshepsut, the adoptive mother, was eagerly awaiting their arrival. Moses clung to Jochebed as they approached the palace. A servant dressed in Egyptian finery opened the huge brass doors and ushered them in. What a contrast the shiny marble floors, tall pillars, and statues of Egyptian gods were to Moses' simple family abode.

In flowing silk robes and a high hat covered with jewels, Hatshepsut greeted them with outstretched arms. "I am so glad to see you, son! I thought this day would never arrive."

After a few minutes of awkward pleasantries, Amram, Jochebed, Miriam, and Aaron said, "We have to go now, Moses. You will be staying here from now on. We love you and will never forget you."

As Jochebed handed her son over to Hatshepsut, he screamed, "Mama, Papa, don't go!" They gave him one last emotional embrace, turned their backs, and walked out. He tightened his body and pushed Hatshepsut away.

Even though Jochebed and Amram's hearts were breaking, they were confident that God had saved Moses for a reason — a specific role in history. And that turned out to be true. But Moses was in a raw place of loss. All that was familiar was suddenly gone. Can't you imagine his adoptive mother reminding him as he grew up of the joyous day he walked through the palace doors? I don't know about you, but

I think Moses would have had mixed feelings, big time.

Isn't this amazing? The craziness that we sometimes feel is the repercussion of abandonment. We're feeling the brokenness of the original trauma of losing our first family, and it's triggered by something in our present-day lives.

Whenever I illustrate mixed feelings when speaking to others about adoption, I ask the meeting planners to come forward. From behind the podium, I pull out five huge candy bars and ask them to show me their favorite bar. Then, without warning, I bend down and pull out a hammer that was hidden behind the podium. With all my might, I pound those candy bars to bits. Then I ask the meeting planners if they'd still like their candy bars. You know what their answer is! Then, without warning, I pull out a quart of vanilla ice cream and ask them if they would feel differently about the candy bars if I mixed them in the ice cream. Smiles come over their faces. Of course. It would be like a treat from Dairy Queen.

That's the way it is with our mixed feelings. That's what makes us feel that something inside doesn't feel right. We need to understand where they came from—from loss of our first family. Our hearts are broken, like the candy bars. However, when we talk about them with someone we love, the pain begins to dissipate, even though it will never go away completely in this life.

WE CAN LEARN HOW TO RECOGNIZE MIXED FEELINGS

Attachment and bonding specialist Gregory C. Keck, PhD, says, "The concept of cognitive dissonance is a tough one even for adult adoptees to understand, and even if they understand it, I don't think that the understanding mitigates the feelings of abandonment. Actually, I'm not sure there is any explanation or reason that adoptees can embrace to resolve their loss. That's not to say that people don't get through it. Obviously, they do."[3]

Dr. Keck makes it clear that cognitive dissonance is one of the highest hurdles we must jump as adoptees. Therefore, our first order of business will be to identify two common markers that may indicate mixed feelings—something that produces a finger-over-the-blackboard sensation psychologically. One of those is hypervigilance.

Hypervigilance

The Synonym Finder says this about vigilance: "watchfulness, guardedness, wariness, caution, forethought, keenness, sleeplessness."[4]

Magnify those words by 100 percent and we have hypervigilance!

Sometimes hypervigilance comes in handy, as when a car is crossing the median and heading directly toward us. Or when a toddler has fallen into the deep end of a pool. We can be "Johnny on the spot," which is a blessing. But at other times, it's distressing. Our systems are constantly working overtime to sort out dissonant beliefs and emotions.

Therapist and best-selling author and speaker Nancy Verrier says, "Although the adoptee might not be consciously aware of the fear of abandonment, which is then felt as free-floating anxiety, there is an attitude which can be readily discerned. It is a kind of watchfulness or cautious testing of the environment, which is called hyper-vigilance."[5]

Lois Rabey, an author and speaker who was adopted at nine days of age, says that one of the ways hypervigilance manifests itself in her life is through the physical reaction of an extremely sensitive "startle reflex." For example, when she's in a room and doesn't know someone has come in, she has an exaggerated reaction. Her family knows not to come up behind her and say "boo!"

Lois believes the major reason for the hypervigilance she experiences in adulthood was a contentious relationship with her adoptive father. "He wanted me to be his *biological* child," she explains. "So even though I didn't know that, there was a tension and a pressure to try to please him. I just didn't succeed because I couldn't. I was always afraid and said to myself, 'Is he going to be mad? What can I do?'"

Lois's innate belief system told her that dads are supposed to love their daughters. When she found in her dad only disappointment that she wasn't his biological child, fingers scraped over the blackboard of her soul.

Authors John and Paula Sanford say, "In the womb, every adopted child has in his spirit experienced rejection from his natural parents. He may have been reacting in his spirit with resentment, *tightening up* in defensiveness. Certainly rest and trust are not formed in him"[6] (emphasis mine).

Another indication that we are experiencing mixed feelings is an undercurrent of anxiety.

Unexplainable Anxiety

I resonate with what author Selma Fraiberg says about adoptee anxiety. She says, "Can a baby under one 'remember' this traumatic separation from his original parents? No, he probably will not remember the events as a series of pictures that can be recalled. What is remembered, or preserved, is anxiety, a primitive kind of terror, which returns in waves in later life."[7]

Many of us experience anxiety but may never associate it with adoption loss. "Oh, I'm just a nervous type of person," we may say to ourselves.

Sue Coons, who was adopted at nine months and found by her birth mother fifteen years ago at age forty-three, says that she developed a panic disorder when she was eight years old and never really understood it or had treatment until the last decade. It was very difficult for her to deal with and created troublesome limitations in both her personal and professional life. She couldn't travel at all.

Lois Rabey links her hypervigilance with anxiety. She says that on an emotional level she has worried excessively about what might happen in the future to those she loves, from the present day to years and years out. She tried everything to rid herself of the worry. Prayer.

Meditation. Counseling. All to no avail.

When she became a grandmother, she grew more and more exhausted with worry about her grandchildren and other family members. Overwhelmed with anxiety, she made a choice and said to God that she was going to commit all that she was worrying about to him and intentionally let go of it every time it came up again. That decision has eased her hypervigilance and anxiety over time.

WE CAN LEARN WELL-INTENTIONED WORDS AND STATEMENTS THAT TRIGGER MIXED FEELINGS

Cognitive dissonance occurs automatically and involuntarily for many adoptees, but adoptive parents and other people in an adopted child's life can inadvertently trigger mixed feelings. I believe that, for the most part, the following types of statements are well intentioned and born out of ignorance; nevertheless, they can have negative repercussions in an adoptee's mind and heart.

Well-Intentioned Statement #1: "Your Birth Mother Loved You So Much That She Gave You to Us."

Trying to equate love and abandonment just doesn't work! I am reminded of the song that says, "Love and marriage, love and marriage . . . go together like a horse and carriage." What if we changed the phrase "love and marriage" to "love and abandonment"? Sing with me now: "Love and abandonment, . . . love and abandonment, go together like a horse and carriage."

Rather ridiculous, isn't it? Is it any wonder that being told that love is what led to our relinquishment produces mixed feelings? Yes, there may have been a loving adoption plan, but to most of us, separation from our birth mothers translates as rejection and abandonment, pure and simple.

Connie Dawson says it translates like this: "I love you/go away."

"Your birth mother loved you so much; she made a loving plan . . . blah, blah, blah." Or, "Your needs are important/don't search for your birth parents or you'll hurt me."

Dr. Keck says, "I think it just confuses kids when people tell them that their birth mothers didn't keep them because they loved them. I think it makes the kids feel even more responsible for inconveniencing their mothers by being born. Also, I think they must feel bad (guilty) about feeling bad, sad, lonely, or abandoned. After all, if someone did this because they loved them, what gives them the right to feel whatever they feel? Also, I think it makes 'loving' someone difficult since love is what 'got rid' of them. If their mothers loved them so much, should they have any negative feelings? Should they love her that much? I do wonder if anything helps kids feel better. Is it better or worse to be 'dumped' by a loving mother than by a hating, abusive, or terrible one?"[8]

Well-Intentioned Statement #2: "You Were Chosen!"

Adoption experts Drs. David Brodzinsky and Marshall Schechter say, "It has long been popular in adoption circles to emphasize that the adopted child is a *wanted* child or, as in the title of Wasson's 1939 classic children's book on adoption, a *Chosen Baby*. This emphasis is a fairly straightforward piece of denial: Usually a child is available for adoption only because he was *unwanted*. It is no accident that Wasson's story neglects to mention the existence of *biological* parents. It is not an easy task to change an unwanted child into a wanted child. This challenge is, however, exactly the task faced by adoptive parents. They must convey to their adopted child that, although he was born to other parents who didn't want him, he is now their beloved child and shall always remain so."[9]

Lori says that she just couldn't believe the line, "You were a chosen child; nobody could love a kid more." She knew that her parents had adopted her in a last-ditch attempt to save their ailing marriage.

A poem by Mi Ok Song Bruining sums up the chosen-child dilemma:

They Said

They said
   smile for the camera
   Open your eyes, they are squinting.
They said
   Stop crying, stop feeling bad.
   Those kids who call you "Chink"
   And "Flat Face"
   Don't know anything
   Besides, you probably provoked them.
They said
   Feel lucky
   You were "chosen"
   Really meaning
   I was also given up.
They said
   We are offended,
   You have everything, so be happy.
   Be appreciative, and
   Never let the tears show.
They said
   You don't belong here.
   Where do you come from?
   Do you speak English?
   Do you like America?
   As if I just landed
   From a distant galaxy.
They said
   Everything I hoped and dreamed

And prayed they wouldn't.
They still do.[10]

Well-Intentioned Statement #3: "Accentuate the Positive!"

Another statement that sometimes causes mixed feelings is "Accentuate the positive." You know—count your blessings, count them one by one. As I've spoken with hundreds of adoptees all over the country, I've discovered that this message is particularly common in religious families. A well-meaning parent, church member, or member of the clergy can unintentionally inflict harm by focusing exclusively on the many positive aspects of spiritual adoption while denying the realities of human adoption. "Oh, we're all adopted." Neither has every person in this world been adopted from a human standpoint, nor has every person sitting in a church pew experienced spiritual adoption.

I believe our places of worship are to be hospitals for people who are hurting. Places where we can bare our souls and find unconditional love and acceptance. In many cases, however, adoptees *don't* experience this freedom and safety when they go to church because the people there don't recognize that adoption is a *mixed* blessing, filled with pleasure as well as pain. Instead, they look at adoption through rose-colored glasses, trying to make it a win/win situation for unplanned pregnancies and infertility, never giving a thought about what effect adoption has on the child.

All too often, an adoptee who voices honest thoughts and feelings like "I felt abandoned" is accused of being "against adoption," "negative about adoption," "giving adoption a bad rap," or "controversial." Do you ever wonder why so many other complex issues and losses can be talked about nowadays—infertility, miscarriage, death, divorce, substance abuse, addictions—while adoption loss remains mostly unacknowledged, even taboo?

Many of us find it difficult to enter new situations to begin with and wouldn't consider entering the doors of houses of worship because adoption is rarely, if ever, mentioned, addressed, or prayed for. Other losses and needs are. But not ours. How meaningful it would be to a hurting adoptee to hear prayers that convey compassion and understanding for the adoption-related issues he or she might be grappling with. How meaningful if our places of worship observed November as Adoption Awareness Month.

The "accentuate the positive" position is also communicated within adoptive homes, which keeps adoptees in bondage to the chaos inside. Ron Hilliard says that when others would try to affirm the positive but he wasn't feeling positive in his own heart, he felt guilty and ashamed. It was confusing to him why his heart would not be in agreement with those who tried to accentuate how fortunate he was. Like the good adoptee, Ron never verbalized the negative—he just smiled and nodded at how "lucky" he was to have such wonderful adoptive parents who rescued him from abandonment.

Scott D. Stephens, LISW, a post-adoption social worker from Cincinnati, knew something wasn't quite right in terms of what he was feeling, but he didn't have words to describe his mixed emotions. The message was somehow communicated that being adopted was a positive blessing and that positive feelings were expected in response. His parents would say things like, "Isn't it wonderful that you were loved so much that your parents chose you?" or "How fortunate you are to have been adopted!"

While all this was true, Ron's heart never quite believed it. All the emphasis on the positive never allowed room for the negative. As a result, the negative was never validated.

Well-Intentioned Statement #4: "You Are Illegitimate."

A word that wounds many is "illegitimate." Some people *still* call us illegitimate and bastards! What a kick in the gut.

Recently I was listening to a well-known preacher talk on the radio about Psalm 139, referred to in the previous chapter, about how God knit us together in our mother's womb and planned every day of our lives before any one of them ever came to be. My heart was so touched

by the way this speaker described the prenatal process.

But then he started calling those children whose mothers had not planned their conceptions "illegitimate." I couldn't believe my ears! I am not the kind of person who writes to radio personalities, but I felt so strongly about this that I did. Little did this man know that the word "illegitimate" translates to many adoptees that we have no right to be alive, that we are mistakes.

He wrote a humble letter of apology.

Well-Intentioned Statement #4: "You Are Special."

Another finger-over-the-blackboard statement claims that we are "special." I believe many adoptive parents intuitively know, even though most of them are not informed, that we are grieving. In perhaps an unconscious attempt to comfort us they may use this phrase. Others who are not educated about how an adoptee thinks and feels may do the same.

Some of us receive the statement with pride and gain a sense of self-worth. However, to many of us it means:

- Others have high expectations of us.
- We must prove our worth by excelling.
- We're not like everyone else in the family . . . we're different.
- Perform!
- Be perfect.
- Conform! Conform! Conform!
- It's not okay to just be ourselves.

Paula Oliver, who through her adoption journey has gained a greater appreciation for God as her loving Abba Father, says that she can remember raising her hand in elementary school and telling everyone that she was adopted. Later on the playground the kids made fun of her by saying stuff like, "Your mom didn't want you so she threw you away." Paula says, "I ran into the school crying and was found by

76

a teacher who told me that being adopted made me special because my parents *chose* me, while most parents are *stuck* with their kids! That was little comfort—it was more like a burden because I didn't *feel* special."

Well-Intentioned Statement #5: "We Love You Just Like Our Own," or, "They Have Two of Their Own and They Adopted One."

Adoptive parents think they are giving us a great compliment with these words, but often they can be like a sword through the heart. When well-meaning parents say, "We love you *just like* you're our own," their child may naturally wonder, *Well, if I'm not their own, whose am I? Where is my real family? Where do I belong?* The parents' statements often translate as "You're *really not* our own. *Almost*, but not completely."

Says one adoptee, "I can't stand it when people differentiate between biological and adopted kids. 'Oh, we have three of our own and then one adopted daughter.'"

Well-Intentioned Statement #6: "You Belong."

Another statement concerns our sense of belonging. Try this simple exercise. Fold your hands together as quickly as you can. Then look. Which thumb is on the top of the fold? Is it your right or left? Let's say, for example, it's your right thumb. Now do exactly the same exercise, at the same speed, but aim at getting your opposite thumb on the top of your fingers. Not as easy as the first time, is it?

Wouldn't you agree that the awkwardness in this simple exercise could be likened to our feelings of not belonging? I can't tell you how many adoptees say in support groups, "I feel like an alien, like I wasn't born. Like I was just dropped down to earth by a stork or something."

Connie Dawson intimates that she's aware of not feeling like she belongs. "I guess I'm a partial belonger," she says. "I was a good 'fitter in-ner' in my adoptive family, in which it was never a topic for discussion. Although I have been warmly received by my birth aunt, I don't really belong there either—at least not the way I imagine other people belong. When I'm visiting her, I feel accepted, but I notice she doesn't throw a family dinner when I visit. One of her nephews (my cousin) will call on the phone and I'm jealous of the endearing and warm teasing they do with one another. I have this persistent feeling of not being entitled to *really* belong, to *really* take a seat at the table, to *really* be heard in a group, to *really* trust myself, to *really* trust others. You probably would be surprised to know this if you observed me in action, but I know I could be so much more."

Richard Curtis says that since he was a total surprise at his reunion, birth relatives gave various degrees of welcoming. He says he deluged them with questions about his birth parents, hungry to learn the details of his heritage. And then he thought to himself, *Now, where does Richard fit into the lives of these people? On the fring*e. "I have this deep need to bond with real blood relatives," he explains, "but I feel like I'm not really a part of either of my families."

Author Corrine Chilstrom, after learning that her eighteen-year-old adopted son committed suicide after leaving home for college, pounded her fist on the kitchen table shouting, "Adoption! These kids never feel like they really belong in this world. Who will ever understand?"[11]

For so many of us, many of the preceding statements and words simply don't line up with what we believe in our heart of hearts is true. Like teenage kids at our first dance, we try so hard to have "good rhythm" with our dancing partners, but instead we seem to step all over their toes. But we can put an end to the awkwardness by making a better choice regarding our mixed feelings.

Our Choice

To claim both our positive and painful emotions as valid and verbalize them. Then, to search for truth.

Ron Hilliard describes our choice beautifully when he says, "As I have learned to accept both the positive as well as the negative, I have had the opportunity to articulate both and can claim my mixed feelings as being valid."

DISCUSSION QUESTIONS FOR
SUPPORT GROUPS OR PERSONAL REFLECTION

1. Do you ever experience mixed feelings? If so, can you describe a time? If not, what is your reaction to the concept of mixed feelings?
2. Do you identify with either of the two symptoms of mixed feelings—a quick startle response or unexplainable anxiety? If so, how? What have you done to cope with these discomforts?
3. After reading the seven well-intentioned statements you might hear from family or friends, did any stand out to you? Which one? Can you remember a time when you heard that statement and how you reacted? If you could do it again, how would you change your reaction?
4. Even if we get to the point of realizing the painful and pleasurable feelings are okay, does it mean they represent truth? Do you think our feelings can mislead us, possibly away from truth and back to old ways of thinking? How might this happen?
5. Write a letter *to* and *from* your birth mother about the broken feelings inside you.

DIGGING DEEPER FOR ANSWERS
TO OUR ADOPTION QUESTIONS

1. Read Psalm 27:10. What does God promise to orphans?
2. A man in the Bible named Job lost his entire family. What impact did this have on his perception of God?
3. How did Job calm himself? See Job 23:10.

Our curiosity about adoption and our beginning might get stirred enough that we want to read about birth parents. We may be asking ourselves why they placed us for adoption. If we could only understand . . . would that help? That's next. Stay tuned.

CHAPTER FIVE

WHY WOULD SOMEONE GIVE UP A CHILD?

The roots of education are bitter, but the fruit is sweet.

— ARISTOTLE

Imagine a sunny Florida beach with a hot and dusty boardwalk leading down to the ocean. You slip on your sandals and walk the length of the boardwalk. As you near the end, you notice several empty pairs of shoes scattered along the boardwalk's edge. Shoes of all sizes, styles, and shapes. Each pair unique. Each bearing the imprint of its owner's feet. Each with a story to tell.

You realize you've never walked in another person's shoes. Never have. Never will. The same is true in adoption. There are three sets of adoption shoes sitting at the end of the boardwalk: the adoptee's, the birth parents', and the adoptive parents'. Each is unique and each has a story to tell.

Like the sunbather realizing he will never wear another person's shoes, we in the adoption triad must respect the fact that we will never completely understand each other's pain or joy. However, through education, we can walk together for a while. By walking side by side instead of apart, we will grow in our capacity to love and be loved. Education enables us to do that.

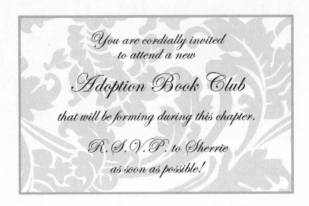

*You are cordially invited
to attend a new*

Adoption Book Club

that will be forming during this chapter.

*R.S.V.P. to Sherrie
as soon as possible!*

Remember when talk-show personality Oprah Winfrey hosted a book club on her daily talk show, motivating millions of people to begin reading thought-provoking literature. She selected the book and challenged her viewers to read it. At the end, she chose six to eight women who had also read and enjoyed the book to join her in her home for a candlelight dinner and a cozy talk about the book.

I'm not Oprah Winfrey, but I *do* have one thing in common with her. I have a love for reading and education and a desire for others to discover the consequent joys and freedom. Books take us outside of ourselves and invite us into the world of another person, or people, where we can learn new viewpoints. We become more developed people who can identify with others who aren't just like us.

Years ago, I would have had no interest in participating in any book club. I was just not a reader. But after going back to college in my midforties to finish my undergraduate degree, I was given an assignment for a creative writing class that required me to weave a few facts around research-based fiction. I knew immediately what my topic would be—adoption. I had the few facts about my adoption and would study the time of my birth and weave fiction around them. I was astounded to find that there was an *entire section* in the university library devoted to the subject of adoption! While sequestered in a reading booth, I'll never forget digging through the archived magazines and research articles, looking for nitty-gritty aspects of life in the 1940s—clothing, cars, food, magazines, and advertisements. Finding this information made it possible for me to dream about what it must have been like during the time when my birth mother carried me.

An interesting phenomenon began as I delved into these books and articles. Thoughts sounded familiar. Emotions rang true. Issues were similar. And much to my astonishment I found *myself* in those pages through the lives of other adoptees! I felt drawn to adoption literature, like a fish to water.

During this chapter, we can have our own little book club. Want to join? Just imagine yourself seated at my dining room table, eating a delicious meal with me and fellow adoptees, talking about our favorite books and why. The people who will be around the table will share their excitement in learning about adoption and also the books that they found most helpful. Their favorite books will give you ideas for when you visit your local library or bookstore.

Renee Mills, a reunited adoptee who was born one week after legislators sealed adoption records, is a great example. Once she started reading, she couldn't stop! She had no idea that so much was written about her *own* life experience. Renee says, "I felt validated because someone *finally* put a name on the lifelong thoughts and feelings I had been unable to verbalize. For once in my life I felt understood and free to be myself!" Her favorite books are *The Primal Wound* by Nancy Verrier and *Lost and Found* by Betty Jean Lifton.

FOUR BENEFITS OF EDUCATING OURSELVES ABOUT ADOPTION

Let's take a look at four reasons why our fellow adoptees are fired up about reading adoption literature. (And keep in mind that when some of them mention my first book, I didn't pay them to do so!)

Benefit #1: "We Might Better Understand Our Adoptive Parents."

I distinctly remember walking the beaches of Destin, Florida, one warm summer day, thinking about my relationship with my adoptive parents. I was in the depths of counseling and examining why a sense of distance existed between my parents and me in my growing-up years. There was an unexplainable sadness that hung over our family, like a dark cloud before a storm.

I subconsciously translated this sadness as disappointment in me even though there was no logical basis for it. My parents would have done anything for me . . . in fact, perhaps too much. Frankly, anything little Sherrie wanted, little Sherrie got. So this unspoken sadness . . . where did it come from?

That day on the beach, after having read a lot about adoption, I realized that my parents had never grieved their many years of infertility. This is a common issue in adoption—an "adoption dynamic." Knowing the era in which they experienced this, with no literature about adoption available, they couldn't have understood this dynamic. They were doing the best they could. How freeing it was for me to learn this! The unresolved sadness in our home wasn't about me . . . it was about them. Knowing this, I was able to love and appreciate them even more, even though both of them had passed away.

One male adoptee says that his parents have so many issues of their own. A therapist has helped him to understand this, along with reading about adoption. They are basically insecure people and this young man has concluded that people who are hurting themselves, no matter how well-intentioned, can't help him.

Benefit #2: "We Know We Are Not Alone."

Remember, we're still around the table. Still talking about adoption dynamics, and someone says, "You felt that way most of your life too?" What do you think they might have been talking about?

Here's a clue: It's one of the secrets we keep well hidden behind our "strong" facades. You guessed it . . . loneliness.

Many of us have carried that secret for years. Even though we may have many acquaintances or friends, we still may feel lonely. This can be equally true of nonadoptees, but I think because of adoptees' "mixed feelings" discussed in chapter 4, it may be a heavier burden for us.

Connie Dawson says she didn't begin to get educated until her husband of twenty-four years and she divorced and she read *Lost and Found* by Betty Jean Lifton. "It was a marvel to find out someone else felt so many of the feelings I did!" Connie says.

Phyllis-Anne Munro, a social worker who has been reunited with both birth parents, says that the books she read helped her know that she was not alone in this journey. Some of the books that have rocked her world are *The Primal Wound* by Nancy Verrier; *Journey of the Adopted Self: A Quest for Wholeness* by Betty Jean Lifton; *The Secret Thoughts of an Adopted Mother* by Jana Wolff; *The Other Mother* by Carol Schaefer; and *I Hope You Have a Good Life* by Campbell Armstrong.

Despite Richard Curtis's concentrated work in dealing with his addictions, the topic of adoption was never discussed with his therapists or in any group setting. The resulting frustration led him to the local library where he located his first adoption-related book — *Being Adopted: The Lifelong Search for Self* by Drs. David Brodzinsky and Marshall Schechter. "I was overwhelmed, finding myself described within the pages of this book. I no longer felt alone," Richard says.

Ron Hilliard began listening to tapes about adoption that gave voice to what he already was feeling. "I began to realize that there were a large number of people who had the same experience as I did. I had always felt alone in my adoption world, and now I discovered that I was no longer alone. I discovered that while each adoptee's experience is unique, there are also common threads among us. The most helpful books were *Twenty Things Adopted Kids Wish Their Adoptive Parents Knew* by Sherrie Eldridge and Ron Nydam's *Adoptees Come of Age*."

Seven-year-old Maggie Backiewicz of Ohio, who enjoys piano,

Girl Scouts, and an open adoption, says that her favorite adoption book is *A Koala for Katie* by Jonathan London and Cynthia Jabar. And why does she like to read it? Because if she forgets, the book reminds her that other kids are adopted too.

Erika Hill lives in Southern California with her family and enjoys reading and taking adventurous trips. She says, "Before I read anything about adoptees, I was alone in a way that I didn't even realize. The more I read, the more astonished I was to find that most of my feelings were common among adoptees. Now I am almost narcissistically drawn to adoption literature. My favorite books are *May the Circle Be Unbroken: An Intimate Journey into the Heart of Adoption* by Lynn C. Franklin with Elizabeth Ferber and *Journey of the Adopted Self* by Betty Jean Lifton."

Lisa Storms echoes the same theme of finding out she was not alone in her feelings about adoption. "Every time I read an adoptee's account of the myriad of emotions [he or she has] dealt with in being adopted, I could totally relate. I stopped feeling 'different' and realized that we share many aspects of our journey."

Sharon McGowan, adopted at six weeks of age and reunited with her birth mother nine years ago, has read all the adoption books she could get her hands on over the years. "I felt like I was alone in my 'issues' and that something was very wrong with me, but after reading the first few books, I understood how adoption contributed to my 'issues' and that I was in good company. I was, in a word, relieved! The first book about adoption I read was *Lost and Found* by Betty Jean Lifton, but I think *The Primal Wound* by Nancy Verrier was one of the best."

Benefit #3: "We Might Feel Compassion for Our Birth Parents."

Another exciting aspect of learning about adoption is that we can walk awhile in the shoes of birth parents. I believe full healing and redemption cannot occur for us as adoptees until we understand how birth parents feel. We first must look at our own pain, but that's only the beginning of the restoration. We need to realize that we weren't the *only* ones who felt rejected or abandoned or who had mixed feelings—many birth parents did too.

"Never in my life did I think about the pain that birth parents go through when they relinquish their babies," Michelle says. "Now, after meeting some birth parents and reading some birth parent stories, I have a better appreciation of their pain. We are all in this together!"

Sandy Garrett says it was truly an eye opener to read the thoughts of birth mothers. She appreciates support groups where she can see firsthand the pain in the eyes of birth mothers. "Now, that was an education for me," says Sandy. "It made me feel like I was that much closer to my birth mother. Now I know that there was a reason behind my adoption. I met a woman who gave up her child and felt pain every single day of her life because of it. It made the people in my life—me, my birth mom, and my adoptive parents—that much more human. My favorite books are *The Primal Wound* by Nancy Verrier; *Twenty Things Adopted Kids Wish Their Adoptive Parents Knew* by Sherrie Eldridge; *When to Forgive* by Mona Gustafson, Ph.D.; and *Reunion: A Year in Letters Between a Birthmother and the Daughter She Couldn't Keep* by Katie Hern and Ellen McGarry Carlson."

Jodi Strathman has educated herself endlessly in the last two years and attended her first American Adoption Congress where she saw all sides of the triad. She's come to understand that while the circumstances in each adoption are different, the emotional repercussions are similar.

Annual conventions of adoption organizations are a great way to educate ourselves. Paige Wilson of California says education was extremely helpful because it gave her a perspective about the adoption triad that she lacked. *The Adoption Triangle: The Effects of the Sealed Records on Adoptees, Birth Parents, and Adoptive Parents* by Arthur Sorosky gave her insight not only into her own behavior but also her birth and adoptive parents'.

"I have always tried to educate myself about adoption even from an early age," says Kim Pittsley. "My favorite book is Hern and Carlson's volume of letters written by birth mothers to the children they placed.

The outpouring of raw emotion and unconditional love in those letters gave me a profound respect for the choices that my birth and adoptive parents made and the strong people that they are."

Benefit #4: "We Might Discover a New Sense of Freedom."

After we find new understanding of our birth and adoptive parents and discover how loneliness need no longer be our emotional reality, a wonderful new sense of freedom comes. We realize that they're struggling people also. Some adoptees benefit from mature, healthy parents, who are able to really listen and hear their children's hearts. The majority of parents, however, don't fall into that category.

Frieda Moore says that she didn't have a clue that there was anything to be educated about concerning her experience of being adopted. But with reading came freedom and she is now very comfortable with who she is. She says that *Twenty Things Adopted Kids Wish Their Adoptive Parents Knew* was a "heart opener" and "hit the nail on the head" in so many ways for her.

Brad says, "Educating myself about adoption through attending adoption support groups made me feel empowered concerning adoption-related conversations, whereas before I was uncomfortable and unable to speak intelligently about my adoption and the feelings associated with being an adoptee."

If you've never educated yourself about the dynamics of adoption, I hope this chapter has whetted your appetite and brought you to the threshold of making another life-enhancing choice for yourself. We can choose to remain where we are in our knowledge about adoption or we can be seekers *and* communicators of truth, looking for every opportunity to educate ourselves and enjoy the freedom that comes with deeper understanding.

Our Choice

To educate ourselves about adoption through reading adoption books, or attending conventions and/or support groups.

DISCUSSION QUESTIONS FOR
SUPPORT GROUPS OR PERSONAL REFLECTION

1. Have you read any adoption books? If so, which books and what are your favorites?
2. Do you believe that adoption struggles are the same for your birth parents and adoptive parents? Do you think it possible that even though the circumstances are different for each person that the emotions are common? Share your thoughts!
3. Write a letter *to* and *from* your birth mother about trying to understand why she placed you for adoption.
4. Review the following resources. Which step will you take to educate yourself about adoption?

ORGANIZATIONS:

NACAC — NATIONAL COUNCIL ON ADOPTABLE CHILDREN
970 Raymond Ave., Ste. 106
St. Paul, MN 55114-1149
1-800-470-6665
www.nacac.org

This organization is a powerful organization, attracting leaders from the adoption field to their yearly conferences. They believe that every child deserves a good home and work tirelessly to help accomplish this goal. Their yearly conventions are my favorite.

JEWEL AMONG JEWELS ADOPTION NETWORK, INC.
This adoption educational organization was cofounded by me and fellow adoptee Jody Moreen and will be revitalized and updated regularly online, with a support group for adopted people only; daily digests, using the archives of newsletters from former years; and coaching tips from me. www.sherrieeldridge .com

MAGAZINES

ADOPTION TODAY
This excellent magazine, published by Richard Fischer, CEO of Louis and Co., offers cutting-edge information about international and transracial adoption. E-mail: louis@adoptinfo.net

ADOPTIVE FAMILIES
Winner of a "Parents' Choice" award, this bimonthly magazine includes articles by Lois Melina, former editor and adoption pioneer. It also features updates on legal trends and book reviews.
1-800-372-3300
Order online: www.adoptivefamilies.com

FAVORITE BOOKS

Boundaries: When to Say YES, When to Say NO: To Take Control of Your Life
Henry Cloud, and Townsend, John
Zondervan, 1992

Destiny and Deliverance: Spiritual Insights from the Life of Moses
Yancey, Lucado, Maxwell, Hayford, Eareckson Tada, Barnett, Boa, Wells
Thomas Nelson, 1998

Esther: A Woman of Strength and Dignity
Charles Swindoll
Word Publishing, 1971

Moses: A Man of Selfless Dedication
Charles Swindoll
Word Publishing, 1999

The Primal Wound: Understanding the Adopted Child
Nancy Verrier
Gateway Press, Inc., 1994
Order by sending $14.95 plus $2.50 handling to:
Nancy Verrier
919 Village Center
Lafayette, CA 94549

The Wounded Healer
Henri J. M. Nouwen
Image Books, 1990

*The Whole Life Adoption Book: Realistic Advice for Building a
    Healthy Adoptive Family*
Jayne E. Schooler
NavPress, 2008

Helpful Links

ADOPTIONINSTITUTE.ORG. This organization, headed by
Adam Pertman, is always providing cutting-edge research. It will
lead you to other reputable research sites.

RAINBOWKIDS.COM. Incredible resources, filled with topics
of interest to anyone in the adoption triad.

TAPESTRYBOOKS.COM. The best place to find adoption
books! Adoption experts are featured on this site also.

MEIMAGAZINE.COM. A bimonthly online magazine with
special emphasis on topics related to those adopted from China;
ages seven and up.

CHOSENINTERNATIONAL.ORG. A biblically based organization, providing online resources, teen camps, and yearly conventions.

DIGGING DEEPER FOR ANSWERS TO OUR ADOPTION QUESTIONS

1. We're all on a quest for truth. Do you believe it is possible to know absolute truth?
2. Where can absolute truth be found? Look up John 14:6. Write your reactions to this statement by Jesus.
3. If Jesus is the Truth, what does this mean for your life?

Another hurdle for many of us is trust. Let's talk about that next.

CHAPTER SIX

WHY DOESN'T ANYONE "GET IT"?

But if I go to the east, he is not there;

If I go to the west, I do not find him . . .

But he knows the way that I take;

When he has tested me,

I will come forth as gold.

— JOB

Have you ever spilled your guts about an adoption-related issue to someone and had that person look at you like you just stepped off a spaceship? It could be a friend, a spouse, an in-law, a colleague, a parent, a therapist, or a physician.

We *try, try, try* to inspire understanding, but more often than not our basic need for connection isn't met. Adoption experts Drs. David Brodzinsky and Marshall Schechter say that adoptees have "a driven need for human connectedness. This craving grows with time, experienced subjectively by some adoptees as equivalent to starvation."[1]

We *need* to connect with others about our experience but it's like we're speaking a different language. It reminds me of a time years ago when my husband's family hosted a German foreign-exchange student. Upon arrival he couldn't speak a word of English. They did various things to help him understand—hand motions, charades, talking louder, then louder . . . but nothing worked.

It's often the same with us, isn't it, when we're trying to communicate our feelings about adoption? We're often misunderstood.

The Synonym Finder tells us that to misunderstand is to "misapprehend, misread, misjudge, miscalculate, miscount, misreckon, read it wrong, get it all wrong, get a false impression, miss the point, see through a glass darkly."[2] To be misunderstood is a disconcerting experience for anyone, but for adoptees it can be particularly excruciating.

Many wounds in life are easy to name. "My mother died when I was five." "I was sexually abused by my brother." "I became a widow a few months ago." But for the majority of us adoptees, our trauma occurred soon after birth when we didn't have the ability to describe our wounds. We had only sensations and feelings.

I believe that our ability to communicate the feelings associated with that trauma remains at an infant stage and when we get too close to pain, tears or anger often come easier than words. We may want to curl up in a fetal position and die, pack our bags and run away, or scream at the top of our lungs in utter frustration. We just don't know what to do with ourselves, let alone communicate what is bothering us to someone else.

Martha says she has adoptive parents and friends who are supportive, but do they "get it"? No! Compounding the problem is that she doesn't "get it" either. She believes her friends might understand more if she could find the words to express it better.

Sandra Garrett, who has been reunited with her birth mom for two years, appreciates her husband's attempts to communicate understanding but the reality is that she feels constantly misunderstood. "Plain and simple," she says, "he just doesn't get it."

Kim Norman, happily married mother of two who has been searching for her birth mother for four years in New York, says that once she was waiting for the results of a court order to open her records in another state. Kim asked everyone she knew to say a little prayer for her and the response was either silence or dismay at why she would be so "overly concerned" about such an "insignificant" matter.

Paula Oliver remembers when she first bared her heart about the thing we all struggle with—fear of rejection from our birth parents. Paula has met hers, yet when she verbalized this fear with what she considered good friends, they put a Band-Aid over her wound with a platitude: "I'm sure they did it because they thought it was the best thing for you."

Ouch!

WISE UP!

Imagine a world where all the people who care about us read every adoption book they could get their hands on. Everyone would ooze with empathy and understanding and we would feel connected as never before. Wouldn't that be wonderful?

Only in our dreams, I'm afraid! The majority of people we know are *not* going to become book hounds on adoption-related matters. And so, what's the answer? Do we *continue* in our feelings of frustration, hurt, disappointment, and disillusionment? Do we isolate ourselves further from well-meaning friends and family members who are only trying to help?

Of course not! Why? Because there is a *better* way. While we may not want to take on the responsibility of educating others, deeper connections can occur *indirectly* as we learn a new method for taking back our power when misunderstood. This method called W-I-S-E Up!* was developed by Marilyn Schoettle, MA, of C.A.S.E. (Center for Adoption Support and Education, Inc.) located in Silver Spring, Maryland. It is designed for children and teens, but I believe it can be equally effective for adults. I've used it myself and it works.

The W-I-S-E Up!* method is taught through the use of the

acronym W.I.S.E. Here's what each letter stands for:

W — WALK AWAY
I — IT'S PRIVATE
S — SHARE
E — EDUCATE[3]

Each option is a way we can first take care of ourselves when misunderstood and *inadvertently* teach others at the same time.

While this is not a guarantee that others will understand or *want* to understand, it *is* a guarantee that by becoming proactive instead of passive when well-intentioned, ignorant, insensitive, or crass remarks come our way, we will slowly regain a sense of control in our lives.

WALK AWAY

The first choice involves the big **W**. We can simply walk away when others misunderstand.

How many of us ever think about options when misunderstood? If you're anything like me, I get so caught up in anger or hurt that the thought of an option never enters my mind (uh-oh . . . there's that victim mentality again).

But now that we *know* we have options, we can take a deep breath and think, "W, W, W, W, W, W!" The "**W**alk away" option provides maximum self-care and communicates a strong message to the sender: "Your remarks were inappropriate and hurtful."

The kids in Brad's class teased, "You don't have any *real* parents. You don't even know who your parents are." According to the acronym, which of the four options should Brad choose?

If I were Brad, I would definitely choose **W** — especially if he was feeling vulnerable at the time.

Cheri Freeman describes a "walk-away time" in her life: "Once I asked my husband's family for their cooperation in writing a book about their collective adoptive experiences. One sister stood up and pretty much told me that if I thought *their* story was worth telling, I couldn't be much of a writer."

Phyllis-Anne Munro describes a "tune-up visit" to what she termed her "treasured therapist of many years." She made an appointment to read a letter she was about to send to her birth mother. In an unexpected turn of events, the therapist proceeded to read her the riot act by saying that even "normal birth families" don't sit around and discuss aunts and uncles or cancer and diabetes. Phyllis-Anne says, "I felt belittled and invalidated. Then I felt really angry! It was disheartening and I have not sought her out again."

Good for Phyllis-Anne! She took her power back and educated her once-sensitive therapist in the process.

See how powerful the choice to walk away can be? Victim thinking and behavior dies and healthy self-care begins.

KEEP IT PRIVATE

The second option—It's Private—also provides protection, yet communicates and educates. A time that we might choose to say "It's Private" is when relatives or friends learn that we're initiating a search for birth relatives. Someone may say, "Why would you want to do *that*?" Or, "Why would you want to open *that* can of worms?"

What can we do? We can simply smile and say, "It's Private. I really don't feel like talking about it right now."

Another example would be concerning those who were adopted at an older age because of serious parental neglect or abuse. "Isn't it wonderful that you have a new family?" someone may say. The adoptee's response could be: "That's a Private subject."

SHARE

The third letter in the acronym, S, stands for "**S**hare." This begins the opening-up process in which we let others hear our feelings and beliefs on a limited basis.

Richard Curtis might have chosen **S**hare in the following situation: "The people who seem to least understand how my relinquishment and adoption have affected me are my adult children. At one point, I eagerly awaited the opportunity to relate new information about my birth family. I'll never forget the looks on their faces when I explained the results of my search and showed them pictures of my birth father. They asked a few questions, were surprised about our Italian background, but showed no further enthusiasm."

Richard says he felt like he'd been slapped in the face. Using the W-I-S-E Up!* method, he might **S**hare with his grown, apathetic children, "Someday I know that your kids are going to want to know about their family history, so I'm going to write it down and preserve it for them and future generations."

When Sandy told her husband that she was going to search for her birth mother, her husband pooh-poohed the idea, asking why she would want to search for another mother—she already had one and that should be good enough.

Okay, Sandy . . . choose **S**! "I have always felt like there is a missing piece of the puzzle in my life. It's very important for me to find that piece through searching."

Even though she has since been reunited with her birth mother, her husband *still* asks her on a regular basis why she wants to go to her adoption support group. **S** again, Sandy! "I need to be with other adoptees and hear their experiences. It helps me stay in touch with my own feelings."

We're getting more and more empowered!

EDUCATE

E for "Educate"—the last letter of the acronym—involves risk but pays great dividends. Here we educate, but only when we are strong, both emotionally and spiritually.

Sharon McGowan says her closest friends either got defensive, insisting that she shouldn't be dwelling on her adoptee status, or dismissive, telling her not to "play the victim." "And these are people who love me!" Sharon says with dismay.

Sharon might seize this opportunity to educate her judgmental friends by saying, "Did you know that adoption experts say that adoptees *are* victims of the gravest kind? We had those initial bonds of trust broken at birth."

Sharon also says that her birth mother incessantly apologizes or takes herself on a guilt trip by saying things like, "I know all of your problems are my fault." In response to her guilt-ridden birth mother, Sharon could educate: "Did you know that many birth mothers feel the same way as you? Placing a child for adoption is one of the most agonizing decisions a woman ever can make. There is a wonderful book that could help you get rid of that guilt; it's called *The Other Mother*, by Carol Schaefer. There's probably a copy at the library."

Leaders in organizations can also be educated. For instance, if our place of worship is having a baby dedication or baptism ceremony and one of the babies is labeled in the bulletin or singled out in the ceremony as "the adopted son of _____," we can educate the secretary and clergy by explaining, "Adopted kids don't like to be singled out or labeled. It makes them feel weird and different. Even though the baby being dedicated or baptized won't realize he's being labeled, older adopted kids in the audience might."

Wising up as adoptees involves practicing new ways of responding to the misunderstandings of others about our adoption experiences. It's educational to others, but not at our expense. Instead of our adoptee fantasy of our loved ones delving into adoption books, *we* become the books they read!

I am reminded of a story about the famous pianist Ignace Paderewski, who was scheduled to perform at a black-tie affair at a great concert hall. Present in the audience was a mother and her fidgety nine-year-old son, who was brought against his wishes in hopes that he would be inspired to practice more.

Before the performance, when the mother turned to talk to friends, the boy slipped out of his seat, walked onstage to the Steinway piano, and began playing "Chopsticks." The crowd was extremely irritated and various people yelled, "Get that boy away from there! Who'd bring a kid *that* young in here? Where's his mother? Somebody stop him."

Backstage the master overheard the sounds, figured out what was happening, grabbed his coat, and rushed onto the stage. Without a word, he stooped over behind the boy and reached around both sides, improvising a countermelody to harmonize and enhance "Chopsticks." And as he did, he whispered in the boy's ears, "Don't quit, son! Keep going. Keep on playing."[4]

Sometimes we are like the boy on the stage of our lives being booed by insensitive people around us who "just don't get it" and who tire of our talk about adoption. But I have found that if we just keep practicing, even if we can only play "Chopsticks," the Master will hurry onstage, bend over us, play a countermelody, and say to us, "Don't quit! Keep on going. Keep on trying."

Our Choice

To be proactive instead of passive when others misunderstand or mistreat us. We can focus on God's care and love for us as orphans.

We don't have to be sitting ducks, or dupes, any longer! We can regain our power and ease the pain of misunderstanding by making better choices.

Isn't this acronym a wonderful tool?

We've covered a lot of territory in this chapter, so let's make sure the information we gleaned gets appropriated.

DISCUSSION QUESTIONS FOR
SUPPORT GROUPS OR PERSONAL REFLECTION

1. Do you ever perceive that others, even those who love you the most, don't "get it" when it comes to understanding your feelings about adoption? Share one incident when you felt misunderstood and how you handled it. Would you do it differently next time?

2. Look at the WISE-UP Method. Which of the four options for making healthy choices and setting good boundaries applies to a situation in your life right now? Tell about the situation and the insights you have for facing it.

3. Write a letter *to* and *from* your birth mother about feeling misunderstood.

DIGGING DEEPER FOR ANSWERS
TO OUR ADOPTION QUESTIONS

1. Friends, we have special needs or emotional vulnerabilities because of the loss of our first family. Learning those vulnerabilities takes us a long way in understanding and accepting how God made us. Then, we can let misunderstandings roll off, like water off a duck's back. Here are our special needs from a biblical perspective:

   • We need to be taught that our life narratives began in eternity past in the heart of God—that he created us to have a relationship with him as his child.

   • We need to understand that adoption is both pleasurable and painful, presenting lifelong challenges and opportunities for growth.

   • We need to know our adoption and birth stories.

   • We need to know all possible information about our first family.

   • We need to be taught that we have deeper needs for emotional and spiritual support and not feel guilty for finding a good support system.

- We need to give ourselves permission to express all our adoption fantasies and feelings.
- We need help in learning how to deal with fears of rejection.
- We need to be prepared for mean things others might say about us as adopted people and about adoption itself.
- We need to be acquainted with fellow adoptees.
- We need to be assured that there is a time for everything. A time to search for birth history and family and a time to give up searching (Ecclesiastes 3).
- We need to accept the fact that some of our adoption questions will never be answered this side of heaven. God holds all the answers in his loving hands and if he wants us to know something, it will be nothing for him to make it known to us (Deuteronomy 29:29).

Just as we need to be W.I.S.E. in dealing with misunderstanding, we also need to learn to whom we can bare our hearts. Who is "safe"? We'll talk about that in detail in the following chapter.

WHY CAN'T WE TRUST
ANYONE BUT OURSELVES?

Do not give dogs what is sacred; do not throw your pearls to pigs. If you do, they may trample them under their feet, and then turn and tear you to pieces.

— JESUS

I remember when we moved from Michigan to Indianapolis and I was hurting, big time. When I went in for "Christian" counseling, the counselor showed me a chart that he claimed was the answer to all my problems. He didn't listen to my feelings but tried to get me to change according to the chart. Being the good little adoptee, I did the best I could, but I was still hurting.

After making some progress, I applied to be an intern in his ministry. He said that I would have to be interviewed first, which the secretary told me was something he didn't require of any other interns. Upon learning this, I feared he was going to "let me down easy" during the interview and say no.

At the interview, I was so terrified that he was going to reject me that I just rambled. His response was to go down a list of behaviors that were not characteristic of someone who was living according to *his* chart. He showed me the items, reading them one at a time and checking every one of them off, saying they described me. It felt like I was being whipped with every new charge he made.

He never got back to me with a decision. I remember walking to the mailbox every day looking for a letter from him, but it never came. That was the time in my life when I was in my "victim mode," so I never followed up with phone calls. The whole experience activated my primal pain of being rejected and not knowing the reason why.

My lack of vocational direction coupled with the move sent me into my first clinical depression. The psychiatrist who evaluated me suggested medication. Bob called the "chart" counselor for advice and he said that taking medicine for depression was sin. I took it anyway.

I remember when the psychiatrist in the hospital asked me what was bothering me, I didn't tell him anything about how the counselor had hurt me — after all, that wouldn't be the "Christian" thing to do. But looking back, I know without a doubt that the counselor was not a "safe" person. He was spiritually abusing me and misrepresenting the God that I love. God never condemns or makes me feel like *everything* I am doing is wrong. Instead, when I'm in a growth process, he gently points out one thing at a time for me to work on. I love the verse in the Bible that says, "God didn't go to all the trouble of sending his Son merely to point an accusing finger, telling the world how bad it was. He came to help, to put the world right again."[1]

Reflecting on that experience has led me to examine various aspects of safety in relationships. What is safety? Who are safe people? How can we recognize them and subsequently develop rewarding friendships with them?

WHY TRUST CAN BE DIFFICULT FOR US

Before we discuss these questions, we need to examine two dilemmas that often keep us from finding safe people and developing healthy relationships.

We Often Trust Only Ourselves

Drs. David Brodzinsky and Marshall Schechter say that the foundation for feeling safe depends on our ability to trust. "Trust allows an infant to feel he can depend on his own behavior as well as that of his caregivers. Without trust, he may grow up doubting his own self-worth, and doubting the motives of everyone he meets."[2]

Ahh . . . trust. The commodity we long for but few of us possess! Reflecting on Brodzinsky and Schechter's comments about the need for trust both in self *and* caregivers, do you think it possible that one half of the equation—learning to trust others—could be missing from our personal trust equations? Do you suppose it's possible that when we were separated from our initial and most intimate caregiver at birth, our infant psyches determined that caretakers couldn't be trusted and that we must rely only on ourselves?

Sharon tests everyone in her life all the time, to prove to herself whether or not they can be trusted. The tests are never fair and she doesn't tell people they are being tested. When they fail, she is secretly glad because it proves her theory that no one can really care for her.

And what is the result of not learning to trust others? This brings us to our second dilemma.

We May Be Stuck Emotionally

Erik Erikson, a German-born American psychoanalyst, was abandoned by his father before birth. Interestingly enough, some say he was almost obsessed with his theory of development (is it any wonder?), which postulates eight stages of development each characterized by a crisis that needs to be resolved. Here's how it works.

At the point of crisis the child is faced with a choice between coping in an adaptive or maladaptive way. Only as each crisis is resolved, which involves an evolution in personality, does the person have the strength to deal with the next stage of development. If a person does not resolve the conflict, he or she will confront and struggle with it later in life.[3] In other words, if we don't get it the first time around, we must go back and learn it.

Some of us already possess trust or may have revisited and resolved the conflict, but others may still have to face it someday. Crystal says she has always had a nagging suspicion that everyone in the world has something in them that makes them able to understand each other, to know what is *really* going on in relationships, and to give and receive love. "I have imagined that I don't have these abilities because I am adopted and missed the developmental stage where most people get blessed with these gifts."

If we never came through this crisis of trust as infants, do you think that means we will remain infants emotionally for the rest of our lives? Do we have to stay stuck?

Absolutely not! Why? Because trust can be *learned*. If we haven't learned it from our initial caregiver (our birth mother) or adoptive parents, we can learn it from others who have successfully passed through that stage of development and moved on toward maturity.

WE CAN LEARN TO TRUST

Authors and professors of psychiatry Malcolm L. West and Adrienne E. Sheldon-Keller say, "The securely attached adult can acknowledge felt distress in a modulated way and turn to supportive and trusted relationships for comfort. Particularly during periods of emotional upset, comfort often needs to be expressed in concrete attachment behaviors that reassure the individual. Put simply, felt security at these times has a lot to do with having someone available who will respond to our feelings and even take supportive action. The special warmth that often accompanies attachment comes just from these tangible reassurances that one is understood."[4]

Now let's translate this into adoptee terms and see how trust can be developed for adopted individuals.

Through a No-Risk Confidante

Connie Dawson has a rewarding trust relationship. She says, "I don't share deep feelings with anyone unless I deem them to be a no-risk confidante. I can talk with other adoptees about adoption issues, but only to a point. If I want to go to a newly discovered place in myself that is related to adoption, I test out whether the other person can go there too. I am fortunate to have a fellow-traveler adoptee for a close friend. I've told him, with tears in my eyes, that I can tell him things I haven't told anyone else—because he is willing to plumb his depths too. In my experience, this is a very rare experience. We have an intimate relationship of a precious kind."

In Clinical Settings

The term "transference" is a clinical term and refers to the unconscious transfer of experience from one interpersonal context to another. In transference, we relive past relationships in current situations. They are repeated over and over, and this can be especially true when we are in counseling. For example, we might unconsciously view our therapist as our father or mother and act accordingly. If we had a poor relationship with our fathers or mothers, we can work through those negative feelings with the right therapist and thus establish trust.

The late Dirck Brown, EdD, founder and first executive director for Post Adoption Center for Education and Research (PACER), former board member of the International Soundex Reunion Registry, former president of the American Adoption Congress, and author of *Clinical Practice in Adoption,* said, "I spent about four years in analysis and let me tell you, transference is a wonderful experience—I've seldom felt closer to anyone in my life than my analyst, John."

Through Friendships

I have learned trust through my friend and colleague, Vicky Rockwell. We met at a women's support group and the moment I saw her, I knew I would love her. She was dressed with western-style boot shoes and I thought it so neat that she had the freedom to express who she really is through her choice of clothes. I longed for the freedom to be myself.

We were in this group for about two years and one time when I was extremely depressed and was supposed to be getting ready for Bob to host his entire staff for dinner at our house, I was overwhelmed. I wept as I told the group how I was feeling, and you know what Vicky did? She came over to help me.

She and I live very different lifestyles, but we love each other just as we are. We are no longer in the group but our friendship has continued for more than ten years. Just yesterday we were talking about the mystery and joy of our relationship, and Vicky observed, "You know, trust is a delicate gift we far too often give when it's not deserved. When we do this, we inevitably get burned, and this restarts the cycle of not being able to trust. Our friendship is unique but not at all surprising. God has taken each of us along very different paths but he has brought us to the same place: his safe presence. I think trust is recognition of the familiar — knowing that we are truly a part of One."

With Wise Mentors

We can also feel safe with the older and wiser men and women who can mentor us.

Irma Forsyth has been my mentor since I was twenty-seven years old. I met her when I attended a women's meeting at church and she talked about Psalm 139. It was at that point that I began to tie in my adoption with the God I didn't know, and to realize that he had been intimately connected to me even before I was conceived in my birth mother's womb. I started to hope that he loved me and might even have a purpose for my life here on earth. Irma and I reminisce about this often and she says, "It was such a joy for me to see that glimmer of faith born in you that day."

At Your Place of Worship

I believe it is also possible to feel incredibly safe in the midst of a group of people. For me, it is the church. Whenever I walk into the church Bob and I have attended for several years, there is a "hello" from someone, a prayer from another, an assuring smile from another. I know I am loved there and feel a little like a newborn baby wrapped up snugly in the arms of my heavenly Father. If I don't attend church on Sunday, I don't feel guilty. That would be legalism. Instead, I know I have missed out on something wonderful.

Through a Personal Relationship with God

Even though there are many religions represented among us, I'd like to share my faith story with you.

Thirty years ago, my husband and I, wanting to be the best parents possible for our two young daughters, started attending church.

The next summer I was invited to be a vacation Bible school helper —a helper, not a leader. One day the teacher asked if I would find a Scripture for her to read to the children. At that point in time, the only thing I knew about the Bible was a little verse I learned as a child: "Matthew, Mark, Luke, and John. Hold your horse while I get on."

Unfortunately, the verse wasn't in any of these books, and even if it were, I wouldn't have been able to find it.

Totally embarrassed, the teacher came to my rescue, and after class she pulled me aside. "Sherrie," she said, "you really ought to go to this Bible study class with me in the fall. It has literally changed my life!"

I smiled compliantly, but was saying to myself, "Lady, you have *got* to be kidding! Me, a with-it, young mother, go to a *stuffy* Bible study? That is the last thing in the world I would ever do."

As we parted ways, I assumed that would be the last I would hear about it. However, this woman had perseverance with a capital "P"! She wouldn't leave me alone.

In the fall, I agreed to go, just to get her off my back. I took my two-year-old daughter, Chrissie, with me because she said they had a children's program. After taking Chrissie to her class, I walked into a church packed with hundreds of women. Up front was a teacher that was saying it was possible to have a personal relationship with God through Jesus Christ.

That did it!

"These women are weird," I said to myself, determining *never* to enter that place again.

Later over lunch, Chrissie told about the children's story she heard, and then with wide eyes, she asked, "Mommy, who is Jesus, anyway?"

I took a deep breath. "Let's see . . . I know they talk about him a lot in church and I know his picture is up on the Sunday school room wall . . ."

I didn't know.

I admitted my ignorance to my daughter and told her that we would go back to Bible study and find out the answer to her question.

As the weeks rolled by, I began to see applications to my life from Scripture.

A year later I faced major surgery and was petrified. I took my brand-new Bible with me to the hospital and happened to turn to Romans 5:3-5: "We also rejoice in . . . sufferings, because we know that suffering produces perseverance; perseverance, character; and character, hope. And hope doesn't disappoint us because God has poured his love into our hearts by the Holy Spirit."

I knew I was suffering. I knew I needed hope. And I knew I needed the Holy Spirit to pour God's love into my heart. On that scary night, when I was at the absolute end of my resources, I prayed, "Jesus, even though you died for me, I haven't wanted you. Please come into my heart. Cleanse me, fill me, and let me be your child. I give the control of my life to you."

Even though extremely painful things have occurred in my life since then, God's grace poured into my heart on that day and every day of my life is more than sufficient for being comforted and finding strength and wisdom for each day.

Even though I have several safe people in my life, inevitably one of them will let me down. They're imperfect human beings, as am I.

My psychiatrist of twelve years, who is one of my safe people, forgot to return a call recently. All my adoptee "stuff" kicked into action. I was sure that I was being a bother, too much to handle, and therefore worthy only of rejection.

In my distress I fell to my knees, realizing that God, the Great Physician, is the only one who will never leave me or abandon me and that he is the only one who can meet all my needs. I will have to say good-bye to all the safe people in my life sooner or later, but not to Jesus. I will always belong to him.

As we gather safe people, God gives us a glimpse of himself through them. In his book *When There Is No Miracle*, Robert Wise wrote about hearing a man named Cecil Henson tell his "death story." In 1940, Cecil was pronounced dead for twenty to thirty minutes. After his resuscitation and recovery he says that during his "twilight" time, he looked fully into the face of Jesus. He described it as a marvelous mosaic made up of a hundred small facets. Each piece added a shade or line to the total picture. So, in looking into this composite face he could see the countenance of Christ. He came to the startling realization that the mosaic pieces were not tile, metal, or glass. Each small section was a cameo of someone he knew who had loved him during his life.[5]

Ultimately our healing comes from God, but I believe he uses safe people to show us what he is like.

RISK BUT BE CAREFUL

We adoptees are learning to trust because we have attached ourselves to trustworthy people and to God. Sad to say, however, not *all* people are trustworthy and we need to always keep that in mind. Trust is not something we ought to dole out like ice cream on a hot summer day to anyone who comes along. Yet because many of us have emotional vulnerabilities and such a deep need for connection, we sometimes throw all caution to the wind and launch into relationships that tear down instead of build up.

Author Lillian Glass, PhD, describes the results of a relationship with such a person. She says, "A toxic person is someone who seeks to destroy you. A toxic person robs you of your self-esteem and dignity and poisons the essence of who you are. He or she wears down your resistance and thus can make you mentally or physically ill. Toxic people are not life-supporting. They see only the negative in you. Jealous and envious, they are not happy to see you succeed. In fact, they get hostile whenever you do well. Their insecurities and feelings of inadequacy often cause them to sabotage your efforts to lead a happy and productive life."[6]

After we've been burned a few times by toxic relationships, we long for the wisdom and courage to listen to the signals of our bodies and souls. However, more times than we care to remember, we don't recognize or heed the warning signs and find ourselves in relationships with emotionally unhealthy people, in undesirable circumstances, or in commitments for which we have neither the time nor the energy.

Can you pinpoint toxic relationships with anyone in your past or present? Jenny sure can. She said she had this "friend" who continually pointed out what she thought were Jenny's shortcomings, one of which was an eagerness to get her nonidentifying information. The person judged this to be impatience on Jenny's part, simply a wild goose chase to figure out her identity. Jenny says, "Maybe it was, but she was *judging* me and playing psychoanalyst. When I finally found my birth mother and had a successful experience, she became jealous and told me so in a voice filled with self-pity. Being with her was a little like rubbing up against a porcupine. She was always prickly and I ended up hurt."

Cheri Freeman says that after her birth mother's rejection, she was really struggling with anger toward God. She sent a list of questions to her brother-in-law who is a pastor and adoptive father, thinking he would understand, but all he did was brush her off. Definitely not a safe person, even though he was a "man of the cloth."

Some of us also become enmeshed in toxic situations and relationships when we share too much too soon. We don't put out the necessary "feelers" or "testers" to see how the other person will react to private information. We dive in the deep end of the pool when we haven't taken beginning swimming lessons.

Richard Curtis describes such an experience. He says, "About a year after my reunion with my siblings in Cleveland I was visiting my two half sisters. While waiting for dinner to be prepared I had an opportunity to spend some time with the middle sister with whom I hadn't had much communication. She asked several questions about my growing-up years as well as my adult life.

"Feeling more comfortable with her, I proceeded to reveal personal stories about my experiences in my adoptive home, my broken relationships with spouses, recovery from addictions, and strained relationships with my own children.

"She became silent, explaining that my behavior was much like her ex-husband's, with whom she has a volatile relationship.

"Oh-oh, Richard, I said to myself. Too much sharing!

"Since that conversation I've sensed a coolness, a backing away, a judgmental, rejecting attitude toward me. I continue to correspond only with my other sister who has accepted me unconditionally."

Richard and Cheri's painful experiences underscore the truth that trust *must* be earned.

THREE WAYS WE CAN FIND SAFE PEOPLE

Wouldn't it be nice if every safe, trustworthy person wore a sign on his or her back that said so? That might qualify as an adoptee fantasy of the highest order! However, there *are* certain characteristics that define safe people, and once we learn them we're much more likely to make wise decisions regarding with whom we share our deepest selves.

They Aren't Dominating and Require a Two-Dimensional Relationship

If we're growing out of the victim mindset and becoming healthier, we can't stand to be in any kind of conversation or relationship in which one person dominates. After the conversation is over, we feel like we've been bound, gagged, and shoved in a corner.

That's far from the kind of relationship we're looking for. There has to be a natural give and take, kind of like playing a graceful game of tennis. One shares and then the other responds in a continual, flowing manner.

A key to this kind of relationship is what David Augsburger calls "equal hearing."

Equal Hearing

I will claim
my right
to be
equally heard.
If I yield
my right to speak,
if I do not claim my time for sharing,
if I do not express what I want in equality,
I am squandering
my privilege of
personhood.
I will respect
your right
to be
equally heard.
You are you.
I want

to hear you.
If I usurp
your right to speak,
if I use up
your time for conversing,
if I do not listen
for what you want in
equality,
I am stifling
your privilege of personhood.[7]

If we've located someone who's not a dominator, but equally as interested in us as he is in himself, we can look for the second characteristic, which is a nonjudgmental attitude.

They're Not Judgmental

Don't you hate having someone point his or her long, bony finger at you and tell you what you should or shouldn't be doing? In my opinion, this is nothing short of playing God.

We are all of equal worth to God. After all, Jesus, God himself, loved us so much that he became man and took the penalty for our sin when he died on the cross. He wanted a relationship with us that much! In our relationships with one another, we are on a horizontal playing field. One of the most effective ways I can spot people who judge are those who give unsolicited advice or counsel. Yes, they may be well-intentioned and even knowledgeable. However, unsolicited counsel is nothing more than a glorified put-down.

Augsburger created a diagram about relationships that I have made myself accountable to for years, and it has literally changed my life. It has helped me sidestep the judgers as well as keep my own attitudes and behavior on track. Notice as you review the diagram that "talking with" is the correct way of relating to others.

Talking down

Blaming

Scolding

Judging

Belittling

Instructing

Supervising

Equal		**Mutual**
give and	**Talking with**	hearing and
take		being heard

Yielding

Ingratiating

Groveling

Apologizing

Placating

Talking up[8]

Once we've weeded out judgmental, self-appointed counselors from our lives, we can put out feelers by observing the reactions of others to our words and feelings. Safe people desire to build up, to reassure us that they care enough about us to invest something of themselves in our lives.

How? Through words and actions.

They Build Up Through Words and Actions

Here are some attitudes and actions of people who build up:

- They accept us as we are—they don't try to "fix" us.
- They recognize our potential.

- They believe in us and tell us so.
- They encourage us to "aim high."
- They assure us that they will always be there for us.
- They seek to neutralize our fears.
- They make us laugh.
- They lovingly and humbly tell us the truth, and they admit their own mistakes readily.
- They give us the freedom to screw up and make mistakes . . . to be human.
- They point us to God and tell us how to know and trust him.

These basic characteristics are "givens" in finding safe people. Being in their presence is like being in the hollow of a tree—we are safe from the storms of life and safe to tell it as it is.

As we apply what we've learned in this chapter to our lives, we will gradually gain the ability to identity safe people and then develop relationships with them.

Our Choice

To begin searching for safe people and for God, to put out feelers, and take a risk.

We must guard our hearts through discernment and simultaneously learn the art of gradual self-disclosure. We need to find a healthy balance between the two.

DISCUSSION QUESTIONS FOR
SUPPORT GROUPS OR PERSONAL REFLECTION

1. Describe a time when you shared too many details with someone who wasn't trustworthy. How did he or she react? How did you feel? How would you reframe it next time?
2. What are some good feelers for adopted people (tests to see if others are safe)? Which statement would you put out as a feeler to see if this person is "safe" for talking about adoption?

- "I have a unique life story."
- "I had interesting beginnings."
- "I was adopted as a child."
- "I was adopted as an older child and I'm hurting so bad."
- Other.

3. Based on the statements above, which of the following indicate a safe person? Why?
   - "Oh, well, we *all* have unique life stories."
   - "Pass the peanut butter, please."
   - "Excuse me, I've got to talk to that person over there."
   - "A unique story, eh?"
   - "I'd love to hear about your story. Would you like to tell me more?"

4. What stood out to you from the indicators of safe people?
   - They're nonjudgmental.
   - They want a two-way relationship.
   - They build us up through truth-based relationships.
   - They want equal hearing.

5. What happens if a relationship is not two-dimensional? Brainstorm some words and phrases. Here's a few to get you started:
   - We become resentful.
   - We enter or continue an unhealthy relationship.
   - We listen constantly while the other person talks. He or she doesn't know our story or listen when we try to share.
   - Other.

6. Write a letter *to* and *from* your birth mother about trust.

Digging Deeper for Answers to Our Adoption Questions

1. On a scale of 1–10, how would you rate your willingness to trust others (10 is the best)? Now, listen to why we might want to consider trusting God. Listen to "The Awesome Legacy of the

Orphan." Underline your favorite promises and for a hard copy of the promises, along with a photo, go to www.sherrieeldridge.com and look in the newsletter archives:

- He does what is necessary to preserve the orphan's life. (Jeremiah 49:11)
- He gladdens the orphan's heart with the bounty of Providence. (Deuteronomy 24:19, farmers were to only glean fields once and leave the rest.)
- He feeds them from the "sacred portion." (Deuteronomy 24:19-21)
- He defends the cause of the fatherless, giving food and clothing. (Deuteronomy 10:18; Isaiah 1:17)
- He hears even the faintest of cries from the orphan. (Exodus 22:22-24)
- He becomes a Father to them. (Psalm 68:5)
- He rescues when the orphan cries for help. (Job 29:12)
- He considers helping orphans an unblemished act of worship. (James 1:27)
- He provides what the orphan is searching for: love, pity, and mercy. (Hosea 14:3)
- He blesses those who provide for the orphan. (Deuteronomy 14:29)
- He has a unique plan for the orphan in history. (Esther 2:15)
- He strongly warns judges who issue unrighteous decrees and the magistrates who cause oppressive decisions against the orphan. (Isaiah 10:2; Malachi 3:5)
- He is pleased when nations and people treat the orphan justly. (Jeremiah 5:28)
- He will draw nigh and be a swift witness against oppressors of the fatherless. (Isaiah 10:2)
- He commands others not to remove "the ancient boundary stone" (could this be their biological history?) or encroach on the fields of the fatherless. (Proverbs 23:10)

Once we've tasted and enjoyed friendships with healthy people and seen a glimpse of God's provision for us as orphans, we may look back at old relationships and see how they have fallen short. This may stir up anger, and we'll talk about that next. Oh . . . that adoptee anger! Watch out!

CHAPTER EIGHT

WHY DO WE GET SO ANGRY WITH OUR MOMS?

Anyone can become angry — that is easy, but to be angry with the right person, to the right degree, at the right time, for the right purpose, and in the right way — this is not easy.

— ARISTOTLE

Anger is a baffling emotion to many of us. Sometimes it seems like a raging lion, seeking to devour everything in its path, while at other times it's like a time bomb, ticking silently, threatening to detonate within our souls. We've all felt it surge through our bodies and minds, possibly escalating into uncontrollable rage. We've also been the brunt of other people's anger and know all too well how that feels. We've felt guilty, victimized, and shamed for having anger. For many of us, it's been an enemy to be sought out and destroyed at all costs.

FOUR REASONS TO WELCOME ANGER

You may be surprised, as I was, to learn that our job is *not* to eliminate anger, but to *welcome* it as a friend carrying a very important message. "How could it possibly be a friend?" you may be asking. Let's look at four reasons why.

It's a God-Given Capacity for Preparedness

Anger can be beautiful because it is a God-given emotion that God wires. It alerts our minds and bodies to flee or fight while energizing us for action in response to either physical or psychological danger. It is a state of physical preparedness.

Todd Beamer experienced its beautiful usefulness. Who will ever forget the horrific tragedy of 9/11? It is burned into our memories forever. Can you imagine how Todd felt when he learned that the plane he was riding in was going to be turned into a missile that would destroy the White House? He must have been terrified in a way that is unimaginable for most of us. He was staring death straight in the face.

Todd told GTE supervisor Lisa Jefferson by cell phone that he and fellow passengers Jeremy Glick and Thomas Burnett Jr. had decided they would not be pawns in the hijackers' wicked plot. The God-given physiological component of anger propelled them out of their seats and helped them rally other passengers to take action.

After assessing their situation, the men decided that they were not going to allow the terrorists to kill anyone else. Believing that there was a bomb on board, the passengers knew that they were going to die that day. But instead of playing the victim role, these three men voted to take action. Armed with nothing but their own courage and a plastic butter knife from their airplane breakfast, Todd Beamer rallied his fellow passengers: "Are you ready? Let's roll." The passengers attacked the terrorists, took over the plane, and forced it to crash outside of Pittsburgh, killing every person on board but undoubtedly saving many other lives.

It's Not a Sin

I have heard preachers pontificate from the pulpit and in the media, "Brothers . . . sisters . . . anger is sin!" These zealots believe they are teaching biblical truth, but instead they are giving a half-truth and short-circuiting the innate purpose of anger, which is to prepare us for danger. They are forcing us into the victim mentality where we sit like dupes, shut down emotionally. The verse they often use to prove their point is "Be angry, and yet do not sin."[1] They get the last part of the admonition correct but disregard the first: "BE ANGRY!"

God commands us to be angry! What exactly does he mean? Another translation of the same verse clarifies: "Go ahead and be angry. You do well to be angry—but don't use your anger as fuel for revenge. And don't stay angry. Don't go to bed angry."[2]

God also tells the proper response — "do not sin." Todd Beamer didn't sin. Sin is when we turn our backs on God. It's not loving God with our whole heart, soul, and mind. We're all born sinful and need to evaluate our dilemma. Will we seek truth? Truth is not just information. Truth is found in a Person, the Lord Jesus Christ. He says if we seek him, he'll let us find him.

It's Like a Scab over a Wound

Another aspect of anger is that it's a secondary emotion, meaning that it's like a scab over a wound. We become angry when we are wounded. The wound has to occur before the scab forms.

The wounding event for Todd Beamer was the news that not only was he facing death, but so too, apparently, were the president and government officials and employees.

If we could talk to Todd today, I bet he would tell us how thankful he is that God wired him with anger, for without that physiological response to danger, he would have sat paralyzed in his seat and our country would have been devastated even more than it was.

It's Evidence We're Not Stuffing Emotions

A therapist friend of mine once said that she believes anger is like a sacrament—something sacred that must be revered and something that can give life. Because of this belief she asks her clients to demonstrate their anger in a way that is unique and safe.

One client brought in a beautiful vase that belonged to her late mother, and during one session in the therapist's office she smashed it to smithereens while shouting all the things she was angry at her mother about. Afterward there was release and freedom. She was moving out of numbness to experiencing a fuller spectrum of her emotions, and she celebrated with her therapist.

I believe Todd Beamer is also an example of how anger can be a sign we are coming to life. You may be saying, "Well, Todd died. How could he have been coming to life?" We can see how from his response. He turned to God, who is the source of all life. Todd knew what real life is. He knew it is not only physical life here on earth, but eternal life with God in heaven. I believe that Todd became fully alive spiritually the moment that plane crashed into the field, because it was in that moment that he saw God face-to-face.

Debra Wood, coleader of an adoption support group in Indianapolis, wrote this intimate prayer about coming to life. I'm grateful for her permission to allow us to eavesdrop on her heart's cries.

> *Beautiful is the day when we realize that the path to the answers of the questions that we have been searching for only come through the pain and tears God has allowed us to endure. In the refining fire, so many times we have cried out in agony to God, "Please turn it down"—not hearing his gentle voice saying, "Trust me, child, I am here."*
>
> *I pray, God, for you to heal me, I pray for you to show me who you are. I pray to see your heart and to learn to love the way you love. In the pain, I forget these prayers.*
>
> *The anger comes when I realize I was created with a wounded heart. Why God, why? Why couldn't I have been placed in my adoptive mother's womb—Why? Why would you allow me to be wounded from the beginning, never knowing peace, never not knowing fear? Why God, why? You tell me that then I would not be me. That I am me because of my wounds. But why God, why?*

The wounds cause ugly, the wounds cause fear. How can I heal from wounds I cannot see, wounds I cannot remember? You tell me that you can remember. . . .

"Show me your ugly," you say. "Trust me," you say. I tell you I am afraid even though you have blessed me with loyal friends who allow me to be me—ugly included. You say again, "Trust me, show me, and I will make the ugly beautiful. . . . One day your ugly will be your beautiful, scars of battles won." I tell you, God, that it is just too ugly. I can't feel. I can't let people in. I can't let people love me. I can't accept the love. I want these things more than life; I just can't seem to get to them. I just can't believe anyone can love me with the ugly. You tell me I do not have to be perfect to be loved.

I tell you I do not have the faith of the great ones; this is too much for me. You say, "It is not the volume of your faith, it is just that you give me all that you have. I know your heart. I know the warfare you are fighting, the wounds. I know. Just give me all you have. That is all I need from you. Whether a mustard seed or a mountain, give me all of it. Give me you and I will give you the desires of your heart."

My desires . . . I want to love. I want to be able to be loved, accept love. "You must first accept mine," you say. I tell you, "All right." I reveal my ugly, the anger, and the resentment. I am afraid. You tell me that you are a big God, you can handle it, it is all right to feel it, express it. I scream, I cry, I explode. The rage is released. You say, "Ah, now you are coming to life!" You tell me that when I show this fear to others it will defeat the lie. I will finally believe I can be loved for me. . . .

Beautiful is the day when we can say, "Thank you for the pain. Please send more so I can know you even better." Beautiful is the day when you say, "Ah, now you can see."

WHAT TRIGGERS OUR ANGER

As we reflect on these aspects of anger, we can conclude that anger, if handled correctly, has the potential for being a *good* thing. As adoptees, I believe it is important for us to know the common triggers for our primary emotions so we will understand the source of our anger and discover healthy ways to manage it.

Being Sent Away by Our Birth Mothers

The best article I have ever read about adoptee anger is written by a birth mother named Carol Komissaroff. She says, "What are adoptees angry about? Lots of things. They're angry with people like me because we gave them away. They need an explanation and an apology. Of course they can't get one because we're nowhere to be found, which frustrates them and makes them mad as hell. Some are also angry because we sent them away from their 'kind,' abandoning them to an environment in which they suffer a chronic, cumulative, vast feeling of unacceptability. The pain, helplessness, and frustration caused by that sort of thing can make a person very mad."[3]

Dirck Brown said, "I spent a year in analysis before I even mentioned that I was adopted, and even then I was very tentative about talking about it. My analyst commented when I began to talk about it that I seemed to be furious and that what he sensed I really wanted to do was strangle my birth mother!"

Anger at our birth mothers may not be evident to us until we begin looking truthfully at how adoption has affected our lives. Until then, we will spill our birth mother anger onto our moms, who more than likely, don't deserve it. It's what psychologists call "misplaced anger." Our birth mothers aren't here to receive our anger, so the closest person possible is our moms. We can become so angry at her in the teen years that we may wonder what is wrong with us. We may have a slight inkling that our anger is out of control, but again, without knowledge and guidance, we mix it with shame. "What is wrong with me?"

Being Treated Like Second-Class Citizens

Another common trigger is being treated like a second-class citizen. Adoptees feel like second-class citizens a lot. The majority of adopted people in the United States can't have our real birth certificates like everyone else, but we can have a nice little amended one that leaves out every detail we want and need to know. Fifty percent of Canadian adoptees have access to their birth records, however. We know what it's like to have birth records withheld and have our hands slapped when we ask for them.

And who are treated like first-class citizens by the system? Our birth mothers. I was told that I couldn't have access to my hospital files, which are public records for everyone else, until my birth mother was dead and I could prove it with a death certificate. Are we still living in a land of slavery, or what?

Fifteen years later, my birth mother died. I called the same woman to tell of my birth mother's death and the hospital files from another state that lend undeniable proof. This woman had another card to trump my new evidence, keeping the files inaccessible to provide confidentiality for my birth mother, who is now dead.

Kim Norman is still very angry about one aspect of being adopted — the fact that she feels like a second-class citizen legally. "I am angry that I am not legally entitled to my *true* birth certificate! The information represented on that piece of paper is about *me*, yet I can't have a copy. I am angry at the way the system is — that there wasn't someone present thirty-two years ago raising these types of questions when I was adopted."

Stacy says that she resents the fact that the privacy of her birth parents is more important in the eyes of the courts than her need to know her history. "I think I understand it, but I feel it's just not fair!" she says. "Adoption is the only thing in my life that I *do* get uncontrollably angry about at times. It's such a personal issue to me. When I get treated by the system like a second-class citizen or as a number, it infuriates me. The feelings are so deep that it brings out fiercer anger than I otherwise show."

Feeling Unworthy to Ask for What We Need

Another injustice is not feeling free to ask for what we need. Do you ever find yourself shrinking back when someone offers you a choice between two gifts—one more appealing to you than the other? Perhaps the person offers you the choice between a silk or burlap scarf. She says, "Go ahead, take the *silk* scarf," and you say, "Oh, that's okay. The burlap one will be fine."

Many of us do that all the time! We don't feel like we're entitled to ask for the silk scarf (what we need and perhaps like). Why is that? Is it because I don't feel worthy?

Connie Dawson says that not feeling entitled to ask for or receive what we need as human beings—unconditional love and connection—naturally leads us to feeling angry. She says, "Hurt? 'You bet I've been hurt and of course I am angry' is what my 'inside baby' wants to say—stomping her foot to claim her entitlement to her feelings."

Cheri Freeman says that she lived a nightmarish childhood with a father who was mentally ill and full of rage. When her parents eventually divorced when she was seventeen, she *finally* expressed some of her pent-up anger toward her adoptive father. The next morning, he showed up at the courthouse and terminated his parental rights and responsibilities. "Of course, he couldn't have done that unless my new stepfather was willing to adopt me, but I felt like I'd been rejected forever and banned from the family for expressing anger."

WE CAN MANAGE ANGER ... HERE'S HOW

Even writing about what triggers some of our primary emotions gets my own adrenaline pumping! But, as I stated earlier, our goal is not to *eliminate* anger. Rather, we need to find appropriate ways to express anger that are not destructive to ourselves or others or dishonoring to God. Here are several to get us started.

Develop Good Self-Talk

When we become angry to the boiling point, we need to pull ourselves back by the scruff of the neck and say, "Self, your anger shows that your pain level is out of control. Now, what can you do to take care of yourself? Run away? No, that won't help. How about a breather? How about a movie? How about working out at the gym? How about chocolate?"

Pause and Pray

It is important to remember that there is a fleeting second between primary and secondary emotions. That fleeting second provides us with a choice. Will we react impulsively or respond responsibly? We're not victims of anger. We have a choice about how to behave!

The old advice to "count to ten" isn't a bad idea. In fact, it's a good one, for as we cool off we can assess what's really happening and determine a wise course of action. Cheri Freeman is trying to learn to respond in the right way by backing off for a "time-out" before sharing angry feelings with anyone. "I can show irritation and frustration easily enough, but anger and fear are harder for me to share maturely."

Todd Beamer had an even better response—prayer. Through the media we learned that the Lord's Prayer wasn't some rote prayer Todd was saying. Rather it was a prayer that he was incorporating into his own life through Bible study.

God is the one who wired us with anger and he best understands it. It's so easy to think that we can talk to him only about "acceptable things" such as Aunt Nell's broken arm. But he knows far more about our anger than we do. He is big and can handle it well!

Refuse to Retaliate

When I allowed myself to feel all my hurt and anger toward my birth mother, everything within me wanted to retaliate, to fight back, even to punish her.

If we blame others for our emotional pain, we give *them* power over what we think, feel, say, and do. Blaming statements such as "They are doing it to me," or "She makes me so angry" reveal a victim's mindset. We have the problem. Nobody can *make* us angry. In any situation we have the power to identify our primary emotion and choose how we will respond in a way that preserves our dignity and safety.

It helps me tremendously to recall that the Bible says, "Don't insist on getting even; that's not for you to do. 'I'll do the judging,' says God. 'I'll take care of it.'"[4] I would much rather have Almighty God deal with my birth mother about her cruel behaviors. I also love the Bible verse that says, "But how is it to your credit if you receive a beating for doing wrong and endure it? But if you suffer for doing good and you endure it, this is commendable before God."[5]

Deal with Past Anger and See Present Anger as a Signal

For many of us, anger has turned inward and become depression. We may have been the good little adoptee and stuffed it. We are shut down. But when we begin to *feel* angry, it's a sign that we're coming to life!

The late Dirck Brown, when confronted by his analyst about his anger, said, "I was able to *begin* to feel my deep, deep anger and resentment over being rejected, abandoned—that Gretchen (my birth mother) did not want me and perhaps didn't want to have me from the very beginning."

Connie Dawson says that when she and her husband separated, she couldn't hold back. "Oh, I was still 'nice,' but I'd never felt anger as I felt it then. I still get angry, but most of the original abandonment anger at being 'put out' as a baby has receded. Now when I'm angry I take it as a signal that there is a *current* problem to solve. I think of all those years I couldn't afford to express my anger for fear I'd be

Our Choice

To give ourselves permission to be angry, but to channel our emotion in a healthy way.

sent away, abandoned again. What a waste of good time."

And so what is the choice we need to make at this juncture?

I'll never forget one of my therapists saying, "Sherrie, you have the right to be angry." I was shocked, for I had perceived in my religious background that I should *never* be angry. What a relief it was to allow my anger to surface so I could learn to deal with it constructively.

DISCUSSION QUESTIONS FOR
SUPPORT GROUPS OR PERSONAL REFLECTION

1. Have you experienced "misplaced anger" at your mom? Please share an incident that immediately comes to mind. Were you aware that your anger was "over the top"?
2. What triggers your anger (people, places, memories)? How do you act when anger is triggered?
3. Do you ever feel like running away from home when you are enraged? Have you ever done it? Did it do any good, or did the anger go with you?
4. Write a letter *to* and *from* your birth mother about the wound beneath your anger and how that has possibly been transferred to your mom.

DIGGING DEEPER FOR ANSWERS
TO OUR ADOPTION QUESTIONS

1. Where is God in all our angry and hurt feelings? Even if we don't believe in him, did you know we can ask him to make himself real to us? Jesus wants to be our "High Priest," meaning that we can run to him and he'll always have open arms and understand our hurts more than any person ever could.
2. For a challenge, read about Jesus as your High Priest in Hebrews 7. Pick one or two verses that stand out like neon to you. Date them!

3. Read Ephesians 4:26. What does God say about anger?
4. Put Ephesians 4:26 in your own words.

As we stop avoiding anger that covers our hurts, we *will* experience emotional pain. Our natural tendency is to run the other way, but being willing to enter our pain is a critical part of our journey. That's what we'll talk about next.

CHAPTER NINE

WHY ARE WE HURTING OURSELVES?

What doesn't kill us makes us stronger.

— ABIGAIL LOVETT

void the pain! Avoid it at all costs. After all, isn't life filled with enough of it? Whether from a failed marriage, the death of a child, the betrayal of a friend, an unwelcome diagnosis, being pulled from your first family because your parents can't love and take care of you, hearing the news that your foster parents have "changed their minds," or the loss of a birth mother at an early age, our natural tendency is to run.

Avoidance techniques for adoption-related pain don't seem to differ much from those people use in response to other painful situations in life. Adopted or not, many of us resort to food, sex, obsession with a certain person, alcohol, drugs, fanatic religion, suicide, or extramarital affairs . . . and the list goes on.

WAYS THAT WE RUN FROM PAIN

As I've interviewed and gotten to know hundreds of adoptees, I've discovered that we use "all of the above" and more — but four styles of running are prevalent for us.

Numbing Out

Compartmentalizing the pain. Throwing ourselves into mindless activity. Checking out emotionally. Acting like everything is fine when it isn't. Holding back tears. Faking a smile. These are just a few of the ways we numb ourselves.

Kenny Tucker, adoption activist, says that he just numbs out emotionally from tough issues so that he can properly digest them later in smaller bits and chunks.

Cheri Freeman says that when simple denial doesn't work, she turns to outright disassociation. If she can't talk herself out of feeling bad she buries herself in a book or series of books or does some marathon sleeping. She knows the pain will still be there when she finishes the last book or wakes up, but at least by then it might be blunted.

Joy Budensiek, author of *Reconnnected—to My Bellybutton*, says, "When something is painful to me, I mentally put it in a box, tie it up tight, and put it on a high shelf in my mind, not to be taken down until the edge of the pain is gone. Or, I mentally shut a door, not to be opened until it is safe. Disassociation may have its 'down sides,' but it may also keep me from falling apart."

We may have been numbing ourselves since early childhood; for many of us it's become a "survival skill." However, the unfortunate result is that we don't develop the capacity to fully enter into life and also *enjoy* the present moment. We're somewhere else instead—in la-la land.

Compulsive Overeating

Another behavior we use to run from our feelings is compulsive overeating. When I was attending a support group years ago someone said, "Food is the number-one addiction." That statement rang true because food is something we *need* in order to live. We can't eliminate it from our lives like an alcoholic can eliminate alcohol. Food is always there, staring us in the face.

Richard Curtis says that whenever he tells his adoption story he always includes his obsession with food. "It is an integral part of my story because it overshadows all my other means of escaping from pain, including addiction to alcohol. As a little kid, as far back as I can remember, I sought food for comfort in dealing with sadness, fear, loneliness, and other painful feelings I couldn't identify. Food became my friend, my solace, and my comforter.

"Compulsive overeating, however, is a silent partner that is overlooked by society and actually encouraged by well-meaning friends and family members. As an adult the cycle of bingeing on food and purging through exercise increased my excess weight, and I kept the bingeing and purging a secret. My behavior destroyed my self-esteem and physical and spiritual well-being. No diets or pills were able to reverse the cycle of eating that was spinning out of control and leading to suicidal tendencies.

"Today, after much counseling, even though I have enjoyed almost ten years of sobriety from alcohol, the addiction to food continues to raise its ugly head from time to time—most recently resulting in a hospital stay for a digestive disorder."

Phyllis-Anne Munro says her specialty was stuffing feelings through overeating. Sad to say, overeating was the only bond with her adoptive mother, since her mother equated food with love.

Compulsive eating not only numbs the pain, it makes the scales go up while our emotional health goes down . . . down . . . down.

Drug Addiction

Another means of escape is drugs, whether legal or illegal, that come in all forms and shapes. While they *temporarily* relieve pain, when misused to run from our feelings they can easily become addictive. Our bodies and minds crave more and more, and we'll go to almost any length to get it.

Lori says, "I was a drug addict for twenty-three years. This was my way of keeping the painful belief away that 'nobody loves me.' I started smoking pot when I was eleven. Over the course of time, I've tried every drug known to mankind except heroin—the only smart decision I made at the time. I knew that if I tried it I would love it and it would kill me."

Courtney asked her psychiatrist to give her something for stress, believing that she just couldn't cope with life any longer. She just wanted something to "take the edge off." Her physician prescribed an antianxiety drug called Ativan. It worked wonders at first, but then its effectiveness began to wear off and Courtney rationalized taking more and more of the drug. Before long she was in a psychiatric ward of a hospital.

Without a doubt, doing drugs is not the answer to our problems.

Workaholism

Neither is workaholism, which can be just as insidious as drug abuse. Workaholism, even more than overeating, is another "acceptable addiction" in our society. Bring the briefcase home every night. Work late. Miss meals. Go into the office early. Climb, climb, climb that corporate ladder. Reach the top. How exhilarating! Success is the goal, and if we obtain it, surely we couldn't have any problems . . . or could we?

Sharon says, "When I was only fifteen, I decided that I would rather work than go to school. I reasoned that the money I would earn would buy my freedom from having to depend on *anyone* for *anything*; I could take care of myself if I had the money.

"I worked as much as possible and became wildly successful, which gave me a false sense of safety, control, and self-esteem. By the time I was twenty, I was a full-fledged workaholic. I couldn't stop overworking. I thought it was the only way for me to have value in my own eyes as well as in the eyes of others.

"When my company was taken over and I was transferred out of the area that I had created, I wanted to die because work was all that was holding me up. I finally sought counseling. Thanks to counseling, prayer, and letting myself finally grieve my early losses, I am much better now, although I know it would be very easy to slip into the old patterns."

Some of us might feel caught in an inescapable addiction right now. We've tried everything conceivable, yet nothing has worked. Is there any solution? Any hope? You bet!

ANOTHER WAY TO THINK ABOUT PAIN

Let me share another way to think about pain through a story about a man named Paul who had some kind of physical ailment that he called his "thorn in the flesh." No one is really sure what it was, but it was so painful that he pleaded with God to have it taken away. Three times he pleaded, but each time the answer was no.

In the years that followed, Paul's "thorn" remained, yet in the process he learned a valuable lesson — rewards come as we move *through* pain and suffering. Paul began to experience a certain kind of strength that came in the midst of weakness and powerlessness. He received profound wisdom about life and death that virgins to suffering couldn't possibly comprehend. He even got to the point of being thankful for the pain because he knew that pain ushered him into the very place where he would be ready to receive these wonderful character qualities. Paul learned to welcome pain as a holy guest in disguise. Ultimately, Paul enjoyed an intimate relationship with God because he learned to embrace his pain instead of running from it.[1]

"Embrace it?" you may be muttering under your breath. I hear you. But there are many blessings that can come from brokenness. There can be joy instead of depression; love for others instead of sick self-absorption; self-control instead of uncontrollable addictions to food, alcohol, and people; contentment and security instead of anxiety; courage instead of panic; deep wisdom instead of shallow, numbed-out living; and knowing God, which is why he created us.

I remember when I was suffering from my second clinical depression. One morning as Bob was driving me to the hospital a new realization came to me about adoption . . . and about God. I at last understood that the missing face I had been looking for all my life wasn't the one my heart had truly been seeking. I thought it was the face of my birth mother, but instead it was the face of God. It was then that I remembered that there was only one person in the course of history who didn't have to wait until heaven to see God face-to-face. How interesting that that person was Moses, the adoptee![2] Perhaps the psalmist David was referring to this when he penned the words: "And I—in righteousness I will see your face; when I awake, I will be satisfied with seeing your likeness."[3] It was at my darkest hour that I learned one of the most precious truths about adoption, about God, and about myself. That was my song in the night, and I will never forget it. I wouldn't trade that time of brokenness for anything, nor would I trade the brokenness I feel every day as I learn to depend more upon the God who made me and loves me dearly.

I know without a doubt that God redeems pain. He takes, as Debra Wood says, "the ugly" and transforms it into something beautiful. Not only will we be rewarded with character, but with new, healthy, and fulfilling opportunities as well—opportunities that will lead us to the unique path created for us. Derek Jeske, who experienced a transracial adoption, has found such rewards. He says, "I have come to embrace pain because I have the knowledge and understanding that I can teach others to accept who they are regardless of where they come from or who their parents are."

It has always been helpful for me when considering the topic of pain to recall a story about a little boy who was watching a cecropia moth break away from its cocoon. The moth's struggle to be free seemed excruciatingly slow to the little boy, so in his pity for the moth he decided to give it some help by widening the cocoon's opening and making it easier to escape.

The boy watched with anticipation as the moth freed itself from the cocoon. He couldn't wait for the wings to fill out so it could fly.

But something was wrong. Instead of the wings becoming strong, they remained shriveled. What the little boy didn't realize was that *struggle is essential* in developing a good muscle system that can pump blood into the moth's wings. The moth was crippled forever because the boy removed the pressures.[4]

So it will be for us if we choose to run from our pain. We'll be removing the struggle needed to develop healthy wings so that we can fly away from our painful pasts. And so, what is a life-transforming choice in regard to the pain we may be avoiding in association with being adopted?

Our Choice

To embrace our painful past by allowing ourselves to feel once again.

DISCUSSION QUESTIONS FOR SUPPORT GROUPS OR PERSONAL REFLECTION

1. Which ways of running from pain resonated with you?
   - Numbing out?
   - Overeating?
   - Drug and alcohol addiction (illegal and/or prescription)?
   - Workaholism?
   - Other.
2. Whom might you share this knowledge with that could help you?

DIGGING DEEPER FOR ANSWERS TO OUR ADOPTION QUESTIONS

1. What does God promise to do with the gaping hole in our hearts? Read Philippians 4:19.
2. What does God promise if we trust him to meet our needs instead of numbing out? See Psalm 22:5.
3. What does God want us to do when we're overwhelmed and don't know what to do or where to turn? See Matthew 11:28.
   - *Tell somebody.* Admit you're running from pain, first to your

Creator, then to a trusted friend, relative, member of the clergy, or support group. I think it must be so hard for alcoholics to attend their first meeting and make the courageous choice to speak up and say, "My name is _____, and I am an alcoholic." But they do it every day all over the world, and we can too! We also need to 'fess up to our physicians if we are abusing illegal or prescription drugs. We can ask for counsel and support while going through withdrawal. We can choose to tell our bosses that we are ruining our lives and family through overworking. If we are compulsive overeaters or alcoholics, we can find an Overeaters Anonymous or Alcoholics Anonymous group in our area and seek recovery.

Once we enter the pain, we may experience feelings of loss at a new level. Let's explore that next.

CHAPTER TEN

WHY ARE WE TERRIFIED OF REJECTION?

You number and record my wanderings; put my tears into Your bottle; are they not in Your book?

— Psalm 56

I magine yourself standing on a cliff at the Grand Canyon. You cup your hands to your mouth and yell something into the wide open cavern. Within seconds you can hear your words echo . . . echo . . . echo . . . until all is silent again.

It's a wondrous experience for tourists at the Grand Canyon but not so for adoptees who hear different kinds of echoes. What if the words yelled down the Grand Canyon of our souls were "I'm gone forever . . . forever . . . forever. You are alone . . . you are alone . . . you are alone"?

Well, it isn't a "what if" situation. Those words *were* yelled down the canyons of our adoptee souls when we lost our birth parents either at birth or later in life. And throughout life, we hear the same echoes . . . in different circumstances, different volumes, and different relationships. The echoes might diminish to almost a whisper but they aren't completely quieted until this life is over.

THE ECHOES OF LOSS THAT WE HEAR

From this core message of loss other messages emerge. While we may not attribute them to our adoption experience, they may be a significant contributor.

Absence Equals Abandonment

It seems a common theme among adoptees that if we can't literally see somebody we love, we conclude that we are abandoned.

A few years ago my husband and I traveled to Chicago to see a play. The next morning I went for a walk before leaving while Bob made business calls. After finishing my walk and returning to the hotel room, the door to our room was locked. I knocked and knocked, expecting Bob to swing it wide open, but no one answered. I knocked again, harder, but still no answer.

My heart was pounding as I quickly scanned the hall. There was a maid across the hallway who reluctantly agreed to open the door. When she opened it I saw the unmade bed and used towels in the bathroom, but *no* Bob. No suitcases. No note explaining why he wasn't there. Nothing!

I ran down to the elevator thinking, *Maybe he wants a divorce and just decided to leave. After all, I've been far from the perfect wife and I sure wouldn't blame him if he did.*

Upon entering the lobby and looking out into the car entrance, there was Bob, *casually* loading our bags in the trunk of the car. He looked so innocent that I wanted to wring his neck!

"Why did you leave without a note or *something*?" I demanded.

"Honey, I just thought I'd save us some time and that you'd be glad we're ready to go," he answered calmly.

I sobbed as we "discussed" the incident on the way home and at one point I admitted, "I thought you left me."

There was that echo again. My husband's unexplained and temporary absence translated to my adoptee heart as abandonment.

Sue has had similar experiences. She says one time her teenage daughter flew overseas for a summer of volunteer work and she thought they were going to have to call in the paramedics for her. As the plane departed, Sue described big, gulping sobs that lasted for a long time. She felt like she was saying good-bye to her daughter forever.

Phyllis-Anne Munro says that she has always feared that loved ones won't return and as a result has made a pact with them to call when they arrive at their destinations. This somewhat soothes her fears.

Five-year-old Katy Puckett seems to always have a crisis when her mom leaves to go anywhere without her. Her mom says, "It's becoming worse the older she gets; the only thing she can explain to me is that she 'worries that I won't be back.'"

Being Alone Is Scary

Another echo involves being alone. Lori says she now knows she has suffered from "abandonment phobia" all her life, and that is why she hates to be alone. After failed marriages she realized she was willing to stay in bad relationships just to be with someone. "I needed people so bad that I would go to hell and back to keep from losing them, even when they were clearly not good for me."

Another echo makes us restless and discontent in relationships and responsibilities.

Don't Tie Me Down

For many of us, our hearts are in a perpetual searching mode. We're looking for something, but we're not sure what. Thus, our contentment and commitment levels fluctuate like a roller coaster.

Paul says that if it weren't for his wife and kids, he'd be a mountain man. There he wouldn't have any responsibility except for himself. Some days he feels like running away, but knows he can't, out of love for his family.

Renee has been through three marriages, but after working through adoption-related issues, she is in a committed relationship.

This tendency toward restlessness has also seeped into her career life. Even though she's always had a career, she changed jobs ten times between the ages of twenty-two and thirty-seven. She says she's still looking for one that "sticks."

Richard Curtis says that with God's help, he began to realize in his previous three failed marriages that he had not allowed his wives to know the *real* Richard. Instead he hid behind the mask of "nice guy." He wouldn't allow himself to fully commit in any relationship without having "one foot out the door."

Conform, Achieve, and Be Perfect

Another message involves conformity, overachievement, and perfectionism. If we're perfect and if we adapt to what other people expect, we won't have to experience any more abandonment, right?

Dr. Rev. Richard Gilbert says that he has needed to excel through work and socialization. He has sought approval and, in countless ways, tried to prove to the world (and himself) that his birth parents made a bad decision.

Sue says she tried so hard as a kid to succeed through overachievement, but to no avail. Nobody knew she had what is now called attention-deficit hyperactivity disorder (ADHD). All she ever heard was that she wasn't achieving up to potential and that she needed to try harder. "If I had tried any harder I would have ground myself into dust. That still makes me sad to think about. Very little that I did was seen as really, really good."

Kim Norman says she has always been an overachiever and that her supergirl efforts were driven by the hope that if she excelled her parents would *truly* love her, even though in reality, they already did. Her ability to receive their love was damaged and so they could never express how much they loved her *enough* to soothe her adoptee heart.

"Overachieving? Yes, of course," says Connie Dawson. "It's how I could deserve to be cared for, because my parents loved pointing to me as successful to prove they were successful. I call it (overachieving) 'earning my keep.'"

Don't Get Too Close

One of the strongest messages that comes from that core experience of loss is a fear of intimacy. Drs. Thomas Patrick Malone and Patrick Thomas Malone define intimacy this way: "Intimacy is derived from the Latin *intima*, meaning 'inner' or 'innermost.' Your inside being is the real you, the you that only you can know. The problem is that you can know it only when you are being intimate with something or someone outside yourself."[1]

Connie Dawson responds, "Surely you jest! If I don't know myself, how can I be intimate with you? If I can't trust you, how can I afford to disclose anything that might make you leave me?"

Renee says she was the classic teen chameleon, adapting her personality to fit in whatever crowd she was running with. As far as achieving, she got straight A's, was in the honor society and student government, on yearbook staff, pom-pom (captain!), and tennis team. "Should I go on?" she says, "Of course I always felt that if anyone knew the 'real me' they wouldn't have chosen me to do those things."

Rose says she wants her friends to like her best, but if they really knew her, they wouldn't. She is critical of her husband, accusing him of not being intimate, but she wonders if the core problem is hers. "With sexual intimacy, I can say that the 'real thing' has never happened because I just can't commit my body to another person—it is not an enjoyable part of my life."

Kasey Hamner says that not only does she expect herself to be perfect, but also her mate. When he's not, she's disgusted and struggles with feelings of hatred and disgust. However, she keeps working on her reactions and is growing each day, even though it still seems really scary to her.

Phyllis-Anne Munro admits that in college a friend constantly confronted her about her inability to be real in front of others. Her fear of rejection was so huge that she allowed hardly anyone to see her pain. "I didn't even know how much pain I was in and how fearful I was until I started going to therapy," Phyllis-Anne confesses.

Patricia DePew says, "I can't handle the closeness others might desire. I have friends but not many close friends because of the intimacy it takes. I don't think they would like me if they really knew me. If a friend and I have a disagreement, I will turn off my feelings and close down our friendship rather than face whatever is wrong between us."

I'll Never Get Out of This Pit

Many of us have struggled with depression. All people do at one time or another in life but for adoptees it seems to be more prevalent. In a research article, a group of adoptees was interviewed and compared to a control group in order to determine the psychosocial well-being of the adoptees. Adoptees in the sample expressed more depression than their peers and exceeded the norm for clinical depression by 30 percent. Despite the higher incidence of clinical depression among adoptees, they were no more likely to have sought counseling for depression than those in the control group.[2]

Jody Moreen of Naperville, Illinois, wife, mother of three sons, adoption triad support group facilitator, and editor of *Adoption Blessings* newsletter, says that her depression first showed up when she was a junior in college and her father decided to take an early retirement and move south with her mom. As clinical depression gradually set in, she lost her appetite, found life joyless despite her faithful friends and boyfriend, and couldn't concentrate on schoolwork, which led to dropping out for a term. During this crisis time her parents were very concerned and sought medical and psychological services for her.

This pattern of depression repeated a couple of times with geographical moves. The loss of family, friends, familiarity, and security that came with these moves shook Jody's emotional foundation "like an earthquake."

Depression has been a major issue for me as well. No matter how hard I tried, I couldn't shake it. I have always been a "perseverance" kind of person and had little tolerance for those who claimed to be depressed. After all, if you're feeling low, all you have to do is pull yourself up by the bootstraps and go on with life.

That belief came to a screeching halt when I admitted myself to a psychiatric hospital for severe depression at the age of forty-one.

As Bob sat at the end of my hospital bed the first night, he asked, "Sherrie, why are you so sad?" From all outward appearances, I should have been the happiest woman alive. I had a husband who loved me, two beautiful daughters, a house in the suburbs, and anything a girl could ever want. I finally told him I didn't know.

Looking back, I am certain that unresolved adoption loss was at the core. But did anyone in the hospital ever mention adoption? No. Did they ask me if I had been touched by adoption in the intake interview? No. Another example of societal and medical ignorance. Twenty years later, I don't believe adoption awareness has increased much in the medical field.

Jan says, "I believe I am suffering from depression right now. I've taken the evaluation questionnaire and five or six symptoms are present. I believe it started years ago. In fact, I believe it may have begun as a child. I remember one instance at school and even the color of dress I was wearing. I was walking down the hall and thinking, 'I just can't take it any more—all this stuff is just too much.'"

Kasey Hamner says she still struggles with depression. Looking at her life on paper is like looking at a dream. Great job. Good income. Devoted boyfriend. Two homes. Good health. Yet still . . . periods of hopelessness and fear that all she holds dear will be lost.

These are just a few of the messages the core echo brings. Perhaps you can add some of your own . . . or maybe you aren't aware of any.

WHY SOME OF US DON'T EXPERIENCE LOSS

I wonder why there is such a contrast in our reactions to loss. I sat next to an adopted woman at a dinner last week. Did she have any painful thoughts? No. Did she feel sad that she was given up? No. Did she wish she would have searched for her origins earlier, since she found her mother's tombstone at the end of her search? No. Adoptees I've spoken with who don't hear the echoes so common to many of us may have had different childhood experiences, or just different coping mechanisms.

Highly Effective Parenting

Some attribute excellent parenting to not hearing echoes. Greg Berger, the graphic artist who created the special edition adoption postal stamp, says, "*Not once* in my life did I consider myself abandoned, even in my simplistic thinking as a young child. This I attribute directly to my adoptive parents."

Melinda Faust, adopted at four months of age from Seoul, South Korea, and now a student at Miami University in Ohio, says that adoption has always been such a blessing in her life and never a burden. She's never felt abandoned, or that her biological family didn't love her, or that she's alone. She attributes this to both sets of parents — her adoptive parents, through their incredible openness and love, and her birth family, whom she believes made the ultimate sacrifice for her good. "Only blessings and love resulted from my adoption, and it feels wonderful to be so blessed," Melinda says.

Perseverance and Resilience

Some of us have suffered more trauma than others. Our resilience to recover from the trauma depends on how God has wired us, the maturity and sensitivity of our parents, and our determination to persevere.

Kimberly says, "Through my experience of an international adoption (Korean into a Caucasian family) I've been able to experience and learn about minorities, discrimination, and what it's like to persevere. I've been strengthened through my adoption experience.

"At the same time, I've dealt with more experiences than what I feel a 'normal' person would go through. I've been dealt a loss that I believe is unique to adoptees. On the other hand, I know that as a result I have worked that much harder to get through these issues. The knowledge I have gained will continue to help me become a more diverse and open person, with much depth. In that regard, I'm so thankful for my adoption; it has brought out my most beautiful qualities and has strengthened me."

The preceding speculations as to why some of us don't experience primal feelings of loss aren't definitive, but nevertheless, good food for thought. For the rest of us who do experience repercussions resulting from adoption loss, we can take heart: The echoes will become fainter and fainter as time goes by if we choose to process them in a healthy manner. They won't go away quickly and can return sometimes in waves. However, if we deal with the past, we'll be better prepared for future losses.

Our Choice

To identify repercussions from adoption loss and grieve them.

For those of us who feel the loss, the only path toward peace and health is to grieve, for grief is to the soul as a fever is to the body. Grief is our heart's way of healing itself. We need to grieve for the life that might have been had we not been adopted. Grieve for the parents we may never lay eyes on. Grieve for the family structure and love we may have missed in our birth families. Grieve for the arms that might have held us. Grieve for the culture we might have known. Grieve over our struggle to be real and intimate with others. Grieve for pushing ourselves to the hilt. Grieve for years wasted on perfectionism. Grieve for pushing away the God who longs for us to run into his open arms.

DISCUSSION QUESTIONS FOR
SUPPORT GROUPS OR PERSONAL REFLECTION

1. If you are depressed, are you willing to seek professional help? Seeking help is a sign of strength, not weakness. Please don't go only to your primary care physician for help. Psychiatrists are medical physicians who specialize in brain chemistry and imbalances. Depression can be an illness. It's not a defect in character, but in chemistry.

2. Write a letter *to* and *from* your birth mother about feelings of rejection, abandonment, and loss.

DIGGING DEEPER FOR ANSWERS
TO OUR ADOPTION QUESTIONS

1. Consider making a "grief box" to work through loss. The steps are outlined here. It's a practical tool for grieving loss. Here are the instructions:

How to Construct a Grief Box

1. Select a box (representative of your life).
   John 1:3: "through him <u>all</u> *things were made."* (emphasis mine)

2. List the losses or hurts in your life (past and present).
   Isaiah 43:26: "Review the past for me, let us argue the matter together."

3. Find an item that represents each loss and put all items in your box.

4. Tell God how you feel about them. All memories. Don't hold back!

Psalm 62:8: "Pour out your hearts to him, for God is our refuge."

5. Ask God to forgive your sins and receive Jesus' gift of forgiveness.
   Romans 10:9-10: "If you confess with your mouth, 'Jesus is Lord,' and believe in your heart that God raised him from the dead, you will be saved. For it is with your heart that you believe and are justified, and it is with your mouth that you confess and are saved."

6. Forgive others.
   Matthew 18:21-22 (MSG): "At that point Peter got up the nerve to ask, 'Master, how many times do I forgive a brother or sister who hurts me? Seven?' Jesus replied, 'Seven! Hardly. Try seventy times seven.'"

7. Thank God (sacrifice) for each loss and how he may cause you to grow from it.
   Psalm 50:14: "Sacrifice thank offerings to God, fulfill your vows to the Most High."

8. Offer box (sinful life) to God.
   Romans 12:1: "Therefore, I urge you, brothers, in view of God's mercy, to offer your bodies as living sacrifices, holy and pleasing to God—this is your spiritual act of worship."

9. Listen!
   2 Chronicles 29:27: "As the offering began, singing to the LORD began also."

Zephaniah 3:17: "The LORD your God is with you, he is mighty to save. He will take great delight in you, he will quiet you with his love, he will rejoice over you with singing."

It's sometimes in our darkest hours that we learn some of adoption's most precious lessons. I'd like to share one I learned with you in the next chapter.

CHAPTER ELEVEN

WHY DO WE COVER INFERIORITY WITH OVERACHIEVEMENT?

Your life is something opaque, not transparent, as long as you look at it in an ordinary human way. But if you hold it up against the light of God's goodness, it shines and turns transparent, radiant, and bright. And then you ask yourself in amazement, "Is this really my own life before me?

— ALBERT SCHWEITZER

Self-worth is a precious commodity that has been foreign to most of us. We don't just have low self-esteem, we've had no self-esteem! It is something many of us want, but it seems to slip through our personas, like Jell-O through a sieve. We may have searched everywhere for it. Overachieving. Perfectionism. Being a smart dresser. Being religious. Looking attractive. Pretending that we have it all together. All are dead ends.

One day my therapist said, "I don't think you have gotten in touch with your adoption loss. I'm giving you an assignment. Go to a local hospital and ask God to show you what you lost when your birth mother sent you away."

You have already read in chapter 2 about my first impressions of the babies my nurse friend saw in the nursery, but on my way home from the hospital I began sobbing uncontrollably. Amid my tears, one word and a phrase came mysteriously to mind: "jewel" and "on the day you were born."

Being the avid Bible student that I am, I rushed home and searched my three-inch concordance (a book that tells where you can find every word in the Bible) for those words. To my amazement I discovered an Old Testament verse that had the same word and phrase in it. I quickly studied the verse to see if I was taking it out of context. I wasn't. God was talking to the orphaned nation of Israel. He said, "On that day when you were born, you were dumped out into a field and left to die, unwanted. But I [God] came by and saw you there, covered with your own blood, and I said, 'Live! Thrive like a plant in the field!' And you did! You grew up and became . . . a jewel among jewels."[1]

I was an orphan, wasn't I? On the day I was born I was "dumped into a field," unwanted. My mother never saw me, never knew if I was a boy or girl. I was named Baby X. It seemed like making application to my own life wasn't far-fetched at all.

As I contemplated the words, a deep sense of peace blanketed me, like newly fallen snow. To think that God loved me enough to be there on the day I was born was something I had never envisioned. My "picture" of my birth was a tiny baby, lying on a stainless steel gurney, like in a morgue. And I was all alone. Not a soul was there to comfort me.

I later learned that I wasn't alone in that delivery room — there was somebody to welcome me into the world. His name was Dr. Fillinger. During my search, I had the privilege of talking to one of his granddaughters. She told me how much her grandfather loved his work and then added, "He wept at the birth of every baby . . . he was an orphan himself, you know."

LEARNING GOD'S OPINION OF US

Another thing I thought amazing about God in this verse is that he didn't say, "Bite the bullet! Put the past behind you and go on as if nothing ever happened." He *validated* feelings of abandonment and called a spade a spade. To hear his opinion of me . . . of us . . . on top of that — "a jewel among jewels" — is simply incredible!

I believe this is what brought the deepest healing from adoption loss for me: validation of the pain, knowledge of God's presence at my birth, and his opinion of me. The result is that I don't struggle much with self-esteem anymore. I know how God feels about me and the circumstances of my birth, and I don't need the approval of others to feel good about myself — not even my birth mother's! This is the extraordinary gift I was given at the bottom of the pit of loss.

CHARACTERISTICS OF LOW SELF-WORTH

I know without a doubt that I am not the only adoptee who has suffered from nonexistent self-esteem. Our friend Moses did as well. When God called him to a prominent leadership position, Moses ran from it like the plague. A close look at his excuses for not stepping up to God's assignment provides a glimpse into the ingredients of low self-esteem.

"I'm Worthless."

Let's set the stage first.[2] God had called Moses by name. Moses was flat on his face in the light of God's holiness and then God said his heart was breaking over the suffering of his people under the wicked pharaoh of Egypt. His plan was for Moses to lead the people out of slavery in Egypt and toward the Promised Land God had determined would be their home forever.

The first excuse Moses gave was: "Who am I that I should go to Pharaoh and bring the Israelites out of Egypt?"

Isn't this a thought we often entertain? "Who am I that I should do _____?"

God answered by giving a promise that hit Moses' most basic adoptee need—reassurance that he wouldn't be alone. "I will be with you."

Because of our loss, we often have difficulty internalizing that truth. Many of us are like Styrofoam cups filled with water that suddenly had holes punched through their sides. We often can't retain what we need to hear and believe! I have a feeling it was that way for Moses too.

"I Don't Have Anything Valuable to Say."

Moses' next excuse came in his announcement that he had no message.

"Well, what if they don't believe me or listen to what I have to say?" Moses argued.

Can you identify? "What could I possibly have to say that would be of any interest to people?" we mutter to ourselves. "How could my life ever count for anything?"

In response to Moses' self-doubt, God told him to tell the Egyptians that I AM (God himself) had sent him.

Still, Moses came up with another excuse.

"I Don't Have the Strength."

God said, "What's that in your hand, Moses?"

"My r-r-r-r-rod," Moses replied.

Then God said, "Throw it down on the ground."

Moses, terrified by this point, threw it down as fast as he could, and when the rod hit the ground it turned into a hissing snake.

"Whoa!" Moses yelled as he jumped back.

Then God told him to pick up the snake.

If I were Moses, I would have been thinking, *You've got to be kidding! Pick up a snake by the tail? I am terrified of snakes.*

However, Moses reached out ever so gingerly toward the serpent's tail and the moment he touched it, it became a rod again. But this time it was a very different rod—it was the rod of God. This meant that Moses wouldn't have to step into his life calling in his own strength; he would have the strength of God instead.

"I'm Not Qualified."

Well, Moses still wasn't convinced. He told God that he *wasn't* a public speaker, and besides, he stuttered a lot.

"Who made your mouth?" God asked, reminding Moses that he created him according to a divine plan.

"I'm just a big chicken, God. Couldn't you find someone with more courage and competence than me to do the job?"

If all Moses' excuses don't show lack of self-worth, I don't know what does.

WHAT FELLOW ADOPTEES THINK ABOUT JEWELS

Like Moses, I needed to be convinced of my worth in God's eyes before I could even consider doing a search for my birth mother or finding my life purpose. Becoming convinced that I was God's own precious jewel was the key to my moving forward. Let me add that just because God met me at this particular juncture in life and revealed this truth to me doesn't mean he will work in everyone's life in the same manner. Remember, he knows us by name. We're the lost sheep and we'll know when he's calling to us. He alone knows how to give each one of us what we need. This is what he knew I needed. However, everyone on the face of the earth needs to know God's opinion of him or her. How God does it is individual. We can't put him in a box!

I asked dozens of adoptees if they believed they are God's jewels. I'm sure you'll identify with at least one of their interesting reactions.

Cheri Manternach says, "Nope, not even a little. Maybe I'm the chunk of coal, and if given enough time, maybe, just maybe . . . I'll become a small diamond. But I have a feeling that's a long way off!"

Issie, on the other hand, agrees with the concept 100 percent. "I think adoptees are indeed God's jewels and he uses them to make the world a better place. Maybe the ones he refines the most are those who are not loved or wanted by their fleshly parents."

Laurie says it's a challenge to imagine that she is so valuable to God when she has been given up by her birth mother. (Remember . . . love and abandonment just don't equate.) "It's comforting to know I am special in God's eyes," Laurie concludes.

Frieda Moore says she is like a diamond in the rough, being refined by God. This is a great comfort to her, for she, like me, had nonexistent self-esteem for years.

"I'm not sure I have believed that I'm a jewel among jewels," says Ron Hilliard. "For so many years I have believed myself to be 'defective,' and as a result I was relinquished. As I grow, I am beginning to understand that the decision to relinquish was not about me. But it takes a while to rewrite the tapes that have been playing in my mind for so long. I am on the way, but not yet there. I'm not sure I would even know what being a jewel would feel like!"

Karen says, "Through a miraculous experience in my life I know in my mind that I am a jewel to God, but there are times, more often that not, that my heart just doesn't believe it. I feel completely unworthy of such a title."

Sharon says, "I believe that statement intellectually, but I struggle with really getting it emotionally. It has taken a lot of work over many years to even really begin to understand that God loves *me*, because of my perception of myself as being deeply flawed and not worthy of love. I now understand that God loves me as I am—which is still pretty flawed! To believe that God sees me as a jewel—well, that's still difficult. But someday, maybe I'll get there. There's hope for me yet!"

Phyllis-Anne Munro wants to believe that she is a jewel to God, to sparkle with the brilliance and beauty he has given her. But that knowledge is still "sinking in." She says that "humbled" is the word that comes to mind when told she is God's jewel.

Lori Pewsey is certain that she is a jewel among jewels. She knows full well that God loved her when she didn't love him. It's been a long road for her to believe that anything associated with the nomenclature "father" could love her for herself and she stands amazed that there was no performance factor attached to it.

I am reminded of the story about a yachting club that hosted a party at a university clubhouse on a lovely lake. One of club members said to a guest, "Come out on the verandah for a moment. I want to show you something."

They walked out the clubhouse door, which opened onto an unlit terrace overlooking the lake. The host glanced at his guest's puzzled face, thrust his hand into his pocket, pulled something out, and held out his opened palm in the light that streamed through the doorway from inside the club.

"Have you ever seen anything like these?" the host inquired.

In his hand lay what first appeared to be ten little pale stones, but as the guest gazed at them he became enthralled, "for each stone was projecting fire-ruby lights, emerald lights, golden lights, amethyst—they were indescribable! It was as if tiny living rainbows had been captured and put into translucent prisons from which they were sending forth rays of fire."

When the guest asked what he was seeing, the host replied, "Mexican opals. I like them so much that I carry them loose in my pocket and put my hand down and feel them, even if there is no time to take them out and look at them. I carry them with me wherever I go."[3]

That's the way I believe God treasures us. We all can choose, in our own time, to believe this comforting, liberating truth. Some of us are so tangled up in our pasts that we haven't taken time to sit down and

Our Choice

To learn to look at ourselves through God's eyes.

analyze where our self-esteem, or lack thereof, is coming from. Is it from other people, from our performance in life, from God, from within? This is what we need to assess.

DISCUSSION QUESTIONS FOR
SUPPORT GROUPS OR PERSONAL REFLECTION

1. Do you believe those of us who were adopted struggle more with self-worth issues than the nonadopted? If so, why?
2. Looking back on your life, can you remember how you felt about yourself? Tell us how you felt as a child, a teen, a young adult, etc.
3. Write a letter *to* and *from* your birth mother, describing how it feels to have no self-worth and how your life may change by seeing yourself through God's eyes.

DIGGING DEEPER FOR ANSWERS
TO OUR ADOPTION QUESTIONS

1. Do you have a desire to know what God thinks about you?
2. What did you learn about God in this chapter that you didn't already know?
3. Read Romans 5:1-5. How could understanding and applying these verses to your life enable you to see yourself through God's eyes?

Now on to one of my favorite topics . . . the joy of friendships with fellow adoptees.

CHAPTER TWELVE

WHY ARE WE RESISTANT TO THERAPY?

Two are better than one, because they have a good return for their work.
If one falls down, his friend can help him up. But pity the man who falls
and has no one to help him up!

— ECCLESIATES 4:9-10

I'll never forget sitting next to an adoptive mom at an adoption carnival where I was speaking. At the end of the day the time came for the children and teens to come on stage to show the parents an adoption art project they had been working on.

When all the kids were in place one of the leaders yelled over the microphone, "Who's adopted here?"

Everyone's hands flew up and squeals of delight burst forth from the little ones. "Me!" they yelled in unison.

The mom leaned over to me and said, "I've *never* seen that expression on my daughter's face. Look at her! When she yelled 'me,' her face absolutely glowed!"

Something unique happened within her daughter that day. What was it? Was it the excitement of being with kids the same age? Was it a sense of pride about her art project or a love of the spotlight?

I don't think so. I believe it was because she had been given a beautiful gift that was brand-new to her—the gift of fellow adoptees. It's a gift adoptive parents can't give. A gift birth parents can't give. A gift adoption and mental health professionals can't give. Only other adoptees can give it to one another. It is a precious commodity!

Something extraordinary happens when adoptees connect with one another. You can't touch it. You can't see it. You can't feel it. But among the adoptees, a sense of connection occurs that is just as real as the clouds in the sky. There is an unspoken bond. A feeling of camaraderie. A reassurance of being understood. A sense of belonging.

It wasn't until I was forty-five that I met my first adoptee friend, Jody Moreen. From the moment we had our first lunch together, we became fast friends. We would sit for hours at our favorite little tearoom, sip spiced tea, and talk about adoption. It was wonderful. As we spent time together and opened our hearts, we discovered that even though the circumstances of our adoptions and adoptive homes were different, common threads united us in almost every sphere of our lives. Jody has since moved to the Chicago area but we remain close friends and stay in contact.

I learned that having an adoptee as a friend is a blessing par excellence. When I didn't have one, I didn't know what I was missing. It was like growing up never having tasted triple chocolate cake!

If we *do* have an adoptee friend, then we realize that he or she is a true blessing, sent our way to strengthen, encourage, and validate all that we are, all that we were, and all that we have yet to become.

WHY WE LOVE TO BE TOGETHER

Why do adoptees enjoy being together so much? What creates that special bond?

This may be difficult for the nonadopted person to understand, but there is something almost mystical that happens when two or more adoptees gather together. Why? Because we are like *family*.

We Are Like Family

Richard Curtis says that we share a common bond that unites us across all ages, genders, races, and religions, bringing understanding that we are there for one another as we seek truth and openness in adoption.

Seven-year-old Maggie Backiewicz says, "My friends are my friends! But, with my adopted friends, it seems like we're related in some way."

Penny Callan Partridge remembers how important it was to her to know that there was a fellow adoptee in her elementary school class. "Even though he and I never talked about being adopted, there was comfort in knowing I was not alone. Then there was my excitement when I was on my way to my first adoption meeting in New York City in 1972. My excitement was actually focused on seeing what other adoptees were going to look like! Soon after that, another adopted woman and I started Adoption Forum in Philadelphia—primarily so we wouldn't have to go all the way to New York to talk with other adoptees."

Now, almost thirty years later, two of Penny's closest friends are adopted women; and her two closest men friends are adopted men. "The adopted are certainly 'my people,'" Penny says, "the way others might identify with an ethnic group. I believe that connecting with other adopted people has been just as important to me as finding my birth relatives. I cannot imagine my life without both."

Kim Norman says that fellow adoptees tend to be some of the most compassionate and understanding people she has ever met and that she feels "a special kinship" with them.

Jody Moreen says that knowing other adoptees has created a wonderful bond of connection because "there is kind of a sisterhood and brotherhood among us." For her, this has filled some of the void that was created by not knowing her heritage.

We Are Drawn to One Another

Not only are we like family . . . we are drawn together, like bees to honey. A friend of mine said that his preschooler seemed to sense when other kids were adopted and whenever he peeked in on her at preschool, she was playing with them.

Kathy says she became good friends with another adoptee, unknowingly. When they got to be good enough friends that they shared secrets with one another, lo and behold, guess what the secret was! They were both adopted. What a wonderful relationship that turned out to be. Kathy says God continues to bring fellow adoptees into her life as the years go by.

"When I was in college, I had three adopted roommates," says Connie Dawson. "I had known my freshman roommate in high school and knew she was adopted, although we never actually talked about adoption. I guess I unknowingly attracted two other roommates who were adopted and I didn't know it until later, perhaps because there was some very subterranean connection or way of being. Who knows? But when I came to learn more about adoption and what it meant to my development, I thought my roommate selection was interesting!"

Kimberly says that her best friend is a fellow Korean adoptee and that she is part of three Korean adoptee support groups. It all started when she went to a gathering for first-generation adoptees from Korea. What a joy for her to find so many people with commonality as well as diversity. She was stretched emotionally and everything she believed about adoption was challenged and is now positive.

We Have a Unique Emotional Language

Renee Mills says she values friendships with other adoptees because she is able to speak about adoption experiences and know that the other person "gets it."

College student Melinda Faust says, "My cousin Kelly is the same age as I am and is also adopted. Always having someone there who completely understands has been really important."

Cheri Freeman says that fellow adoptees can "read" each other from just a few words or their body language, which makes us feel like we belong to each other. "And that's a good thing when you don't feel you belong anywhere else," she concludes.

Bob Blanchard stresses the importance of these relationships because he has found much insight about personality traits that are common among us. He has found it so beneficial to be able to discuss these things with others who have "been there."

Jody Moreen says that even though adoptees' circumstances are unique, we share some of the same feelings and emotions. She has become more keenly aware of this since attending and leading adoption support groups with other adoptees. When one is sharing his or her adoption story, you can look up and see the heads of other adoptees nodding in understanding and agreement. "There seems to be an 'emotional language' only understood by another adoptee who has walked a mile in our shoes."

Deb Bryan was amazed at the immediate connection she felt to fellow adoptees upon first meeting them—more of a connection than to folks she had known for years.

We Can Vent Feelings

Not only do we feel comfortable in communicating with one another, but we can also blow off steam in safety. Kim Norman can be brutally honest with her fellow adoptees, and being with them surfaces issues that might otherwise be neglected, ignored, or denied. Going to support group meetings keeps her in touch with the tough issues she wants to resolve.

Paula Oliver says that it's so much easier to explain what she is feeling to someone who has been through it personally. She finds relief when talking with fellow adoptees who can wrap words around her emotions and give her the freedom to express all her feelings and frustrations.

We Don't Need to Explain Ourselves

Another wonderful benefit of our relationships is that we don't need to explain ourselves to one another—there's just kind of a "knowing."

"As an adoptee, my friendships with other adoptees have been wonderful because we understand each other and can easily have empathy for each other," says Joe Soll, CSW.

Connie Dawson agrees that it's a relief not to have to explain herself or protect herself from the judgments she feels are so often there when someone "finds out" she's adopted. "It's very subtle," Connie says. "It may have something to do with adoptees being 'rejects' or something. Sometimes I think people feel, at some primitive level, that we have experienced abandonment and they pull back because their worst fear is being abandoned. And we've already experienced it."

Phyllis-Anne Munro says that her adoptee friend gave her a sense of security and safety in his presence, even though they didn't talk about adoption.

Alex brings up a crucial point. He says that it is truly a joy to be with fellow adoptees but under one condition: that they are growing, open, aware, and eager to know about the complexities of adoption. These dynamics, he says, produce the "knowing" about one another that needs no explanation.

If you don't have a fellow-adoptee friend, you don't know what you're missing. It *is* like going through life not knowing that there is such a thing as triple chocolate cake!

WHY WE PREFER ONE ANOTHER'S PRESENCE OVER THERAPY

Now let's shift gears a bit and focus on the title of this chapter—"Why Are We Resistant to Therapy?" In preceding chapters, we've discussed loss issues at length and I think it is safe to conclude that the majority of us struggle to one degree or another with fears of rejection and abandonment. Why do I bring this up *again*? Because many of us find help for these fears in psychotherapy.

Psychotherapy certainly has its place in helping many of us become whole, and often creates an environment where we have the guts to let down the I-have-it-all-together facade and be real. That's a beginning in itself. Therapists can also teach us the necessary tools for handling difficult situations from the past and the present. If we can find the right type of therapist and therapy, we can come a long way in letting go of our "baggage" and becoming all that we were created to be.

However, there are distinct limitations involved in psychotherapy that are not inherent in adoptee-to-adoptee relationships and support.

Therapy Is Only Temporary

The first is the fact that therapy is temporary. You know what I discovered after seven *long* years of therapy and thousands of dollars under the bridge? At the end of one-hour appointments, all I could see was his or her backside leaving the room for the next appointment! I was just one of many clients and this was a business relationship to him or her, whereas for me, it was personal and I had become extremely attached.

Yes, I learned what it meant to feel safe. Yes, I learned how to open up. Yes, I learned to trust. Yes, my life was changed tremendously by professional coaching and mentoring. But eventually, whether it is after seven months or seven years of treatment, the relationship ends. For many adoptees, the "good-bye" at the end of therapy can be a huge trigger for abandonment issues.

Therapy Can Be Limited

It is vitally important for the therapist to help us grieve the loss of that trusted relationship. But even that process can fall short. Why?

First, because "termination," no matter how well done, often translates as loss and rejection for many of us. For that reason, we are much more likely to handle stopping therapy with peace of mind if it doesn't feel so final. Fellow adoptee Joyce Maguire Pavao, EdD, LCSW, LMFT, suggests what I suspect is the best way for adoptees and therapists to part. "There is a completion of each stage of therapy, but no 'termination,'" Pavao advises. "The word 'terminate' is too loaded for those who have suffered the losses associated with adoption. The therapist or team of therapists . . . remains available for consultation and therapy. This avoids the emotional cut-off and loss that are primary issues in adoption."[1]

The second reason therapy can fall short is because most physicians and therapists haven't been specifically trained to know how loss impacts adoptees. Dr. Pavao said in an article in *Family Therapy News*: "There is no real training in professional schools regarding adoption. In social work programs, there is perhaps one case study. Certainly, there is nothing in marriage and family therapy or psychology graduate programs, unless someone makes it his or her dissertation. Even then, it is hard to find faculty who understand the issues and have experience in this field. In the American medical school curriculum, there are only two or three paragraphs about adoption. The American Association for Marriage and Family Therapy (AAMFT) occasionally offers one or two workshops on adoption at its national conference. But this subject is under-represented at all mental health conferences."[2]

I must add here that there *is* a national association of adoption pediatricians. I didn't know that until I attended a recent conference. So, the medical field is coming along! Still, I don't believe there is any doctor or therapist who can understand an adoptee like a fellow adoptee *unless* that professional just happens to be an adoptee. And not just *any* adoptee, but one who is dealing with adoption-related issues on a personal, ongoing basis.

One of my friends entered a therapy relationship believing that because the therapist was also adopted, she would "get it." But she didn't. This therapist had not done her own emotional work. The result was that my friend terminated therapy and found what she needed through adoptee support groups and friendships.

The crème de la crème therapist is a fellow adoptee who *has been* and *is currently* learning and growing from his or her adoption experience. Not only can that person relate to our issues on a personal level, but also can weave in appropriate, psychological principles that provide insight that's tailor-made for an adoptee. However, these individuals are rare and difficult to find. Connie Dawson, Dirck Brown, Joe Soll, Joyce Macquire Pavao, and Betty Jean Lifton fall into this category and have been such a blessing in the therapeutic world.

Adoptee Friendships Last

Even if we're fortunate to have the most effective therapy and closure possible, we still need a huge safety net to fall into, like the kind they have at the circus for tightrope walkers. That safety net is relationships with fellow adoptees. Certainly the tools I was taught in therapy are ones I will always use. But as far as relationships go, adoptee friends are my *permanent* source of support.

Adoptee friendships are great because we never have to say goodbye. We can seek out one another and stay connected indefinitely because our relationships are not business related, but personal.

Richard Curtis has found this to be true and has put it into action. Last spring seventeen male adoptees from around the country met at the annual session of the American Adoption Congress. At the end of the session they realized what a rare experience their annual all-male meeting creates for ninety minutes. But it was so temporary because once the convention was over the group dispersed and didn't have contact until the next AAC convention.

"But this year was different!" says Richard. "We created an ongoing e-mail system (AACMA—American Adoption Congress Male Adoptees) linking us to each other, whereby we can correspond any time with the entire group or with individual members."

After reflecting on the potential depth of our relationships with each other and the limitations of therapy, wouldn't you agree with

Our Choice

To connect in meaningful, supportive relationship with at least one fellow adoptee.

me that an hour with a fellow adoptee who's growing as we are can far surpass weeks of psychotherapy? Besides, it's free!

DISCUSSION QUESTIONS FOR SUPPORT GROUPS OR PERSONAL REFLECTION

1. Do you have a fellow-adoptee friend? If so, tell about the friendship and the blessings/challenges of it.
2. Did you realize the need we have as fellow adoptees for one another before reading the stories? What is your reaction to the chapter? At least ten words!
3. Are you, or have you been, in therapy? What was it like? Did the therapist really understand adoption issues? Did you feel "heard"?
4. What are some ways you can connect with fellow adoptees? Online? Start your own support group of all adoptees? Consider using Under His Wings Workbook, free for downloading at www .sherrieeldridge.com.

DIGGING DEEPER FOR ANSWERS TO OUR ADOPTION QUESTIONS

1. Let's take a look at what the Bible says about friendship. Look up these verses, write them down, and star which one(s) are your favorites:
   • John 15:13
   • John 15:14

- Proverbs 27:10
- Proverbs 27:17

2. What adopted person was a personal friend of God? Look up Exodus 33:11.

Yes, there's something unspoken that draws us together, like magnets to metal. We share a common interest and we can huddle together in amazement as we see our common, ordinary lives gradually transform into something extraordinary, like the bud of a flower opening into a full bloom. Whenever we see each other and enter into that secret place of mutual understanding, every moment is cherished and we are invigorated in ways we never dreamed possible.

As we hear the stories of other adoptees and how adoption as well as reunion has impacted their lives, we may begin thinking about the possibility of a reunion with our own birth families. However, there is an obstacle we must overcome before considering that possibility. We'll cover that next.

CHAPTER THIRTEEN

WHY THIS UNQUENCHABLE THIRST FOR A CONNECTION WITH OUR BIRTH FAMILY?

True guilt is guilt at the obligation one owes to oneself to be oneself. False guilt is guilt felt at not being what other people feel one ought to be or assume that one is.

— R. D. Laing

Connection! Connection with our past, with our heritage. This is one of our *most* basic needs as adoptees. But because we can become so enmeshed in false guilt, our innate need for thinking about a reunion with our birth families is shoved beneath our consciousness.

Drs. David Brodzinsky and Marshall Schechter say, "Connectedness to an adopted person is like water to a person in the desert. You spend your whole life having it hidden, denied, and desecrated."[1]

Do you think this is true? Is it true that we *keep it hidden*? Oh, yes. Many of us don't think we should have such a desire, so we hold it close to our chests, like a good hand in a card game. It's another one of our adoptee secrets.

Is it true that we *deny* our need? I believe this is true also.

How? By putting up smoke screens. "Oh, the only reason I want to search is for medical reasons. I don't want a relationship with my birth mother/father."

You know what I say to adoptees who say this to me? "You really want to find your birth mother but are afraid to admit it." There is a deep yearning within us to connect. Getting medical information is important but secondary.

Brodzinsky and Schechter say that they are often asked what percentage of adoptees search for their birth parents. Their answer: "One hundred percent. In our experience, *all* adoptees engage in a search process. It may not be a literal search, but it is a meaningful search nonetheless. It begins when the child first asks, 'Why did it happen?' 'Who are they?' 'Where are they now?' These questions may be asked out loud, or they may constitute a more private form of searching—questions that are examined only in the solitude of self-reflection. The universal search begins during early school years, prompted by the child's growing awareness of adoption issues."[2]

And how about the *desecration* part?

First of all, what does that word mean? My dictionary says, "To divert from a sacred to a profane use or purpose."[3] What is it that is sacred? I believe it is our very lives and life purposes. Would it be correct to assume that connection with our birth families is sacred? I have never thought about it that way, but I think it is a beautiful concept.

Just think back to chapter 3, where we shared our innermost thoughts about our birth parents. Love in the purest human form came through the words on those pages. No matter what the circumstances of our conception or our experiences with our birth parents after birth and on into life, a deep love for them still exists, which results in a need for connection in *some* form. Because we have dual identities (adoptive and birth parents), it's impossible to think about our life purpose without including our birth families.

Why, then, is our desire for connection hidden, denied, and desecrated? I believe it's because of a phenomenon called "false guilt." This is not psychobabble, but instead a psychological reality hidden in the deepest regions of our adoptee hearts. It's irrational and illusive and the constant companion of many throughout life, even though we may not know its name.

False guilt is something we feel responsible for, over which we have or had no control. Dr. Paul Brand, a missionary physician and author, likens false guilt to phantom pain. He says, "Amputees often experience some sensation of a phantom limb. Somewhere, locked in their brains, a memory lingers of the nonexistent hand or leg. Invisible toes curl, imaginary hands grasp things, and a 'leg' feels so sturdy a patient may try to stand on it. Doctors watch helplessly, for the part of the body screaming for attention . . . does not exist."[4]

THE MESSAGES OF FALSE GUILT

What is it that we are truly responsible for? For many of us, that question leads to the messages of false guilt. How can we recognize these condemning messages and then, once we do, how can we get rid of them?

"You Are Responsible!"

Responsible for what? The message is so vague, yet haunting. Dr. Richard B. Gilbert says, "There is the innocence of a child, even an adult child, to hold on to what isn't in order to fix it."

False guilt takes a sacred purpose—our lives—and tells us that we are responsible for the circumstances surrounding our conceptions and births. "YOU were conceived in rape!" "YOU were an unplanned pregnancy." "YOU are illegitimate." "YOU may think this reunion is going well, but it's painful for me." "YOU were the reason your birth mother's life was ruined." "You were a mistake from day one."

The result? We subconsciously believe we have no right to be alive.

"You Have No Right to Be Alive."

The truth, of course, is that we had *absolutely no control* over the circumstances of our conceptions and births. Our parents did.

Kimberly Steiner silently blamed herself for her conception and being abandoned, concluding that there was something wrong about her that made her mother give her up. Either she did something wrong, wasn't large enough, wasn't pretty enough, or wasn't quiet enough. Somehow she didn't measure up to her mother's standards.

What has given me comfort about this is a verse in the New Testament that says God created *all* things. In fact, it says, "without him nothing was made that has been made."[5] This reassures me that I am not a mistake; I am supposed to be here; I am included in the *all*. That's true for each and every one of us.

"Justify Your Existence by Meeting the Needs of Others."

If we take another step into false guilt, we believe that we must prove our worth. This often takes the form of unhealthy caretaking—tending to others' needs and desires at the expense of our own well-being. If we were to use a psychobabble term, we would be flaming "codependents," deriving our worth and reason for existence by serving the needs of others.

Do you ever want to say to a parent who expects too much of you, "Can't I just be your daughter/son? I don't want to have to work to meet your needs."

Connie Dawson says that if she were to speak realistically about her parents, she would say that they were emotionally immature and needy. They complained about their lives, but did nothing to deal with what they were complaining about. She thinks this is important because her mother had suffered three unsuccessful pregnancies before Connie was adopted and she doesn't believe her parents ever grieved their losses. They had so much repressed grief that Connie picked up their pain and tried to take care of it, never wanting to be the cause of their "feeling bad."

Her mother also shoved responsibility on Connie for her dad's anger and anxiety. "No wonder I learned to stake my existence on how well I could relieve the stress of others," says Connie, "to the exclusion of myself, of course. The trouble with adapting by being so 'helpful' is that I didn't develop *my* identity aside from being the helpmate."

Richard Curtis says he was the caretaker in all of his relationships. But why not? He had learned those traits well in his adoptive home, desperately seeking to be loved by an adoptive mother who herself needed help in dealing with the loss of her husband and two stillborn children. As a child, Richard could not provide this kind of help, of course. He lived in terror and felt that survival in his home depended on taking care of his emotionally broken mom.

"Our Pain and Shame Are Your Fault."

Another lie of false guilt is that we are responsible for our birth parents' pain and shame.

After the unsuccessful reunion with my birth mother, whenever I told my story I felt a heaviness come over me, like I was at the funeral of someone I love. One day I realized how erroneous some of my beliefs were. I said to myself, "Sherrie, you're accepting your birth mother's pain and carrying her shame. You don't have to do that any longer." So now when I tell my story, I say, "I have no relationship with my birth mother." And I leave it at that.

Even now, after my birth mother's death, her granddaughter, after clearing out her condo found something I had written about adoption. "Her life was never the same after that," she said. "It (me) ruined her life."

I know now I didn't ruin her life. She died a miserable and lonely woman because of the choices she made.

"You Are Guilty, Guilty, Guilty."

If we are people of faith, we may confess everything possible before God, yet retain an indefinable sense of guilt. We may even believe that God has forgiven us, yet this nagging guilt plagues us. I know one adoptee who begins practically every sentence with "I am sorry but. . . ."

Sandy Garrett says that she treated her adoptive mom horribly as a teen and later her mom died, leaving Sandy with a lot of guilt, wondering if her mom ever knew Sandy loved her. What made it doubly confusing for Sandy is that now she is reunited with her birth mother and she treats her like she *should* have treated her adoptive mom. Sandy says, "I constantly worry that my adoptive mom is watching over me and is hurt by how nice I am to my birth mom."

I have learned to bypass false guilt by choosing to believe what the apostle John says in the New Testament: "If we claim that we're free of sin, we're only fooling ourselves. A claim like that is errant nonsense. On the other hand, if we admit our sins—make a clean breast of them—he won't let us down; he'll be true to himself. He'll forgive our sins and purge us of all wrongdoing."[6] If I confess my wrongs to God and guilt keeps haunting me, it's a dead giveaway that I'm carrying false guilt.

It's also possible to be caught in a cycle of performance-based acceptance with confessing sin. We religiously confess every sin and are nervous we've missed one. What would God do? Would He club us over the head? What about the sins we can't see?

What good news to know that when Jesus said, "It is finished," he was talking about our sins, past, present, and future. Every one of them he took to the cross and paid the penalty for by his death. When unfounded guilt overwhelms us, we need to remember his work and those words.

HOW TO BE LIBERATED FROM FALSE GUILT

Maybe now is the time to change from buying into false guilt. False guilt can and does keep us from making that connection with our birth families. Even though you have missing history, there are ways that you can make that sense of connection and face your greatest fear. Some adopted people never follow through with a search even though they have all the information. Nonetheless, they have allowed themselves to think deeply about the possibility. I believe that's facing your greatest fear. I have seen it happen time after time in adoptee support groups. People listen to the story of Moses and other fellow adoptees, and when they hear various reunion stories they start to feel free to think about their own.

Hearing Another Adoptee's Story Brings Freedom to Consider Searching

That's what happened to me. When I read about how God himself brought Moses' birth brother, Aaron, back into his life in response to Moses' whining about being incompetent for the task God had set before him, I was encouraged. God told the stuttering Moses, "I know he can speak well. He is already on his way to meet you, and his heart will be glad when he sees you."[7] Moses had a choice at that point. He could either open himself up to a reunion with his birth brother—and to fulfilling God's will with his brother beside him—or he could continue to hide out in the desert. Moses made the right choice, and God honored it in countless ways.

Jody Moreen had a similar experience. She says that attendance at a local adoption support group gave her the gumption to go forward with her reunion. It was at those meetings that she gained confidence that searching for her birth mother was not wrong or selfish, but instead a very normal desire and valid emotional need.

"Being a person of faith, I needed to surrender this desire to God," Jody says. "I desired a confirmation that it was indeed his will that I search for my birth family and history. In time I felt assurance when I read in the Bible, 'Then you will know the truth, and the truth will set you free.'"8

KNOWING GOD LOVES YOU AND WON'T WITHHOLD ANY GOOD THING FROM YOU

Eventually, we have to do battle with the old ways of thinking. We need to know what true guilt is. True guilt is the result of moral and spiritual failing.

Often, we adopted people feel false guilt for what we have lost, but this is false guilt. For every loss, God promises gain—a deeper relationship with him. See if you can identify with any of these:

- I didn't appreciate the acceptance of Christ until I had been utterly rejected.
- I didn't appreciate his strength until I allowed myself to become weak.
- I didn't appreciate his loyalty to me until another betrayed me.
- I didn't appreciate his grace until I fell flat on my face.
- I didn't believe my Lord's belief in me until I felt the sting of persecution.
- I didn't appreciate the light of his countenance until I sat in darkness.
- I didn't appreciate the little things in life until I looked death straight in the face.
- I didn't appreciate the healing balm of Gilead until I had been deeply wounded.
- I didn't appreciate the shoulder of a friend until my heart had been broken.
- I didn't appreciate the indwelling Holy Spirit until I felt totally abandoned.

- I didn't appreciate intimacy with God until I spent time in the desert.
- I didn't appreciate the hope of heaven until I buried a loved one.
- I didn't appreciate the privilege of prayer until I had no one to whom I could turn.
- I didn't appreciate Jesus as Lord until my life became unmanageable.
- I didn't appreciate Jesus as my Life until I came to the absolute end of my own resources and strength.

If any of the preceding rings true, how can we heal and move forward?

Our Choice

To weed out false guilt and begin thinking about how to meet our basic need for connection with our heritage, but ultimately, with God.

DISCUSSION QUESTIONS FOR SUPPORT GROUPS OR PERSONAL REFLECTION

1. Which of the following do you believe adoptees feel the most false guilt for?
   - For being alive (my life was a mistake).
   - For not being the fantasy child their parents desired.
   - For not living up to parental expectations.
   - Feeling like I don't belong in my family.
2. Do you ever feel like you're "intruding," or are unwelcome? If so, could this be indicative of false guilt?
3. Write a letter *to* and *from* your birth mother about false guilt.
4. False guilt is just that—false. How would you separate it from true guilt?
5. How do you think false guilt ties in with perfectionism? How often do you say, "I wish I woulda, coulda, shoulda . . ."

DIGGING DEEPER FOR ANSWERS
TO OUR ADOPTION QUESTIONS

1. Read Ephesians 1:3-4. Do you believe there is a difference between being adopted by your parents and being adopted by God?

2. Read Ephesians 1:5-12. What do these verses say that Christ did for you?

3. According to Ephesians 1:13, when is a person "included" in Christ?

4. What happens to those who hear the word of truth (verse 13) and believe it?

5. According to Ephesians 1:14, once you are "included," can you be shut out? How does this make you feel as an adopted person who has suffered abandonment?

Even though we've learned the difference between true and false guilt, we still may feel twinges of false guilt when we talk about our birth families in the presence of our parents. We'll discuss this next.

CHAPTER FOURTEEN

WHY ARE WE AFRAID OF TALKING TO OUR PARENTS ABOUT OUR BIRTH FAMILY?

Adoptees are caught between the loyalty they feel to the adoptive parents who rescued them and the invisible loyalty to the mother who gave them birth.

— BETTY JEAN LIFTON

Have you ever stretched a rubber band between your hands as far as possible? You pull in opposite directions, taking a deep breath because you're afraid the band is going to break. When you're near the breaking point, you let go because you don't want to get snapped.

Well, what happens if *you* are that rubber band and are being pulled in opposite directions out of loyalty to both sets of parents—adoptive and birth? This is another issue that involves our dual identity (adoptive and birth), and coming to terms with it means that we must learn that it's all right to talk about our birth parents to our adoptive parents.

Struggles with whom we should feel loyal to are common among adoptees; in fact, some of us may be experiencing those feelings right now. So let's take a look at what loyalty issues really are and how they affect our relationships with our adoptive parents.

A loyalty issue occurs when we feel we must be protective of our adoptive parents. We perceive that any verbalization of our feelings about our birth parents would hurt them or make them perceive that we are ungrateful for what they've done for us. Yet we naturally long to know our birth families. We wonder, *Is it permissible or possible to be loyal to both?*

Synonyms for "loyal" are: "faithful, allegiant, true-hearted, devoted, pledged, dedicated, steadfast, unchanging, firm, stable, solid, supportive."[1] Knowing this, where does our struggle originate? Is it just "built in" to us as adoptees because of the dynamics of adoption, or could negative reactions of adoptive parents be a contributing factor?

Lori Pewsey knows full well that asking even a few questions about her birth family will cause problems, so she hasn't told her mother she is searching. As a child, when Lori *did* ask her mother those few questions, she got the quivering-lip, teary-eyed response. Her mother would say in a hurt tone, "Why would you ever want to know?" Since that time, Laurie knew that her desire and quest to find her birth family would have to be her secret.

Kenny Tucker says, "My adoptive parents have chosen not to meet my biological parents, so there's some sense of ignoring the 'pink elephant [unspoken but obvious subject]' in the living room when I'm with my adoptive parents or my biological family comes up in conversation."

WHAT WE BELIEVE ABOUT LOYALTY

Kim Norman felt the tug of loyalty at an early age. She says, "I do remember feeling guilt about expressing thoughts about my birth parents to my adoptive parents when I was young. I felt insecure about how they would react to my initiating a discussion out of my curiosity."

Melissa started thinking about her birth mother when she learned about her adoption at age sixteen. Although she felt she had the right to think about her birth family, she also felt guilt, fearing she was being disloyal to her adoptive parents. She was fortunate to have a loving family with the added bonus of being raised with a biological sibling, but she still felt guilt. No wonder Melissa felt guilt—her parents didn't tell her she was adopted until age sixteen! Through their actions, they made it quite clear to whom loyalty was due.

Loyalty issues can also begin as we contemplate searching. If they have begun by then, they often intensify as we move closer to reunion.

Even though Renee Mills's adoptive father has been dead for thirteen years, she hasn't told her adoptive mom that she is going to meet her birth father in just a few months. She describes her mother as "fiercely protective of my dad's memory" and Renee is sure her mother would say she was betraying her dead father by seeking out her birth dad.

We Feel We Must Choose Between the Two Families

As adoptees, we may be confused about to whom we are supposed to be loyal. Many of us have a special place in our hearts for our birth parents, yet we fear that talking about them—or even thinking about them—is an act of disloyalty to our adoptive parents. We feel caught between a rock and a hard place because we believe we must choose between the two.

Rebecca L. Ricardo says, "I can remember thinking as a young child of six or seven that my birth parents could come and find me and that I would have to choose between them and my adoptive parents. This was a choice I did not feel I could ever make."

Lisa Storms says she doesn't feel safe talking about her roller-coaster emotions with her adoptive parents since she has started searching. She says they are more interested in the facts of the search than in how she is feeling. This has caused her to hold back emotionally, the result being that she feels she has to choose between her two sets of parents.

We Fear We Might Create Misunderstandings

It took Jody Moreen a year after starting her search to share the news with her adoptive parents. Because her relationship with them was warm and loving, she feared creating a misunderstanding. However, after the initial shock, they encouraged her to carry on.

Paula Oliver says that she didn't want to hurt her folks but when she finally decided to go ahead with her search, much to her delight her parents were very supportive and even expressed that they wished they would have had more information to give her.

Emmary Nicholson says, "I haven't told my adoptive dad that I was reunited, even a year after my birth mom passed away. I *do* want to tell him though. Loyalty to my adoptive dad is also why I haven't pursued a relationship with my biological dad. I've written him a letter that went unanswered. I haven't done anything since then to contact him."

We May Appear Ungrateful

We are in the midst of loyalty issues when we are struggling with thoughts like, "They have given me everything when I had nothing." "I was an orphan and they gave me a roof over my head and plenty of love." "I long to talk about my birth parents but I feel I owe all my allegiance to my adoptive parents."

Sue says that when she found her birth parents, she didn't tell her adoptive parents, concluding that they would see it as an act of betrayal on her part, an example of her not having any gratitude for the great life they had worked hard to provide. Guilt plagued her. "Yet I *needed* to search," Sue says.

We Feel Sneaky and Guilty

Another loyalty issue is the feeling that we are being sneaky. We feel like traitors.

I can't begin to tell you how sneaky I felt that day I drove out of my dad's driveway, turned the car as if heading for Indiana, but went instead to the county courthouse. There I was, a grown woman, still feeling like she had to sneak around like a child. I felt like my parents were in the living room and I was in the kitchen trying to quietly get my hand in the cookie jar for a treat. How dare I sneak around looking for a cookie when I had a dad who loved me so much he would have done anything for me? What would Dad do if he found out? I was afraid he might become angry. After all, I was their one and only child and I didn't think he would want to share me with anyone.

Cheri Freeman felt sneaky when she found her birth mother's last name on the "receipt" for her adoption. She didn't mention it to her adoptive parents, but years later when she was ready to search she asked a friend to pose as her birth mother at the hospital where she was born to illegally verify the last name and obtain the first name of her birth mother. As she began her actual search, Cheri wondered if her late mother would approve of her decision. In preparing for a move, Cheri's daughter found Cheri's birth mother's name written on the inside of her baby book, which was proof that her mom knew the name all along. This brought Cheri great peace, believing that this was her mom's way of giving permission for her to search for her birth family.

Connie Dawson says, "Would it be enough to say I waited until my dad had died and my mother was in a nursing home? When I contacted my birth family, I did so without telling my mother. I felt so sneaky but my counselor helped me realize that my belief that I had to protect [my adoptive parents] at the cost of my own needs was like a 'condition of life' for me. As an adult, I could, of course, make different decisions from those I made as a child, but I've been surprised by how strongly I felt I was being disloyal and untrue to them and to myself."

HOW WE CAN RESOLVE LOYALTY ISSUES

After listening to these struggles, wouldn't you say that it's time that we gain some kind of peace and autonomy? As adoptees, we have the *right* and oftentimes the *need* to be loyal to *both* sets of parents. Having a dual identity is a fundamental fact of our uniqueness.

If we're allowing ourselves to be pulled in both directions, what is the answer? Do we live in a state of stress and tension all our lives, feeling like we have to walk on eggshells when it comes to the topic of our birth parents? No, we don't!

Let's go back first to the opening illustration of the rubber band. We have determined that we know what it feels like to be that rubber band. But what would happen if we could cut that band? What if we made the decision to verbalize our thoughts and feelings to our adoptive parents without reservation? Talking about our birth families is *not* tantamount to mutiny! Instead, it's a sign that we are beginning to integrate the dual aspects of our identity . . . and that's good!

Resolving loyalty issues is a difficult task because we have an ingrained belief that we need to take care of our adoptive parents' feelings. We need to consciously remind ourselves that they are big people and can take care of themselves. In addition, we need to give up trying to control them for fear they will reject us. We can't control anyone's responses, except our own. Accepting that fact is taking a big step toward maturity.

When loyalty issues come up, we can use self-talk to remind ourselves, "This is a loyalty issue and it feels very uncomfortable. But giving up control of how my parents react is what I must do in order to grow. Do I want to grow? Yes . . . but I will experience growing pains along the way, especially regarding this issue."

I am reminded of a passage in the New Testament that talks about what true love is. Part of it goes like this: Love "takes pleasure in the flowering of truth, puts up with anything, trusts God always, always looks for the best, never looks back, but keeps going to the end."[2]

Is loving like this going to be easy? Read on with me. "When I was an infant at my mother's breast, I gurgled and cooed like any infant. When I grew up, I left those infant ways for good. We don't yet see things clearly. We're squinting in a fog, peering through a mist. But it won't be long before the weather clears and the sun shines bright!"[3]

It isn't going to be easy for us, but Maggie, age seven, gives us hope that adoptees *can* work through this conundrum of divided loyalties. She says, "I don't feel guilty for thinking and talking about my birth family. It doesn't mean I love my adoptive family any less!"

I would imagine that those of you who have grown up in totally open adoptions, with ongoing relationships between your birth and adoptive parents, might not have as many loyalty issues. However, even in the healthiest of families, there are bound to be some, for we are all fallen human beings. No birth or adoptive parent, no person on the face of this earth, can claim perfection. And so what is our choice about loyalty?

Our Choice

To freely discuss our birth families with our adoptive parents

The rubber band has been cut by our own choosing! The pressure is off. We are moving toward more and more freedom! Every time we recognize a loyalty issue, we can give thanks that we are unique creations with a dual heritage, and that even though it is often difficult for others to understand or accept, we can feel confident that this is our life path.

DISCUSSION QUESTIONS FOR
SUPPORT GROUPS OR PERSONAL REFLECTION

1. Make a list of statements and behaviors that create "rubber band" feelings and reactions. Following each statement, write a healthy response. Here are several to get you started:

- "Why would you want to meet *them*?"

  "Because they are a part of me and not knowing them makes me feel empty inside."

  "The puzzle of my life is missing pieces and I need to find them to complete it."

  "They gave me my body and my first home. Why wouldn't I want to meet them?"

- "Leave us out of this . . . you can search, but we don't want any part of it."

  "That's fine, Mom and Dad. I respect your choice."

  "You are free to do whatever you want."

  "The decision is up to you."

- "Why would you want to do *that*?"

  "I want to talk about and meet my birth parents because they are an integral part of my life."

  "Because they gave me the gift of life."

  "Because I have a special place in my heart for them."

- "I guess it means that we didn't do a good enough job as your parents."

  "It's not about your parenting; it's about my needs."

  "Parenting skills have nothing to do with my choice."

  "I wish you didn't feel that way."

- "Why would you want to open *that* can of worms?"

  "I don't consider it a can of worms. I consider it a bouquet of flowers."

  "It hurts me when you refer to my birth family as a can of worms."

  "When you refer to them as a can of worms, I feel ashamed of myself. Please don't say it again."

- "Do whatever—it's no big deal to us. We really don't care."

  "It may not be a big deal to you, but it is to me."

  "That's a pretty unloving thing to say."

  "I wish you did care, but I can't control your thoughts."

- Complete silence when we talk about birth families.
  "If you don't want to talk about it, that's okay with me.
  "Your silence speaks volumes."
  Walk away.
2. Write a letter *to* and *from* your birth mother about this issue of loyalty.

DIGGING DEEPER FOR ANSWERS TO OUR ADOPTION QUESTIONS

1. Read Romans 8:28-29. What does God promise to do in and through the confusing things of life for those who belong to him?
2. Read Romans 11:17. How could you liken this verse to adoption? Who is the wild olive shoot?
3. What does this verse say happens to those who trust in Jesus? What specific word describes the shoot's relationship to the true (hint: starts with "g")?
4. What does God promise you will become? See Isaiah 61:3b.

We have determined that talking about our birth families to our parents is not disloyalty! Thus, we are now at a fork in the road where we must decide what path we will take—the narrow or the wide way. We'll see what's involved with both paths in the following chapter.

CHAPTER FIFTEEN

WHY DO WE FIND IT SO HARD TO GIVE OURSELVES PERMISSION TO SEARCH?

Two roads diverged in a wood

And I took the one less traveled by

And that has made all the difference.

— ROBERT FROST

We're at a fork in the road now and there's a sign pointing in two directions. One part says "Familiar" and the other, "Unknown."

The path called "Familiar" looks appealing because it's broad, smooth, and well traveled. The other road, "Unknown," is narrow, infested with crabgrass and dandelions, and appears long unused. Ahead is a forest of trees that looks impenetrable.

The road called "Familiar" represents the opinions and feelings of others about what we should say or do in regard to the option of searching for and reuniting with our birth families. "Unknown" is the path that leads straight into our hearts and speaks to us with a still, small voice.

What road will each one of us take? Will we take the familiar road by listening only to the voices of others, possibly ending up with a heart full of bitterness and what-might-have-beens? Or will we take the road of Robert Frost, the narrow one, and be true to that still, small voice that says, "This is the way; walk in it"?[1]

I am a strong advocate for searching, for I believe that *through the process*, no matter where it leads, we grow. In grace. In love. In forgiveness. In peace. It's a win/win situation because positive personal growth occurs regardless of the outcome. Every fear must be faced and every stone overturned as we seek clues to our past.

Some of us might not be able to make a literal search, but we can search in other ways in order to connect with our past. For instance, Susan was left on the steps of an orphanage in Romania with only a diaper to her name. She can't obtain any history, but she could still do some searching by visiting her birth land and seeing the orphanage she lived in. Or she could make a "life book," filled with images of her native land.

There comes a time for many when we *know* we want to search. Every time we dream about the possibility, we are pumped! We have gone too far down the adoption road to turn back. What is the driving force behind all that adrenaline?

The quest for truth, plain and simple. Truth about ourselves. Truth about what is written on our sealed adoption certificates and hospital records. Truth about how adoption has impacted our lives. Truth about our "other" parents and family out there somewhere. Truth about how our adoptive parents *really* feel about a possible reunion. Truth about what life is all about. Truth about what Truth really is.

Bob Blanchard says, "It really doesn't matter if the outcome of your search is good or not — it's just important to know the truth."

We have this burning desire to know because truth brings freedom. Freedom from the adoption baggage we have carried around for years. Freedom from the paralysis of not being able to be ourselves and know it's okay. Freedom from shallow living and compromise.

Even though we have this wonderful promise of growth and freedom that results from discovering truth, it's scary to embark on the narrow road and, as a result, our search may wax and wane as the years go by. But that's okay.

Laurie says that her search flickered on and off like a lightbulb, but beneath the flickering was a steady desire to know truth.

"It took me a long time to decide to go ahead and begin searching," says Ron Hilliard. "I had actually begun the process about five years earlier only to decide not to proceed. At that point I think I was mostly afraid of what I would find, and especially afraid that if I did find my birth mother, she would not want to have anything to do with me."

Paula Oliver remembers being excited, scared, hopeful, and wary all at the same time. "Mostly I felt like I was on a treasure hunt."

THE RISKS OF SEARCHING

Why does the narrow path often feel so scary? Because every single thing we encounter will take us into territory we've never traveled. Those ominous woods that lie ahead on our path may be filled with either life-giving redemption or heart-wrenching rejection. Therefore, we must count the cost before we begin to determine if we are willing to expose ourselves to such risk. It really hurts to be rejected and we must make sure we're ready to withstand that pain. We must have a good support system in place of friends, family, and clergy who will hold us up as we work through the indescribable disappointment and loss.

We May Experience Disillusionment

The illusion of many is that if we search and find the long-lost relative and ultimately have a glorious reunion, we will instantly feel "normal" and *not adopted* anymore. All the pain from our past will magically disappear.

There's that adoptee fantasy again! Many adoptees in support groups chuckle when another member returns fresh from reunion.

"Do you still feel adopted?" we ask.

The answer is always yes, accompanied by a red face!

Feelings of being adopted *don't* go away! Remember, we are engaged in a lifelong process of growth and the particular path for us involves adoption and learning to grow from the wounds of being relinquished by our first family. Searching and reuniting are not the panacea—the God who is ready to hold us in his everlasting arms is the only one that is the panacea, the one who can comfort every aching abyss of our hearts.

We May Be Rejected by a Birth Parent

Another risk of reuniting is rejection from a birth parent.

"Fear? You betcha!" says Connie Dawson. "When adoptees consider searching (getting what they need), they are faced with huge risks."

Connie's fear was that if her birth family (her birth mother was dead) "rejected" her, and by contacting them she might put her relationship with her adoptive parents at risk, then she would have no one. She would be nowhere. "I would have seen to my own exile. This is the same fearful space I faced when my birth mother 'sent me away' and I felt that every connection I had was severed. I was like any animal who is born, who is helpless, and whose mother walks off."

Lorraine says that her birth father refuses all responsibility and that opening herself up to a reunion with him would be a crisis waiting to happen. She wouldn't be able to withstand the heartache and rejection.

Fear of Not Being Able to Handle the Emotions

Another risk we must face is that overwhelming emotion may occur. As I anticipated meeting my birth mother, I didn't know if I would laugh or cry. It's totally new territory we're traversing.

Penny Callan Partridge says, "Many of us don't want to risk having strong feelings, or particular feelings, stirred up. Ultimately, we are probably choosing between one set of feelings and another: the feelings that go along with not knowing versus the feelings that may be stirred up if we choose to try to learn more. Neither way is comfortable! But none of these fears is enough to stop the majority of us. The need to know about ourselves, to know our own stories, is just too great."

Our Adoptive Parents May Feel Hurt

The most pressing concern for Jody Moreen when she contemplated searching was that she would alienate her adoptive parents. Though she had an open, honest, and loving relationship with her adoptive mother, the whole story of her birth and adoption was not a topic ever brought up for discussion. She had always been a very pleasing and compliant child and desired her parents' approval. Therefore, it was difficult for her to give herself permission as an adult in her thirties to search for the missing pieces of her past. She didn't know how her adoptive parents would interpret her search and was concerned about hurting them in any way.

It took Renee Mills nine months to finally tell her adoptive mother that she had been matched with her birth mom through the International Soundex Reunion Registry. She was terrified of hurting her. She was flying to Florida to meet her birth mom and didn't want to lie to her adoptive mom about her destination. Renee asked her adoptive mother to sit down because she had something very important to tell her. It was then that she began showing pictures of her birth family sent to her by her birth mother. Tears flowed, but at last it was all out in the open. Sometimes she senses her mom getting defensive when she talks about her birth mother, but her mom has encouraged their relationship. Renee's birth mother and adoptive mom have now met each other and both express appreciation for the role the other plays in Renee's life.

THE REWARDS OF SEARCHING

Obviously, searching entails some significant risks, and each of us must make our own decision. It's our choice to make, no one else's.

But now on to the good part of searching—the rewards!

We May Experience Feelings of Completeness

"I am complete," says Kasey Hamner. "I know who I am and what I want in life. No more secrets and lies. No more wondering where I got my funny-looking knees or if depression is part of my family history. Knowledge is power, in my opinion."

Some of our adoptive parents will be threatened when we tell them we feel "complete." They will wonder why we didn't feel complete with them. However, if we think of the completeness as the missing piece of our life's puzzle finally being found and put in place, it may be easier for them to understand. I just tell you this as a warning to tread lightly if your adoptive parents are struggling and not supportive of you. You may want to share your feelings and joy from feeling complete with your supportive people.

Phyllis-Anne Munro has gained a much greater sense of wholeness. For years she never believed she could be or deserved to be a mother. After meeting her birth father, for the first time she felt she could parent. "I feel a much greater sense of who I am. What a gift!"

Richard Curtis says that if growth is accomplished through truth and knowledge, then since beginning his search and reunion process, eight years of healing have occurred in his life. The results, he says, are a sense of peace, serenity, and an understanding of where he fits in the universe.

"Understanding my adoption experience," Richard says, "has allowed me to bring authenticity to my relationships with family, friends, and others in my life. I no longer hide my thoughts and feelings—the veil of secrecy has been lifted. People now get the real Richard since I've uncovered my past, understand how precious the present is, and perhaps have an idea of where I'm going and who's going with me in the future. Perhaps these are the blessings I can also offer to others."

We May Feel More Self-Confident

I remember one twenty-something adopted female sitting with her newly found birth mother. Sipping tea in my kitchen, she said that now that she had found her birth mother, she knows how "to be."

"I think that searching was more about finding myself than it was about finding my birth family," says Ron Hilliard. "The process of finding my birth family led to the realization that 'this is who I am.' A whole part of me was discovered, and I have found that the process of finding my true identity is still going on. I 'found my voice'—I now speak out of a real authenticity because I have a clearer sense of who I am."

For Kenny Tucker, meeting both his birth parents was life changing. "I am more secure in who I am. I feel I can accomplish anything since I waded through the fears of rejection to the other side. I am humbled by the magnitude of it all."

Laurie's search has helped her to accept her beginnings. Before searching she had so much anger about not knowing her past. She found a tombstone at the end of her search for her birth mother but has been able to glean information about her from relatives. As a result, she is better able to accept herself.

We May Be Able to Finally Put a Painful Past to Rest

Issie came to the conclusion that she couldn't help the circumstances of her childhood, but that she could still create her own life. She was placed with parents who were dirt poor and tried to poison her mind about her birth parents from day one. "White trash," they called them. Mentally ill. No morals when it came to sex. Issie doesn't know who her father is even though her adoptive parents know and could tell her if they were the least bit loving.

Issie used to be terrified of rejection, but no longer. Why? Because she made a life-transforming choice to say good-bye to the lies and abuse of the past and determine instead to be all God created her to be. She is a beautiful woman of faith who loves God and doesn't have one ounce of bitterness in her heart. She believes that those who are rejected not only by birth parents but by adoptive parents are very special to God — the object of his tender love and care. She is a blessing to others who read her writing on various Web sites.

Increased Ability to Love and Be Loved

After Frieda Moore talked with her birth mother, she finally felt like she belonged in her adoptive family. She says the love and acceptance were there all along, but she couldn't receive or give love the way she longed to until she completed her search and reunion. She was finally able to be vulnerable enough to love and let others love her.

Deepened Love for Adoptive Parents

Just about 100 percent of the reunited adoptees I've met have a deeper appreciation for their adoptive parents. If adoptive parents could only realize this prior to and during reunion, what a difference it would make for everyone. When Jody Moreen found her birth family, both parents were deceased, but she had three living sisters. Not long after a successful reunion with the sisters, her adoptive parents met them and everyone was warm and welcoming.

Jody says, "The most precious gift my adoptive mother has ever given me was when, unbeknown to me, she bought a bouquet of flowers and suggested we drive to the cemetery to visit my birth mother's grave. We walked silently to the unmarked grave and I wept as my mother gently laid the flowers down at the site. Never in this world have I felt closer to my mother. To think that she would honor my birth mother like this has forever deepened my love for her."

We May Experience Spiritual Growth

Frieda Moore says her growth comes from God, not the acceptance or rejection of her birth mother. Her birth mother's rejection just pressed her closer into his arms, and realizing she has been adopted by her heavenly Father is so much more precious and valuable than any earthly relationship ever could be.

These are just a few of the rewards of surviving the wintery times of our souls. I can assure you that you will grow tremendously, whether the outcome of your search is positive or painful. Even though my reunion turned sour and I had no relationship with my birth mother whatsoever until her death in 2006, I have grown in ways I never dreamed possible. In fact, I believe I have grown *more* as a result of being rejected! I have learned that people can't meet my needs. Only God can. I have also learned that God's comfort is so much deeper than any rejection life can throw at me.

Our Choice

To tune out the input of others and listen to our own hearts, but especially to God.

And so, in light of all the blessings —some wonderful, some painful—of search and reunion, what choice do we need to make?

DISCUSSION QUESTIONS FOR SUPPORT GROUPS OR PERSONAL REFLECTION

1. Make a list of pros and cons about searching.
   The only person who needs to be convinced that it is time to search is you. Right now your heart may feel overwhelmed with some of the feelings that our fellow adoptees have discussed. What is needed is an objective look at the whole idea of search and reunion, and a list such as this will help accomplish that purpose.
2. Define in your own words what it means to be true to yourself.
   This phrase "true to yourself" may seemingly go against your

religious beliefs. If you are a person of faith, the One you want to always be true to is God. Philippians 2:13 says: "for it is God who works in you to will and to act according to his good purpose." It is his voice we need to heed—not other people's, which we are prone to do if we are overly compliant adoptees. We need to listen to that still small voice within so that we can do what he wants us to do.

3. Write a letter *to* and *from* your birth mother about the topic of searching.

DIGGING DEEPER FOR ANSWERS TO OUR ADOPTION QUESTIONS

1. Read Ecclesiastes 3:1-8. Which of these verses stand out to you? Which verse typifies where you are in life right now?
2. Read Isaiah 49:15-16. Who will never reject you?
3. Read Jeremiah 1:5. Who knew you before you were in your birth mother's womb?
4. Read Psalm 139:16. Who planned your life before you were born?
5. Read Psalm 139:13. Who was with you in your birth mother's womb?
6. Considering all these verses, what does this tell you about how God feels about you?

Now that we've considered the risks as well as the rewards of searching, it's time to begin thinking about taking some concrete steps. We'll cover that in the following chapter. We're on the upward swing now in our journey, so hold tight.

CHAPTER SIXTEEN

WHY ARE WE TREATED LIKE CHILDREN WHEN WE SEARCH?

Any search for information no matter how "high" or "low" the purpose — whether it is baseball statistics or philosophy — is valid because it is a search for truth.

— MONA MCCORMICK

I f your list of pros and cons encouraged you to go ahead with your search, this chapter is for you. Nothing is impossible. It may *seem* that way, but you will be surprised at what may show up when you start digging.

Most of us have an "amended" birth certificate, meaning that the names of our birth parents have been removed and only nondentifying information is available. This information may include whether or not they have other children, their occupations, and residence. I know this is more than frustrating — to think that our birth parents' names have been removed and that we're given "bogus" birth certificates.

Some of you may have much more information to start with than others. Because of the wonderful efforts of the American Adoption Congress, One Voice, Bastard Nation, Origins USA, and similar groups, a few states now have open records—Alabama, Alaska, Delaware, Kansas, New Hampshire, and Oregon. Some states also have registries through which birth parents and adoptees can register to let the other person know they are interested in reuniting.

Others of you may be experiencing an open adoption and have no need to search. You are in direct contact with your birth parents. Let me warn you, however, that as great as open adoption is, it's not the panacea. I have a friend who has experienced an open adoption and fell apart when she went off to college. The issue of grief remains the same for those of you who know your birth parents because you don't know them in the way that you would have had they chosen to parent you. This is a great loss that needs to be grieved.

Realize that the suggestions I make for searching are from my own experience. Each state differs in adoption laws and regulations, so my counsel is only a springboard to get you thinking and moving forward with some sense of direction. How sorry I am not to have known about the wonderful resource book on searching by Jayne Askin titled *Search: A Handbook for Adoptees and Birth Parents*. She goes into much more detail than I will here.

CONCRETE STEPS FOR SEARCHING

Based on my experience, here are steps to take in searching for your birth parents, starting in logical sequence.

Find Out If Your State Has a Registry

Some states have adoption registries through which both birth parents and adoptees can file a document stating that they would like contact with the lost loved one. Contact your county courthouse for this information.

Contact the Adoption Agency

Mine was a private adoption, so I didn't have the resource of an adoption agency, but the majority of you do. Were you adopted through an agency or were you a ward of the state?

If you don't have your birth mother's name, ask the current social worker at the agency through which you were adopted. Even though they're not allowed by law to give out names, they sometimes do. A friend of mine kept calling and talking to the same social worker every time. The social worker began to feel compassion for my friend and eventually revealed bits of information and eventually the name of her birth mother.

I am not implying that you manipulate the social worker, but "the squeaky wheel gets the grease." There is nothing wrong with consistent contact. Remember, you have the moral and human right to know your history. I gained much confidence when reading the genealogy of Jesus in the first chapter of Matthew in the Bible. Jesus knew his birth history!

Request a Nonidentifying Release of Information Form from Your County of Birth

The next thing is to contact the probate judge in the county where you were born (if you know it) and request the form for nonidentifying information. You might be given this kind of information:

- Age information on your birth mother
- Education background of your birth mother
- Her religious affiliation
- Her physical description
- Medical history of your birth mother
- Your family nationality
- Professions of the birth mother and her birth parents
- If the birth mother and father were single or married
- Hobbies
- Why you were placed for adoption
- Ages of the birth grandparents

- First names of grandparents
- Additional historical information

This can be a somewhat frustrating method for obtaining information, but at least it's a start, and you will likely not have to pay for this information. You can also obtain forms online at www.searchadvisor.com.

Request Your Original Birth Certificate from the State Health Department

The majority of us have "amended" birth certificates, with the names of our adoptive parents listed in the parent category. When you write to the state health department of your birth state requesting your original birth certificate, you may be denied outright, funneled to another office, or simply receive another amended certificate.

Does that make you as mad as it does me? Jayne Askin quotes an individual who echoes my sentiments, and possibly yours.

> We are not separate or different than those born with a heritage they have always had knowledge of . . . and the freedom to investigate further if they so choose. Being denied information concerning myself that is not denied a non-adoptee is degrading and cruel . . . what an invasion of humanity! . . . (to) close up a human life as a vault somewhere and say, "you may not know about yourself—you have not the right to even ask . . . Your anxieties are neurotic, your curiosity unnatural."[1]

At the counsel of the adoption professional I hired, I wrote to the state department of health and requested my birth certificate under the only name I had—the one my adoptive parents gave me (not "Baby X," as the hospital nurses had "named" me). This was a different document than my dad had given me. His was an adoption certificate. What I was seeking was my *original* birth certificate. Why did I want it even though

I already knew my parents' names? Because I wanted proof that what was written on Dad's certificate was the truth. In addition, I wanted with all my heart to break the secrecy. I hate secrecy! We all do.

In my letter I didn't say that I was adopted. I didn't lie in any way; I simply asked for what any other citizen has a legal right to obtain. Within weeks I had my original birth certificate in my hands . . . and I didn't break the law!

You may want to try this if your circumstances were similar. If you want to do this online, write to the National Center for Health Statistics: www.nchs.com.

Contact the Hospital for Birth Records

Next, make a stop at the hospital where you were born. If you can't travel there, write a letter requesting your birth information. Again, don't use the "A" word — "adoptee"! Don't tell them you are an adoptee. The doors will immediately slam in your face.

When I contacted the hospital where I was born, I began a long battle with the superintendent of records for my birth records. I will tell you about it in more detail in the next chapter.

Some hospitals readily release records and some remain rigidly closed, like the one where I was born.

Ask Your Physician to Request Release of Hospital Records

My next line of attack was to ask my current physician if he would write a letter requesting hospital records, which he did. He requested not only my birth records but also those of my birth mother.

Asking for these doesn't require a medical emergency. An emotional hurt needs to be resolved, and if your physician won't write a letter for you, maybe it's time to find another physician.

Conduct Your Own Research at the State Library

Your next step may be to visit the state library in your birth state. The library contains city directories from the past, which can be amazing resources. For example, in the 1940s when I was born, they contained not only the name and address of the person, but also his or her occupation and other details. These are even more pieces you can put in your puzzle.

Usually you'll find librarians at such a facility who specialize in genealogy and are more than eager to help you find information. You can even say you're an adoptee without discrimination! Don't be afraid to ask these professionals for assistance.

Hire an Adoption Professional

Sometimes it's difficult to find someone who won't charge an arm and a leg to do a birth parent search. But I was lucky. I learned of a professional in a town near my place of birth and I was able to hire her for $100. I don't suppose you'll find anyone that inexpensive nowadays, but it's an option well worth considering if you're running into roadblocks in your search, or simply want an experienced guide throughout this process.

If you are having difficulty finding a professional, contact adoption support groups in your birth locale and ask who they would recommend. They usually know the possibilities better than anyone. If you can't find an adoption support group, contact the American Adoption Congress and ask for help: www.americanadoptioncongress.org. They have many helpful links on their site.

Comb Death Records at the Church of Jesus Christ of Latter-day Saints

The professional I worked with believed that we would be able to narrow down our search further by seeing which of the people I found in the library's city directories were already deceased. We went to the local branch of the Church of Jesus Christ of Latter-day Saints, which has the most extensive death records in the United States. We went through the microfiche and found several possibilities whom the professional believed could be my grandfather and grandmother.

Visit the State Health Department

The last stop was the state health department, where we obtained death certificates of the people who may have been my grandparents. Within an hour we had identified my grandfather's certificate, which contained valuable information, such as the funeral home that took care of the arrangements for his burial.

Let me warn you that my search took place fifteen years ago. Times have changed and funeral homes are savvy about adoptees trying to find information. I recently found out about the death of my birth mother. Of course, I wanted the death records. Even in death, we can learn valuable truths about health for ourselves and future generations. When I called the funeral home, I was told that I had to be the "designated person" on my birth mother's death certificate to obtain information. When I asked how someone without a will (my birth mother), who gave no history in the hospital, could have designated a person, there was no concrete answer. Just a flat no. Eventually, I obtained her death records from the hospital where she died because I could prove I was a blood relative. I had my original birth certificate.

You will have to pay a fee and fill out a form for each death certificate you order. We ordered more than needed, but it narrowed down the search to the final clue. To find out the particulars and expedite your search online, go to the National Center for Health Statistics: www.cdc.gov/nchs.

Contact the Funeral Home for Survivors

The name of the funeral home where arrangements were made listed all survivors by name and address. This is a part of my story I'm not proud of, but I have to declare complete ignorance about the approach my adoption worker took with the funeral director. When we found the information about the funeral home, she just told me to go home and wait for her call. Never did it enter my mind whether or not what she was doing was ethical. I think she introduced herself as a family friend. In other words, she lied. But the funeral director was very cooperative and had no problem in giving names and phone numbers of family members who were still living at the time of my grandfather's death—including his daughter, my birth mother. Times were different then. This would not happen today.

Whether we are taking our first step toward uncovering our pre-adoption history or our tenth, we need courage. Courage to face our past history, whether the details are pleasant or painful. Courage to stand up for our rights, even if we have to haul someone to court to get information. Courage to fight for the unsealing of records. Courage to keep on keeping on when treated like an errant child. And courage to believe that this is all going to be worth it in the end.

I was terrified seventeen years ago when I began my feeble attempts at searching. But looking back I can say confidently from my experience that courage comes when we need it.

Our Choice

To take our first or next step toward obtaining our birth certificates, medical records, and other information about our birth families.

The late Corrie ten Boom, once a Nazi prisoner of war, asked her father when she was young how she would ever have the courage to face death. Her father's answer was simple. He said something like this: "Corrie, when do I give you your ticket to get on the train?"

"Well, just before I get on, Pappa," she said.

"That's the way it is when you die," her papa told her. "You will have the courage when you need it."[2]

That's the way it will be for us as we take one concrete step after another.

I still remember when I scratched out a letter to the probate judge in pencil on simple notebook paper. Bob and I were vacationing in northern Michigan. The rest of the family was out on the beach, but that flame for truth had been ignited within me so that even the beach I loved didn't seem as inviting as taking my first concrete step toward gaining information about my past.

I wish you the best as you begin your search! Remember that you will grow no matter what the outcome. So step forward with confidence.

DISCUSSION QUESTIONS FOR
SUPPORT GROUPS OR PERSONAL REFLECTION

1. How do you feel about starting a search? If you're working with a group of adoptees, come up with one word that describes everyone's feelings.
2. How do you think your birth family would react if you contacted them? Have you thought about that? Please share your thoughts.
3. Write a letter *to* and *from* your birth mother about your feelings about having to search so hard to find her.

DIGGING DEEPER FOR ANSWERS
TO OUR ADOPTION QUESTIONS

1. Read Jeremiah 29:11. What does God promise for your future? How do the words of this promise affect you as you contemplate searching?
2. Go back to Psalm 139:16. Who is already in your future?
3. What are we to do when we are at our wit's end when searching? See Isaiah 50:10.
4. If the worst-case scenario occurred and you experienced rejection, who could you run to that would understand? Read Isaiah 53:3-6.

As we begin to take concrete steps, at times we will feel overwhelmed with emotion. Fear. Confusion. Frustration. Disappointment. Exhilaration. In fact, you may be feeling that way right now after reading this chapter. Perhaps you haven't begun your search and the whole thing sounds incredibly intimidating.

Remember, we're on a path toward life transformation by God's power. It's one step at a time. I assure you that there is light at the end of the tunnel!

When we are feeling overwhelmed, it is time to pull back a little and be gentle with ourselves. We'll talk about that next.

CHAPTER SEVENTEEN

WHY DO WE PUSH OURSELVES BEYOND OUR LIMITATIONS?

You number and record my wanderings; put my tears into Your bottle — are they not in Your book?

— PSALM 56:8 (AMP)

The more we hurt, the more we push ourselves and deny what is really happening inside ourselves. We were "given up" by our birth parents, so by golly, we're going to be the best parents possible. We push ourselves to the limit—past the limit—because we want our life and the lives of those we love to not feel the pain we've felt.

The battle for my records had been going on for *twelve* years. After going through all the steps in the previous chapter, I went to the hospital where I was born *again*, explaining how important authentic birth information is for an adoptee. I hoped that perhaps a little education about adoption would help the superintendent soften her position.

This time, instead of patting me on the knee and condescendingly asking if "we had an adoptee here," she invited me to go down into the hospital basement where the records were stored. My heart was beating like a drum! Maybe she was going to have a little compassion and relent. Why else would she have gone to the trouble of taking me there?

She left me at the door to the records vault and went to look for my file. To think that moments later I might know my missing information made my heart soar. After a few minutes she returned and said that my records were there but that I couldn't see them. "Confidentiality," she said, dangling the bait and then taking it away.

My body began shaking with deep sobs as she stood at a distance, like a marble statue. She walked away as I wept in that cold, dark hospital basement.

Not long afterward my husband called her and explained the importance of having my records. She pulled them out of my file, read them to herself, and announced to Bob that there was *absolutely nothing* significant about the birth. Why would I want such records so badly? (Silly little adoptee!)

Folks like this lady have no conception of why we want such information. We know why we do! We want to know when we slept, ate, and pooped. Significant? Maybe not to the outsider, but to us with adoptee hearts, those facts are proof that we are real. We were real babies, who had a real birth, in a real hospital, with a real mother.

I finally hired a lawyer who wrote an "ex parte order." The judge replied that there was no reason why I shouldn't be treated as any other person in regard to confidentiality provisions of the law, since I already had my original birth certificate and had been reunited with my birth mother. The hospital superintendent's response was that "this will be the last we would hear of this" and that I could not have my records. Another hand slap!

A few weeks later I wrote to the probate judge saying that I believed the superintendent was in contempt of court. The reply was that "they had done all they could for me." That was the letter I received while trying to write this chapter.

I remembered Jayne Askin's words about our rights as adoptees: "Under the American system of government, citizens (either as individuals or organized into groups pursuing defined interests) can raise a challenge to any federal, state, or local statute or administrative policy affecting them that appears inconsistent with the guarantees contained in the Constitution of the United States."[1]

I got fired up, thinking I could now appeal to the state.

But then a new thought dawned on me. *Why?* Was it *really* birth information I wanted? Was it *really* the desire to be treated fairly by the law?

No, I think there was much more. It was all about control. My birth mother had the final word about sending me away and I was determined not to let her have the *last* say. As I write these words fifteen years later, God would have it that I did have the last say by obtaining her death records which provided invaluable medical information for my family.

Since writing this book originally, I have become an adoptive grandmother. Our five-year-old granddaughter struggles often with "big feelings." Lisa, her wonderful mom, does everything within her God-given power to help her through the feelings.

As adopted adults, we have big feelings also. Anger and rage that sometimes seem uncontrollable.

Just know, friend, that it's not unusual to feel overwhelmed when you're searching, when doors are being slammed in your face, and when the scars of the past are ripped open through present-day circumstances.

WHY ARE WE OVERWHELMED AT TIMES?

At times we can get absolutely crazy and obsessed over searching. Once we've turned onto the "narrow path," all we can think about is what lies ahead. Sheila Rounds says, "When you are searching and you keep hitting roadblocks, it's exhaustingly painful."

Sharon McGowan feels overwhelmed several times a year and throws a pity party. She also tries to get moving — to do something . . .

anything—so that she can feel more in control of the uncontrollable.

Oh, the uncontrollable. How we adoptees hate that old feeling of having no control! It's so hard when we're in a rage to remember that God is in control of our lives.

Lack of Information

Wanting to proceed with searching but having absolutely no information to go on can be incredibly frustrating.

Laurie spends endless hours at the computer or looking over the information she does have. Often it seemed impossible to her to make any progress.

Richard Curtis is furious about his time spent researching and frustrated that adult adoptees are still being treated like children. He laments the fact that those who were adopted many years ago usually don't have the legal advantages of younger adoptees.

Concern for Our Children or Grandchildren

Whenever my children or grandchildren have health problems, I always feel irritated that I know only half my history. None of my descendants will ever know their complete health histories. My eighty-one-year-old birth mother took that information to her grave. My doctor calls that "cruel." I agree.

Derek Jeske has similar feelings. There is always that unknown factor, which scares him, especially when it comes to having children. To not know if there are any health-related issues in his background and then to have children and wonder if he's passing along any diseases is unsettling for him.

Society's View of Adoptees

Up until recently, I dare say that 99 percent of American media reports demonstrate ignorance and denial concerning adoptions and adoptees. For example, when someone commits a heinous crime and he *just happens* to be an adoptee, the press snatches it up and makes sure that the public knows that the murderer was adopted.

How often do we hear about all the highly successful people who were adopted, like Nancy Reagan, Gerald Ford, Dave Thomas, and Melissa Gilbert? The media doesn't say, "Adopted President Gerald Ford"! On Wendy's commercials, the late fast-food chain founder didn't say, "Hi, I'm adopted Dave Thomas." Come on, now!

Jodi Strathman agrees that many media stories associate adoptees with criminal acts. She says, "Let's get real . . . the majority of adoptees are not mentally ill or murderers!"

The media is starting to come around. One example is the Hallmark Channel's series on adoption on Sunday evenings.

There is also a new "romanticism" afloat in our society about adoption. If parents adopt a child with a bloated stomach and flies buzzing around its head, they're heroes. A wise person said, "Maybe we should dress the foster children we see in the newspapers shabbily and have flies buzzing around their heads." There is a craziness surrounding adoption now. I don't mean to imply that there's anything wrong with international adoption, but many adopted people I've interviewed lately can't stand the way the media romanticize the movie stars who bring children home from other countries. It's not the parents or the children — it's the media!

I also am aware of well-intentioned organizations in the U.S. that tell children from abroad that they're coming for a vacation to the U.S. Meanwhile, they've lined up potential parents and families to see if the child is a "fit." If the child isn't deemed a "fit" after a few days of visiting, he's sent to the next set of potential parents. The child is then sent back home and the decision is made by the potential parents. This breaks my adoptee heart as I know it must break yours. Children are so intuitive. They know what's going on! Potential parents are on perfect behavior, and kids too. After all, if they're not, they won't be chosen. If they are chosen, parents are shocked to see feces smeared on their living room walls. The poor parents and poor children! It almost seems like we're back to the Orphan Train days when orphaned children were auctioned off. The intentions of the organization may be sincere, but they're sincerely wrong.

Karen says, "The insensitivity of the media and all the hype about the movie stars adopting is frustrating. I am glad that they are making it acceptable and mainstream, but it seems to be at the same time trivializing of the child and the "adoption" piece of it is overemphasized. (Look, she adopted a poor baby from Cambodia, isn't she so sweet to do that?) Is this new baby of Tom Cruise's *really* his first? The news makes it to be that way. If he is any kind of real father (and he probably is), it must really hurt him that the media has disregarded his "adopted" children as his "real" children."

Stigma

The warped views of society in general naturally spill over to individuals in our lives. Karen says, "I'm tired of having the feelings that are so close to my heart be something that makes others uncomfortable. Most people don't want to know about it. As soon as you bring it up, you've got 'the plague.' It's very hard to cope when very few people have compassion for the most difficult challenge in my life."

Teresa Armor, a transracial adoptee, says that the cultural factor is definitely involved in stigma. She says answering questions about her adoption from ignorant yet well-meaning people can feel a little overwhelming. In response, she tries to educate whoever is asking and show them why the difference they observe in appearance and personalities within her family is not because of their mixed culture, but because of the uniqueness of every individual.

Discouragement

Ron Hilliard says that there are times when he just wishes he were "normal"! As he has become aware of how early-life loss has impacted him, he sometimes gets discouraged. He says that it seems as if he keeps dealing with the same adoption issues over and over again, with no permanent relief. "I somehow believe that I should get over it, or move beyond it, and when I find I haven't it's discouraging and frustrating. I feel as though there is something wrong with me for still being impacted by the issues. I feel overwhelmed about adoption in the midst of relationships. I guess I believe that some of my relationship struggles wouldn't be going on if I weren't adopted. And it takes a lot of energy to work through the issues I have related to adoption."

Whenever Sharon McGowan sees a baby on television whose parents are thrilled about its arrival, or a baby who's not wanted, she becomes a baby emotionally for a few minutes and is overwhelmed with pain, loneliness, and hopelessness.

These comments remind me of a story I once heard. It was advertised that the Devil was going to put his tools up for sale. On the day of the sale, they were marked for public inspection, each with a sale price. The tools were hatred, envy, jealousy, deceit, and pride. Apart from the rest was a very harmless-looking tool, very well worn, but expensively priced. "What is the name of this tool?" asked one of the purchasers. "Ah," said the Devil, "that is discouragement." When asked why he priced it so high, he said, "Oh, because it's more useful to me than all the others. I can pry open and get into a man's heart with that when I can't get near him with any other tool. And once I'm inside, I can do with him whatever I choose. It's badly worn because I use it on almost everyone, but few people know that it belongs to me."[2]

Uncooperative Birth Mothers

Something else that can feel overwhelming to adult adoptees is uncooperative birth mothers.

Cheri Manternach's birth mother wants nothing to do with her after forty-one years, and Cheri is experiencing an illness that is hereditary. Her mother won't give her even the most basic medical information about her family of origin.

A few years ago, I woke up on a hospital gurney after having a grand mal seizure. Of course, the first thought that came to mind was, *I wonder if this is hereditary.* At this point my mother would not talk to me and so my husband called. She just laughed at my request for medical information and expressed disapproval of the contact for such an "insignificant" matter.

Overextending Ourselves for Others

Another avenue that can lead to feelings of no control is when we become overactive in trying to help others. We try to pour out to others from an empty pitcher and it just doesn't work. If we can keep pouring into others, keep overextending, then we won't feel our own pain. We become "flaming codependents"! We depend on helping others to keep our own issues at bay.

Just ask Kenny Tucker. He often feels overwhelmed by his activism activities and helping other adoptees search.

Dawn Saphir says, "At first I couldn't get enough information, I couldn't meet enough adoptees, and I certainly couldn't learn enough about Korea, my birth country. As I have gotten older, I have been overwhelmed with feeling *obligated* to do this work and confront these issues to help others."

Many of us have chosen to go back into the system that has injured us in hopes of helping others. Phyllis-Anne Munro works in the foster care system, which triggers her own issues at times. She does the best she can but sometimes she just comes home and cries, while at other times feels rage about the injustice she continues to see.

So what do we do when we feel overwhelmed? To put it simply: We nurture ourselves.

HOW WE CAN NURTURE OURSELVES

Dr. Paul Brand, a missionary physician in India who has worked with children with clubbed feet, learned that if he could draw the child's attention to an urgent need, such as intense hunger, the deep satisfaction of having that need met would set up a barrier for pain and he could easily correct the clubbed feet.

The child's mother was to refrain from nursing until the exam. When the time came and she sat opposite Dr. Brand, laid her baby across her knees, and opened her sari, her breasts were swollen with milk. As the baby sucked greedily at her breast, Dr. Brand removed the old splint and washed the foot, then began to move it around "to test the range of movement." Sometimes the baby would turn its eyes toward him and frown, but eating was the overwhelming priority. If the baby quit nursing in order to yell, that meant Dr. Brand had gone too far and forced the foot into a position that would put tissue under too much stress. At the first cry of protest, doctor and mother would have to wait, unwrap the plaster, and start over with a new bandage while the baby went back to the breast. Dr. Brand says, "If we crossed the pain barrier, even though we could see no obvious injury, swelling and stiffness would later appear. Using this technique we got dramatic results of total correction without resorting to surgery. The correcting influence had to be both gentle and persistent."[3]

Just like Dr. Brand's patients, our emotional "feet" often feel clubbed by adoption-related issues. If we are not gentle with ourselves when feeling overwhelmed, we may cross our own pain barriers and get into trouble emotionally. Many of us have suffered from severe depression.

But how can we be gentle with ourselves? Here are some ideas from fellow adoptees.

Rely on Prayer and a Good Support System

The late Dirck Brown relied on prayer and key people, especially his wife Molly and his Episcopal priest. Dirck once said, "It also helped to create Post Adoption Center for Education and Research (PACER) and have almost weekly sessions of our triad support group—a powerful experience to be able to share your joys and frustrations with others facing the same issues." Dirck also used PACER to educate professionals and others about the long-term issues related to adoption that the public generally discounts.

Joy Budensiek says God brought people into her life who have given of themselves by sharing their own joy and pain. As a result, she can grow emotionally and blend into life rather than be consumed by her own broken heart.

Soak in Unconditional Love

"Part of nurturing myself is simply allowing myself not to be perfect," says Ron Hilliard. "To realize that I am a work in progress and to not fall into believing that being relinquished is something to 'get over.' This is who I am, and it is okay to be who I am."

Phyllis-Anne Munro's husband makes her feel treasured and safe by letting her be in whatever emotional space she is and loving her unconditionally. Their relationship has healed some very deep wounds she has carried for years.

Read Your Bible

I have been a person of faith for more than thirty years, but when my beloved dad died a few years ago, it was a tremendous loss for me. I remember planning his funeral. Sitting in his living room with my Bible and a notepad, I began looking up verses I wanted the pastor to read for the service. Prior to that time, I was so overwhelmed with grief. As I read the verses, however, I was energized by them. I had known the power of God's Word for years, but never had I so literally seen its power. It was like I'd been hooked up to an IV with God's life-giving power and presence dripping into my veins.

If you've never read the Bible, I encourage you to purchase one. Start with *The Living Bible* and the book of John.

Learn to Play

One of my therapists told me years ago that I needed to learn to have fun—that, she said, is the final step of healing.

Recently, my husband, Bob, and I were "playing house" with Livy, our five-year-old granddaughter. The dollhouse was resting on a huge leather ottoman by the couches and we were all on the floor. Livy designated who Bob and I would be—he was "Gramps" and I was "Mimi." She started the play, and as we developed our fantasy story line together, Bob and I became hysterical in our responses to one another's characters. Livy looked at us, trying to figure out what was so funny. It was proof to me that both Bob and I have come a long way in healing from hurts of the past.

Our Choice

To lovingly accept our limits and nurture ourselves.

And so, what life-transforming choice can we make when we feel overwhelmed by issues related to being adopted?

Don't you feel a little relieved, knowing that we have similar limitations and irritations? After we have learned to accept our limits, we can nurture ourselves by one or all of the following.

DISCUSSION QUESTIONS FOR SUPPORT GROUPS OR PERSONAL REFLECTION

1. When do you have "big feelings?" How do they manifest in your life?
   - "I get so angry I can't stand it. I don't know what to do with my anger."
   - "I run away from home."
   - "I get really mean to the people I love the most."
   - Other:
2. What triggers your "big feelings," your feelings of being overwhelmed? Can you name specific situations or comments?
3. Write a letter *to* and *from* your birth mother about being overwhelmed because you try so hard.
4. What can you do to nurture yourself? What can you choose that is healthy?
   - Get a massage.

- Listen to inspiring music. Find the local Christian music station and keep it on all day.
- Read the Bible or listen to it on CD.
- Pray and tell God how you feel. Journal your thoughts and date them.

DIGGING DEEPER FOR ANSWERS TO OUR ADOPTION QUESTIONS

1. What does God say we should do when overwhelmed? Read Psalm 37 and write the words and phrases that stand out to you. You will know God is speaking to you through the Scriptures when one or two pop out, as if they're written in neon. Record them! They're his love letter to you.
2. What does Hebrews 4:12 say about the Bible, God's Word? Do you believe it could be powerful? What makes it powerful?
3. What will ultimately nourish our souls? Read James 4:7-10. Can you put this verse into your own words and make application to your current life situation?

Now that you're nurtured, it's time to turn again to a subject nobody likes to talk about—rejection.

WHY DO OUR BIRTH RELATIVES REJECT US?

Can a mother forget the baby at her breast and have no compassion on the child she has borne? Though she may forget, I will not forget you! See, I have engraved you on the palms of my hands; your walls are ever before me.

— ISAIAH 49:15-16

Rejection.

Just the sound of the word sends chills up my spine!

Rejection is the dark side of the search and reunion process. The agonizing side. The side that is rarely, if ever, talked about. We don't see it talked about on television shows. Only the happy, happy stories, which if truth were known, are the furthest thing from reality and a form of stress for those touched by adoption. To be reunited with a person you have a physical relationship with, but no history, is awkward and forced at the beginning. To be put in the spotlight is even worse.

How many of us are rejected? Statistics, like most aspects of adoption, are sadly nonexistent, but many claim that only a minority of adoptees are rejected by a birth relative at reunion. During the years I have been researching and talking with other adoptees, however, I have found that number to be significantly incorrect. Many of us have been rejected but we're so ashamed and feel so responsible that it's not talked about often. We'll break silence in this chapter. Remember, we're in a safe place with one another.

Why do birth relatives reject some of us? Does our physical appearance remind our birth mothers of our fathers, whom they have no positive feelings for? This could be. Does seeing us trigger issues in them that they have never dealt with? This is a good possibility. Are they emotionally and mentally unbalanced? Oh yes, this could be true. Or are they just downright mean? This possibility doesn't escape the radar screen either. You could probably add a few of your own personal reasons.

I will never forget when I was reeling from my birth mother's rejection. While attending my first American Adoption Congress, (a wonderful annual event that I highly recommend), Dirck Brown asked me to tell him my story. I got to the part where I was going to say, "All I wanted was for her to say the words 'I love you,'" and I began sobbing uncontrollably. He looked me straight in the eyes and with such compassion said, "It really hurts, doesn't it?" I knew by the tone of his voice that this wasn't some platitude—it came from his heart. Dirck took me into the lobby of the hotel and told me how he had experienced the same type of cruel rejection from his birth mother years ago. Still, after many years had passed and she had died, he wept telling me his story. The pain of being rejected by one's birth mother is a pain that goes deep and lasts for a lifetime.

Before discussing the ramifications of rejection, let's define it. *Webster's* gives us a good start. "Refusing to have, take, or act upon. To refuse to accept a person. To rebuff. To throw away or discard as useless or unsatisfactory. To cast out or eject. Something rejected as an imperfect article."[1] I love what the onlinevisualthesaurus says about rejection: reprovation, excommunication, exclusion, censure, disfavor, renunciation, defection.

Ron Nydam, PhD, gives a vivid illustration from a client's encounter with his birth mother. She told her son: "If you want answers, see a psychiatrist; if you want a companion, get a dog."[2]

I don't know about you, but parents who make those kinds of remarks to their children are incomprehensible. Many times when holding a newborn baby, we adoptees might wonder how anyone could ever give up this child. This is something we'll rarely admit, but it's a common thought among us. I didn't know people like Dr. Nydam cited existed prior to my experience with my birth mother.

HOW ADOPTEES DEFINE REJECTION

"We Are Dispensable."

What is the message beneath the words? I believe it's, "You're not important to me. You are dispensable, and I can surely go on with my life without you."

When I reunited with my birth mother, my therapist suggested that I do left-handed drawings every night to process my feelings. It sounded a little weird when she suggested it and it might to you as you read. Apparently the idea behind the exercise is to take away your sense of control that you normally have when using your dominant hand. I did what she said when I was away at reunion and they are remarkably revealing. You might want to try it sometime. After fifteen years I still have them and one of them shows a huge birth mother saying, "You weren't important to me." On the floor beside her is a little baby on her knees, crying buckets of tears. Another drawing shows my mother dumping me as a baby into a garbage can.

I wrote above the drawing, "It hurts. Deep inside it hurts. I wanted her to say she thought of me often but instead she didn't even know my birthday."

"We Are Their Dirty Little Secrets."

Karen says that her birth mother rejected her "right out of the gate." She didn't even give Karen the dignity of getting to know her first before making up her mind. Karen was her dirty secret and she couldn't stand the thought of others knowing. She told her that her mother (Karen's grandmother) would also reject her.

As Karen reflects on the rejection, she says, "She didn't just reject me—she wanted nothing to do with my son, *her own grandson*! When I found her, my son wasn't even one year old, a beautiful baby. How could she reject him? The only time I met her she reviewed pictures I had brought of him with detachment and terse comments."

"We Don't Want an Unknown Sibling."

When birth siblings learn that a parent conceived an unknown child, their reaction may be to reject us as well. This was the case with my half sister, who hadn't been on speaking terms with my birth mother for five years until I came on the scene. She was on the next plane to Sun Valley, Idaho, to meet me. The first words out of her mouth were incredibly rejecting. Looking back, I guess she wanted to share in giving the "blessing" of rejection that she knew was coming.

Laurie's birth half sister found it difficult to speak with her since she was told that Laurie was her half sister. Laurie, like Karen, was her birth mother's secret. Laurie has tried to make contact, but her birth mother wants nothing to do with her. She is hoping that one day she will speak to her, or that at least she will eventually develop a relationship with her half sister.

"They Just Don't Know What to Do with Us — Relegated to the E-Mail Address Book."

Richard Curtis says, "Even though I have not been overtly rejected by birth relatives, I have the feeling that I'm being ignored or at least overlooked by family members who just don't know what to do with me. Both of my birth parents were deceased when I finally conducted my search and so my 'reunions' have been with siblings and cousins. That being the case, after the initial shock and curiosity of discovering a secret birth relative, most members of both families have relegated me to receiving a card at Christmas or an occasional e-mail. At first I tried to take the initiative and keep in contact, especially with my siblings; but I've gotten little response."

Thus, the person(s) we may have searched a lifetime for couldn't care less about us. Words can't describe the pain. How do we react when we're rejected?

OUR NATURAL REACTIONS TO REJECTION

If we've received hostile responses from birth relatives, how do we usually react?

We Isolate Ourselves

Isolation and rejection silence us. We are frozen in fear and don't want another soul to know our experience. We feel we have been branded for life.

We *do* need isolation from the rejecting birth relatives, but not from fellow adoptees who have had similar experiences. In their company we can find a *good* kind of isolation and refuge, where we experience protection, comfort, strength, and validation.

David, a man who lived in biblical times, experienced this kind of safety in a group of people who had experienced rejection. He was terrified and running from the wrath of King Saul. He had no alternative but to adopt the life of a fugitive. Adoptees can do that when rejected. We can become fugitives from anyone who wants to love us. We are wounded and want to crawl away and lick our wounds. A cave in a nearby valley gave David the shelter he needed. We seek a cave too. Maybe not a literal one, but a cave, nonetheless. For David, it was like a dark vault and it was there that anyone in distress could flee. Four hundred men came to join David. Together they became a mighty group of warriors, able to overcome their enemies, including their deepest fears.[3] For us, our cave can be an all-adoptee support group. No one, I mean no one, understands rejection like a fellow adoptee who has experienced a similar scenario. I will always be grateful to the late Dirck Brown for providing a "cave" for me when I needed it. How did he do it? By sharing his story and shedding tears with me.

If we go through rejection and have no one to share with, it is a dangerous place to be. Don't let yourself go there, friends. Read about rejection. Learn that others—many others—have experienced the same. You are not alone and there is nothing wrong with you. And, you didn't bring it about. Don't lay that guilt trip on yourself.

We Accept Shame

Another natural reaction to rejection is to believe the lies told about us. We put on a pretty face and hide the pain, for shame tells us that what our birth relatives have said or done to us is true, or that we deserve it.

I remember my first visit to my therapist after my rejection. She said, "You know, it was going to happen sooner or later." I was stunned. I interpreted her words as, "You deserved it."

Then she explained, "No, Sherrie, I meant that sooner or later *she* was going to get in touch with *her own* buried feelings, which led her to react in the negative way she did. It has nothing to do with you."

It took a few months, possibly years, for that truth to become real, when I realized it was not about me, but about my birth mother, who could have chosen to deal with her issues at reunion, but didn't. She took the easy path—to send me away once more.

THE FOUNDATIONAL FEAR

Beneath our natural fear of rejection is a foundational terror of being forgotten. Forgotten by the one who gave us birth. Forgotten by the biological father whose name we may never know. Forgotten by blood relatives who went on with life without us. But perhaps most of all, forgotten by God. As I personally became aware of this fear of being forgotten and shared it with the adoptees in my support group, eyes welled with tears and you could have heard a pin drop.

In my search for wisdom I learned that far from being forgotten, we, as orphans, are the object of God's special care and protection. Here are a few things the Bible says he does for us:

- He does what is necessary to preserve our lives.[4]
- He defends our cause.[5]
- He hears even our faintest cries.[6]
- He becomes a Father to us.[7]
- He rescues us when we cry for help.[8]
- He provides what we are searching for — love, compassion, and mercy.[9]
- He blesses those who provide for us.[10]
- He strongly warns judges who issue unrighteous decrees and the magistrates who cause oppression against us.[11]
- He has a unique plan in history for us that no one else can fill.[12]

While studying the subject of being forgotten, I saw a poster-sized reproduction of a U.S. commemorative stamp. Two words grabbed my attention — NEVER FORGOTTEN. The poster depicted an army dog tag on a chain, inscribed with the words, "MIA and POW — NEVER FORGOTTEN."

I thought about it a lot in the days to come. Aren't we as rejected adoptees a little like prisoners of war? Aren't we missing in action in many ways? I took this as a sign that I will never be forgotten by God. I even purchased a gold ID bracelet with a chain like a dog tag. On one side I had the jeweler inscribe "Baby X." On the other side were the words "Never forgotten." But, there is something far better and deeper that will never be lost and will never tarnish like a bracelet will over time. It's the inner assurance from God's Spirit that we belong to him. If we trust in Jesus for our salvation, he will tenderly carry us through every valley, including the valley of the shadow of death, to the home that he is preparing for us right now, as you read this book.

I am reminded of a story about a young American Indian man who was about to go through "the rite of passage into manhood." Prior to this event, he was prepared to defend himself in every way. On the day of the rite, he was blindfolded and led, gun in hand, into a dark forest and left alone overnight. The blindfold remained all night.

During the night, whenever the wind blew a leaf or an animal scurried through the underbrush, he was sure it was a wild animal seeking to devour him. He was terrified. When morning dawned he removed his blindfold and saw a path leading off to his right. He thought he saw someone at the end of the path. As he contemplated the figure, he realized that it was his father, aimed and ready to shoot anything or anyone that would hurt his son.[13]

I believe that's the way it is for us when we're rejected. We're not alone, and there is someone greater and stronger taking care of us—it's Jesus. Remember the verses about who knew you before you were born? Remember who was in your birth mother's womb, creating you to be the incredible person you are? Remember who warned that your birth mother may forget you but that he never would? Remember the nail-scarred palms with your name written on them?

THE SILVER LINING IN THE CLOUD OF REJECTION

There is always a silver lining within the dark cloud of rejection, but it may take years for us to discover it. The pain doesn't go away overnight. In fact, does it ever *really* go away?

Recently I talked with one of my pastors whose thirty-two-year-old son died suddenly of a heart attack. I asked him if it was possible to get over such pain. His response? "It hurts just as much today as it did the day it happened."

It was then that it dawned on me that as an adoptee who has lost a loved one *and* been rejected I don't feel *I* have the right to say that it hurts just as much today as it did the day it happened. It's not socially acceptable. If we do, we're labeled angry adoptees. Why don't we just get on with life? If they only knew that adoption produces a wound that is deeper than death or divorce.

My seven-year-old grandsons, Austin and Blake, know in a child's way that my birth mother rejected me. "Why doesn't she like you, Mimi?" they ask. I have to tell them I don't know. I can frankly say, "It still hurts very much and probably always will this side of heaven."

This has been a real "aha" awakening for me. I have heard others say that adoptees have an irreparable wound. When I first heard that, it felt like a relief because it was consistent with my own emotional experience. But later in my journey, I started to believe that all the hurt should be gone once I'd "finished" grieving, and I judged others who said theirs wasn't. That is, until my pastor candidly shared his pain. We can grieve our past losses as best we can and that will help us not "go under" with future losses, but we'll always have scars.

I can live a fulfilling and even joyous life, however, when I recognize that there is something called "redemption." *The Synonym Finder* says this about *redemption*: "Retrieval, saving, freeing, liberation, deliverance, emancipation, rescue, release, reprieve, escape, regeneration, reformation, rebirth, reconstitution, and comeback."[14]

So what do I mean by "redemption" in terms of my experience as an adoptee? First, my pain is being used for my good and God's glory. Second, the comfort I receive from God outweighs the pain. Third, I am now a "warrior" and can defend myself and others, knowing all the while that I am being defended by the One who loves me passionately. Doesn't all we've learned about how much God loves us make you a little homesick for heaven? A few years ago, my husband and I visited a mansion like I'd never seen—the largest estate in the U.S. As we began our tour, our imaginations ran wild, envisioning what it might have been like to have lived as a resident there. It was a grand old place, containing anything and everything you could ever want on this earth. A library with 10,000 volumes, an indoor pool and bowling alley, and thirty-three guest rooms. We laughed thinking what a privilege it would be to even be a servant there.

We came to the banquet hall. There were sixteenth-century Flemish tapestries hanging on the walls, three fireplaces, and a table to seat sixty-four. What festive gatherings must have happened there.

As we marveled at the exquisite furnishing, our minds quickly turned to another banquet that is yet to be. A heavenly one. The wedding banquet, planned by Jesus for those who love and belong to him through faith. The table is all set. The time is near. Look closely at the table. There is a place reserved there just for you.

As we gazed at this earthly banquet room, we realized that it is nothing compared to what Jesus is planning for us (Ephesians 3:20-21)! What joy filled our hearts as we thought about sitting at the heavenly feast someday, elbow to elbow with our brothers and sisters in Christ from ages past and future. What a glorious day that will be (Revelation 19:7-9).

Continuing through the estate, we came to a room with walls lined with family portraits from generations past to the present-day family. Just use your imagination and think about our heavenly Father's home. There may be family portraits hanging on the walls. You and I will be included! We are family because we've been adopted a second time by Jesus.

As we completed our tour, we listened to the curator share his perceptions of the owners of the mansion. He told of their kindness and graciousness. His admiration for them could be clearly seen. I prayed that my love for Jesus will be as evident to the people I meet or those who read my writings.

Yes, the mansion our heavenly Father has waiting for us is like none we've ever seen! We will live there not as servants, but as heirs . . . as sons and daughters. John 8:35 says, "Now a slave has no permanent place in the family, but a son belongs to it forever." We will be able to see Jesus face-to-face. We will enjoy all he has planned for us from eternity past. It will all make sense. All our adoption questions will fall away. There will be no need or desire to go anywhere else. Every need will be met, every tear wiped away by those nail-scarred hands. Doesn't the thought of it make you homesick?

Until that day, we can have peace because we know that this world and what we can see isn't all there is to life. Life and peace are found in a relationship with Jesus, which can begin now, and last forever.

Our Choice

To focus on God's promises to provide for us as orphans and to remember Jesus' nail-scarred hands as proof we'll never be forgotten.

Viorel Badescu has experienced rejection that few of us will ever know. Now a student in Hawaii and a member of Youth With A Mission, Viorel says, "I was born in Romania and my father killed my mother when I was five. I saw it all—it was all blood. He went to prison for eighteen years and we four children ended up in a communist orphanage, which is much like a concentration camp. Rejection was all you got—there was more than you could stand and many children went nuts."

Viorel says that even this kind of tragic experience can have a silver lining, but it's certainly not easy to see. She says, "I became a Christian when I was twenty-one. It wasn't easy to forget all the rejection I'd experienced, but one thing that really helped me was to remind myself every day of who I am to God, over and over again—to read the Word of God [the Bible] and choose to believe it. Believing that I am his child is like replacing the negative with the positive in my mind. It's a fight, a hard one. It is painful and I lose lots of fights. I have to work hard at it. But it's worth it."

DISCUSSION QUESTIONS FOR
SUPPORT GROUPS OR PERSONAL REFLECTION

1. As you've thought about the possibility of reunion, have you considered the possibility that you might face rejection? On a

scale of 1–10, with 10 being the best, how prepared are you for rejection?

2. What are some good ways to prepare for possible rejection? (Please see the Jewel Among Jewel Archives at www.sherrieeldridge.com. There is an entire issue there on rejection by fellow adoptees.

3. Write a letter *to* and *from* your birth mother about rejection, both past, present, and future.

4. Make a drawing with your nondominant hand, expressing in a picture and words your perception of adoption and reunion.

DIGGING DEEPER FOR ANSWERS TO OUR ADOPTION QUESTIONS

1. Did you know that God knew you long before you were born? Just as the prophet Jeremiah had a "prenatal" calling on his life to belong to God, love him, and serve him, so do we. "Before I formed you in the womb I knew you, before you were born I set you apart."

2. If God knew you in the womb, how would you draw your time line? Do this in your journal and put where you will be at the end of life on earth.

3. Guess who else was rejected by birth relatives? This was so validating to me. Look up John 1:11. If you're in a group, read this aloud. Then put your name in the verse. Personalize it like "(your name) came to that which was his own, but his own did not receive him."

One of the benefits of being in an adoption support group is that we learn truths from one another that are yet undiscovered in our own lives. A great blessing came to me when someone in my group uttered words I had never heard. Let me share what they were with you in the next chapter and how a new season dawned in my life as a result. It can happen to you, too!

CHAPTER NINETEEN

WHY KEEP SEARCHING AFTER ONE BIRTH RELATIVE REJECTS US?

Home is the place where, when you have to go there, they have to take you in.

— ROBERT FROST

Once while attending an adoption support group meeting, I heard a statement I'd never heard before. "If your birth mother rejects you, it doesn't mean that the *rest* of your family will."

As I thought about that comment, I concluded that the same blood that pulses through their veins pulses through mine. I have every right to contact other family members as my birth mother does. I am family even though she doesn't want me to be. It was high time for us to start claiming our birthright.

A few months later I received a call. "Is this Sharon Lee Eldridge?" a woman whispered.

I paused, for no one *ever* calls me Sharon Lee—except when I was a kid and got into trouble.

After acknowledging that I was indeed Sharon Lee, she introduced herself as my birth cousin, Sharon, from Bay City, Michigan.

After giving me a few basic facts about our family, I realized that she was reaching out in love. We talked for at least two hours as she gave me her perspective of the family, specifically my birth mother. My cousin had heard about me through "the family grapevine" after I had been rejected by my birth mother. She contacted me out of pure love, hoping that she could restore to me some of the feelings of belonging to my birth family. She told me during our phone call that she wished she could have known me sooner so that she could have warned me prior to meeting my mother about her history of negative behavior.

One week later I received a package from her with black-and-white matted photos of my birth family, going all the way back to the 1800s. As I looked at the faces of my relatives I felt like a little child peering from *outside* a window on a cold, wintry night, watching a happy family around the fire. After carefully examining the photos I saw no resemblance and concluded that I must look like my birth father, whoever he is or was.

One of Sharon's hobbies is investigating and recording our family's genealogy. She sent me a notebook filled with pages detailing each generation—date of births, how many children, where and when they died and were buried. She also sent a thick book written by a distant relative that contained a detailed description of who belonged to whom. When I came to the part about my birth mother and supposed father, there was no mention of me. None. As far as the rest of the family was concerned, I didn't exist.

Sharon must have anticipated the effect that would have on me, so she inked in my name where it should have appeared. We were reunited soon afterward, and a close friendship developed between the two of us over the years.

CLAIMING YOUR BIRTHRIGHT

Because of that positive experience with Sharon, I reflected once more on the statement I had heard at the support group meeting and concluded that it must be true; so I continued my search for other relatives.

Reaching Out to Other Relatives

I learned from my cousin that we had an aunt living in Michigan, my birth mother's older sister, who was dying of cancer. I decided to contact her via letter.

> *Dear Barbara,*
> *You don't know me but I am the firstborn child of your sister Marjorie Elizabeth Clark that she gave up for adoption in 1945. A few years ago we had a reunion but unfortunately have no relationship now. I have come to realize that not only is she my birth family, but you and many others are as well. It would be such a joy to meet you. I don't want anything from you—just a chance to meet you face-to-face. Would you be interested?*
> *Best regards,*
> *Sherrie Eldridge*

When my birth mother found out that I had contacted her sister, she went ballistic, which was no surprise. Regardless, my aunt invited my husband and me to visit her in Michigan. We sat together for an hour as she shared memories of the family. Before Bob and I left, Barbara struggled out of her La-Z-Boy, oxygen tank in tow, walked into the dining room, and carried out a beautiful china bowl, laced in gold leaf. "This was your grandmother's," she said. "I know if she were here she would want you to have it."

After photos and hugs, we said good-bye. That was the first and last time I would see her, for she died a few months later. However, the contact with her set off a chain of events that would open more doors in the future.

You May Be Surprised by Other Doors That Open

A few years later I got an e-mail that didn't make much sense. It said, "So, you've written a book! Congratulations and welcome to the family."

Welcome to the family? I thought. Who is this, anyway? Is it a fellow author congratulating me on the publication of my book? I didn't reply because I didn't know what to say.

A week later I got a phone call from a woman who asked, "Hello, is this Sherrie Eldridge? The Sherrie Eldridge who wrote *Twenty Things Adopted Kids Wish Their Adoptive Parents Knew*?"

"Yes," I replied, thinking it was a call from someone who had read my book.

"This is your Aunt Marge—I'm the wife of your Uncle Dave from Nashville! Did you get our e-mail?"

"What e-mail?"

"The one that said, 'Welcome to the family!'"

"Oh my goodness!" I gasped. "I had *no* idea that it was from *my* family! Thank you for following through with a telephone call! I would have never put two and two together."

"We thought maybe that was the case so we decided to pick up the phone and call."

After a few minutes of chatting, Aunt Marge asked if I would like to talk to my Uncle Dave. *What would he say to me?* I wondered, suddenly nervous. *Would he reject me like his sister [my mother] had?*

A friendly, jovial voice boomed through the phone lines and for the next forty minutes he relayed fascinating things about my birth family. "Your great-grandfather and your grandfather were U.S. Coast Guard lighthouse keepers on the Great Lakes from the mid-1800s through the mid-1900s. I even lived in one of the lighthouses. Your grandfather carved miniature ships, and one of them was bought by Henry Ford and now is in the museum in Greenfield, Michigan. It's too bad your grandparents didn't know you. They would have loved you and been so proud of you."

You May Be Overwhelmed with Kindness and Love from Other Relatives

A few months later Bob and I met my aunt and uncle in southern Indiana where they were vacationing. Over a leisurely dinner they showered us with family stories and gifts that once belonged to my grandparents.

Afterward, Bob and I climbed into the backseat of Uncle Dave's shiny yellow Cadillac, and as he pulled into the hotel parking lot he turned up the radio and the old gospel song "How Great Thou Art" filled the air. I got a *huge* lump in my throat. We exchanged hugs and said good night at the elevator.

"Can you believe it?" I said to Bob, leaning my head on his shoulder as tears dripped down his shirt. He hugged me close and said, "It's pretty awesome, isn't it? God really does bring blessings from buffetings."

The next morning when we were walking to the parking lot to say good-bye, Uncle Dave put his arm around me and said, "Sherrie, I love you, and don't you *ever* forget that you're a Clark!"

I choked back the tears, for that was something I had never heard. Something deep down inside me was healed when Uncle Dave said those words. At last I felt connected to my birth family and like I belonged!

Since that time I corresponded and spoke often with my aunt and uncle via e-mail or phone. When I turned on my computer and opened a message from Uncle Dave, he always said, "Hello, beautiful! Top of the morning to you and Bob!"

Uncle Dave began connecting me with other family members—two cousins, Sally and Larry. Sally invited us to her home to meet her and her brother, and when we got to her doorstep she swung the door wide open and *ran* to give me a hug. The three of us compared physical features and decided we share the same nose. She gave me a pine cone Christmas tree that my grandmother made years ago that sits on my dining room table as I write this chapter.

Larry sent me two videos of the family from the time he was a child. I got to see my grandma and grandpa as they really were. Not just black-and-white lifeless photos, but *real* people! How strange to think that my life was unfolding just a four-hour drive from these people who were my family but knew nothing about me.

DISCOVERING OUR ROOTS

The following autumn Bob and I met Uncle Dave and Aunt Marge for the Michigan Lighthouse Tour and made a whirlwind trip to the Upper Peninsula to see the lighthouse in Brimley, where Uncle Dave once lived as a child. He kept saying, "Sherrie, how many women your age can say that their great-grandfather and grandfather were lighthouse keepers? You have a very special heritage. You are one of us, you know. You can't disown us!"

We Climbed Sacred Steps

As we climbed the same steel, mesh spiral stairway of the Brimley lighthouse that my grandfathers walked every day generations ago, each step seemed sacred. Silently we gazed upon majestic Lake Superior and the multicolored fall leaves on the shores of Canada. Uncle Dave told of his childhood experiences to other tourists in the room that once was his. I listened with pride to my sweetheart of an uncle.

We Heard Healing Words

We headed toward Cheboygan where I met two other cousins and saw the old homestead where my birth mother and family lived. We also visited the gravesite of my grandparents. Prior to going, I asked Uncle Dave to take me to the florist to buy flowers for their graves.

As we approached the headstone, Uncle Dave said, "There it is. That's where your grandparents are buried, Sherrie."

We exited the car in silence and I took a few steps forward, bent down, and placed two red carnations and baby's breath on their graves.

Sobs came from somewhere deep inside me. I realized for the first time what I had missed in not knowing my birth family. I ran to Bob's strong arms once again.

"They would have loved you so much," Uncle Dave kept saying. "They would have been so proud of you, Sherrie." I felt like a newborn baby, being bathed in love by Uncle Dave.

Three Generations Connect

A few months later Uncle Dave and Aunt Marge came to visit us in Indianapolis to celebrate Aunt Marge's and my birthdays and also to meet our daughters, our sons-in-law, and our four grandchildren.

At the restaurant that night, as my beautiful adult daughters, Lisa and Chrissie, came through the door and Uncle Dave swept them up in big hugs, I couldn't hold back tears any longer. More sobs! To think that this was the *first time* my children and grandchildren had ever touched the skin of a blood relative other than me—well, it was more than I could take in. Of course, no one else could understand my tears, but that's the way it is sometimes.

Your Story May Keep Unfolding

Five years later, when refreshing this book, my Uncle Dave is gone. Aunt Marge is in an Alzheimer's unit in another city. Uncle Dave had three heart surgeries before he found me. I know I'm not the only reason God left him here on earth a while longer, for he has children and grandchildren who loved him dearly. However, I know without a doubt that finding me was one of the reasons Uncle Dave was granted the length of life he had. One day, he was sitting at his computer listening to Aunt Marge, and the next moment, he was face-to-face with the Lord he loved.

I always encourage those who are searching, or contemplating it, to not wait too long. Life changes so quickly. If you're thinking about searching, consider moving forward. None of us know how much more time we have left here on earth, nor those we're searching for.

Our Choice

To reach out to other birth relatives if our birth parents or siblings reject us.

Time is of the essence.

When I realized that I had just as much a right to be a member of my birth family as my rejecting birth mother did, a totally unexpected series of blessings came my way. Any of us can make a choice that can be truly life changing when we realize that our extended family may welcome us with open arms.

DISCUSSION QUESTIONS FOR SUPPORT GROUPS OR PERSONAL REFLECTION

1. Would you like to begin your process of searching, or continuing your search after a rejection? Here are some "first steps":

   - *Write a letter.* I believe this is the best way to make an initial contact with any birth family member. Make it short and sweet. Be sure and tell them that you want nothing from them, just to meet.
   - *Brace yourself for a blowup.* Many of our rejecting birth mothers are emotionally unstable, so we can expect a strong reaction from them whenever we cross into what they consider "their territory." Don't allow fear of what your birth mother might say or do stop you from reaching out to extended family members
   - *Have someone else answer the phone, if possible.* Setting healthy boundaries can keep you safe from further abuse.

2. Write a letter *to* and *from* your birth mother about this topic.

3. What relative would you reach out to if rejected by a birth parent? Do you know any other relatives? Maybe it's time to start searching for some.

4. For those who never will have any hope of a reunion, I encourage you to make a "forever fingerprint," using the concepts from my

children's book by the same name. We all have that deep need for a sense of connection — that's what we're after. The fingerprinting exercise will help you feel connected to your genetic past, but even more so, to the God who created you.

DIGGING DEEPER FOR ANSWERS
TO OUR ADOPTION QUESTIONS

1. Read John 17. This is Jesus' prayer for you. Underline meaningful verses and share them with one another.
2. Do you think finding birth parents, whether a positive or painful experience, will fill the needs in our lives as adopted people?
3. Look again at Ecclesiastes 3:11b. The Amplified Bible says: "He also has planted eternity in men's heart and mind [a divinely implanted sense of a purpose working through the ages which nothing under the sun, but only God, can satisfy]." Do you ever feel hungry to know God?

The next chapter deals with letting go of our birth mother's original decision to send us away. That decision brings a welcomed result.

CHAPTER TWENTY

WHY DO I NEED TO FORGIVE MY BIRTH PARENTS?

Leave the irreparable past in God's hands, and step out into the irresistible future with him.

— OSWALD CHAMBERS

As adopted people who have experienced rejection, we can do everything within our power to bring about reconciliation. Reconciliation involves two people and when the rejecting birth relative doesn't respond, we're responsible to forgive and move on.

By this point in my personal search, I realized that the only peace and clear direction is found in the Scriptures.

After many failed attempts at reconciliation, I was studying about Abraham in the Old Testament.[1] God promised him that he and his ninety-something-year-old wife, Sarai, would have a baby together. Both Abraham and Sarai thought this impossible, so Abraham slept with Hagar, his wife's handmaiden, got her pregnant, and she bore him a son that they named Ishmael.

It wasn't long after the birth of Ishmael that Sarai became pregnant and delivered the promised son, naming him Isaac. The whole crew lived together under the same roof. Hagar (the birth mother) and Ishmael (Abraham's birth son) were causing great discord within the household. Finally, Abraham (the birth father) made an incredulous, no doubt agonizing, decision: he sent Hagar and Ishmael away. It was amazing to read. God himself told Abraham (the birth father) to send away the birth mother and birth child. What a new thought, with new eyes, after having been rejected.

It dawned on me that *I don't have to take my birth mother's abusive behavior anymore. I don't have to keep turning the other cheek. I don't have to keep trying.* When there's continual abuse, to keep on trying to reach that person is a bit like banging one's head against a brick wall. It hurts! After realizing that God himself told the patriarch Abraham to send away his birth child and mother, it became permission for me also. It was okay to say good-bye, which I did. Never in my wildest dreams did I think I'd find the answer in Scripture, but God has the answer for any problem life can throw at us. It felt like a grand piano had been lifted off my back. I was free at last to move into the future, for I had let go of her original decision to relinquish me as well as her subsequent rejections. I felt like the alpine climber who was preparing to ascend a high mountain. His load became extremely heavy and early in the climb he was physically overcome. The guide said that the climber must make a choice, for he was not only hindering his own climb, but also the climb of others to whom he was roped. He must either give up hope of reaching the top or give up the weights. The question he finally had to answer was, "Do I let go of all these things so that I may gain the summit?"[2]

When we choose to let go of what hinders our climb to the summit—the need for our birth mother's love—we are freed. Now, when I tell my story, I say that I loved my birth mother but that she couldn't receive, or refused to receive my love for her. I have forgiven her, which began with a decision but has taken years to become experiential in my emotions.

It wasn't until I had seen myself apart from God, no different from my birth mother, that I was able to forgive her. He loves her just as much as He loves me, but for a long time, I didn't want it to be that way.

CUTTING OURSELVES LOOSE FROM THE NEED FOR OUR BIRTH MOTHER'S LOVE AND ACCEPTANCE

Many of us must face the issue of forgiveness.

Author and speaker Beth Moore vividly illustrates what happens when we aren't willing to forgive. She says it is as if we have the very person we resent roped to our backs. Ironically, we bind ourselves to that which we hate the most. Beth illustrates this truth by bending over and having her audience imagine the offending person tied to your back. Just think of the negative messages this person would be screaming as you walk through the day. Think of the weight of the person's body on you. What a burden.[3]

If we are Christ-followers, he commands us to forgive others. After looking at the cross and seeing what we've been forgiven for, how can we withhold it from someone else?

Cheri Freeman carried her birth mother on her back for years. At a New Year's Eve service at her church in 1999, the pastor urged individuals to let go of old baggage before going into the new millennium. Cheri went forward, and as her pastor prayed for her, she envisioned her birth mother on a cliff, miles across a deep gorge. "For the first time in my life, there was no string between us, nothing tying me to her," Cheri says. "I not only felt strong enough to stand, but I felt safe. That's the first time I realized how afraid I had been of her. Suddenly, all the anger, hurt, and bitterness simply disappeared, and I was able to pray for her and to ask God's blessings upon her for the first time. To me, to be able to sincerely ask for God's blessings upon her is the meaning of forgiveness!"

Though forgiveness is a mystery to many, and to others an order from a demanding God, perhaps you had never considered it being for your own good. Knowing now the self-destructive effects of not forgiving, are you warming up to the idea of forgiveness? Are you willing to go on to the next step with me?

FORGIVENESS IS A DECISION, FOLLOWED BY A PROCESS

Forgiveness is rarely a one-time event. It's not pretending that a hurt didn't matter or is okay. It's not tolerance. It's not make-believe. It's a *process*, which I hope this book has helped us journey through.

Author David Augsburger says, "To 'forgive' is, in the English language, an extended, expanded, strengthened form of the verb *to give*. By intensifying the verb we speak of giving at its deepest level, of self-giving, of giving forth and *giving up* deeply held parts of the self."[4]

Considering the true meaning of forgiveness, let's see how it fleshes out in everyday life for fellow adoptees. How did they let go? How did they forgive?

We've Realized We Can't Change the Past

Karen says letting go of her birth mother is *accepting* that she was adopted and can't change that fact. She says, "It would have been much easier to 'let go' if she had told me, when we met, that she had missed me, wanted to know how I was doing, or any of those things you think a mother separated from her child for twenty years would want to know." But Karen accepted her birth mother's response—or lack thereof—as well . . . because she couldn't change it.

We've Learned to Be Content with the Unknown

This is difficult, to say the least. Dawn Saphir believes that many years ago when her mother chose adoption, it was a very loving act. She explains that in Korean culture, the reasons for giving children up for adoption are often harsher than what Americans would be able to understand. "I have explored many if not all of those options and have come to terms with the fact that any one of them may have been my birth mother's reasons for giving me up." She has chosen to let go of the details she will never be able to know.

We've Given Up the "What Ifs"

Richard Curtis says his birth mother's decision to give him up had an incredible impact on his life. But long ago he stopped dwelling on the "what ifs" and went ahead with life according to a plan that still is unfolding. "Now I can simply live each day to the fullest with all of the energy, love, and truth that I can put forth."

We're Grateful That She Tried Her Best

Theresa Armor is quite sure that her mother wanted to keep her and that she lived with her at least a year before being abandoned outside of an orphanage in Seoul, South Korea. She's made peace with whatever situations or factors led her birth mother to realize that she couldn't care for Theresa anymore. She is happy and fulfilled in her life, which might not have happened had her birth mother chosen to keep her.

Derek is thankful that his birth mother at least made the decision to create an adoption plan for him. He is reminded of this every time he reads about an infant being found dead in a Dumpster.

We've Realized It's Not About Us

Ron Hilliard's interpretation of being relinquished was that it was mostly about him . . . something *wrong* with him. Letting go of his birth mother's decision required coming to the place of realizing that the decision wasn't about him, but was about her and whatever was going on in her life. For Ron, letting go of her decision has involved forgiving her, which is an ongoing process.

Uncovering part of the story of his relinquishment has been a part of that process because it has helped him understand some of the circumstances and influences that led to her decision. Verbalizing his experience and feelings within a safe place and being open to the entire story (not just his own interpretation of what happened) have helped a lot. As Ron has processed this, he has begun to understand that his birth mother's decision might have actually been prompted by love, having his best interests at heart.

We've Taken Personal Responsibility

There are a multitude of teen and adult adoptees who are stuck in anger and bitterness. Just go to an online chat room and listen to the conversation. It's just not worth the price, to us, to those we love, to hang on to anger and an unforgiving spirit.

For Sharon, letting go and forgiving means "giving up the adoption excuse" — that being adopted is the reason for all of her problems. It means having sympathy for her birth mother, especially at the time of relinquishment.

We Can't Forgive Her Apart from God's Help

The late Corrie ten Boom had to ask God to make her willing to forgive her Nazi perpetrators. During World War II, she and her family were arrested for concealing Jews in their home in Holland, thrown into a concentration camp at Ravensbruck, and brutally tortured by the guards. Corrie was the only member of her family who survived.

Years later, during a speaking engagement, she mentioned having been in Ravensbruck. Afterward a man came up to shake her hand and when she looked into his face she remembered him as one of the former Nazi guards who tortured her. She struggled to move her hand toward him but felt frozen. She told God that there was no way for her to forgive this brutal murderer. Finally she asked God to help her.

She raised her hand, almost mechanically, and recalled, "From my shoulder along my arm and through my hand a current seemed to pass from me to him, while into my heart sprang a love for this stranger that almost overwhelmed me."[5]

As adopted people, we can experience the same sense of God's power and presence as we choose to forgive those who have hurt us, especially our birth mothers. Here's a poem I wrote to celebrate our freedom that comes from letting go of anger and bitterness.

Letting Go

Letting go
    How can it be?
    Of she who was supposed to care for me?
Why did she do it?
    I'll never know
    But someday the other side of the tapestry will show.
Not knowing she loves me
    Or, that she even cares
    Has set me on a path filled with pain and snares.
But now the ifs and what-might-have-beens have to go
    No matter the process,
    No matter how slow.
We're adopted people who've chosen to let go of our birthmothers'
    original choice
    We're no longer bound
    We've found peace and can finally rejoice.

I hope you're thinking deeply about the issues of letting go and forgiving. Perhaps you are ready to make a life-transforming choice. You'll never regret choosing to forgive. Anger and bitterness can become so familiar that we don't realize how destructive they are.

Author C. S. Lewis told a story about a ghost arriving at heaven with a lizard on his shoulder. Apparently this lizard was the center of the ghost's life—they were intimate friends. The ghost had been preoccupied with the lizard for years.

The truth of the matter, however, was that the lizard was

demanding, burdened the ghost with fatigue, and left scales all over his clothes. Nonetheless, the lizard continued to live there with the ghost's permission.

On the day the ghost arrived at heaven's gate the gatekeeper said, "You must kill that lizard. No lizards are allowed in heaven."

How could he possibly part with his lizard? Yet he wanted heaven so much.

Our Choice

To let go of our birth mother's original decision and rejections and choose to forgive, no matter what our feelings tell us.

Finally the ghost tore the lizard from his body and threw it to the ground.

The lizard cried pitifully and then died ... but then an amazing thing happened. The dead lizard transformed into a beautiful horse that carried the ghost into heaven in triumph.[6]

That is exactly what happens as we let go of the lizard of resentment and hatred that has taken up residence in our hearts.

DISCUSSION QUESTIONS FOR SUPPORT GROUPS OR PERSONAL REFLECTION

1. Are there birth relatives that need forgiveness from you? How do you feel about that possibility?
2. If the other person doesn't respond, are we to keep trying? When do we give up and let go?
3. Has the lizard of anger and resentment been living on the shoulder of your life? How can you detect his presence?
4. Write a letter *to* and *from* your birth mother.
5. Read some good books on forgiveness. David Augsburger's book *The Freedom of Forgiveness* is a good place to start.

DIGGING DEEPER FOR ANSWERS
TO OUR ADOPTION QUESTIONS

1. What do you think about Abraham sending away the birth mother and birth son at God's command? It's an amazing account. Read Genesis 21:8-15. What was Ishmael doing to Isaac? (verse 9)
2. How did God take care of the birth mother and son after Abraham sent them away? See verses 11b-19.
3. Would reading a story and principle like this from the Bible give you the courage to do the same with a rejecting birth relative? Help us to understand your answer.
4. What do you believe about the Bible? Read Hebrews 4:12 and write in your journal.
   - An interesting book?
   - A book for religious people?
   - A book they have in churches?
   - The authority for my faith and life?

We've jumped one of the highest hurdles and now we're ready for the rest of our lives. That's what we'll talk about next.

CHAPTER TWENTY-ONE

WHY AM I AFRAID TO STEP OUT INTO THE FUTURE?

Lives of great men all remind us

We can make our lives sublime,

And departing, leave behind us

Footprints on the sands of time.

— LONGFELLOW

I magine a beach where the sand is pure white and the seascape absolutely breathtaking. Early every morning a crew rakes the beach with power machines, leaving only "rake lines" behind.

As the day wears on, sunbathers and joggers come to the beach, each living out his or her plans for the day. By sunset, the rake marks are gone and all that is left are the imprints of feet.

This world was once an even more spectacular beach that was combed clean early in the morning and *each one of us*, whether we know it or not, is currently making footprints across it during this time in human history. And each one of our footprints is like none other. Custom-designed. Distinctive. Exclusive. Matchless. Irreplaceable.

And what does that mean? I believe it means that there is a unique purpose for each of us in human history that no one else can fill. This is exciting for those of us who once believed our lives were a mistake.

WE WERE ADOPTED FOR A PURPOSE

First, if God "created our inmost being," then our lives are not a mistake. We are God's creation, "fearfully and wonderfully made."[1] Second, if he knew all about our destiny before we were even formed, then he also knew who our birth and adoptive parents would be. And third, if he ordained every day of our lives before we were born, then he must certainly have a unique plan for our lives.

Not all of us are going to be a Moses! We can be doing equally important things whether we are in the spotlight or behind the scenes. Living out our life purpose isn't necessarily an activity; rather it is *who we are* as people—and as adoptees we are people who have come through the fires of sorrow and are now shining like gold. We can have an impact whether we're up on a stage lecturing, talking to a neighbor, being a parent or spouse, studying in college, or waiting in grocery lines. Because Jesus Christ lives in us, he is living out his life in and through us. Richard Curtis says his mission in life is simply to show up every day—to bring a healthy, centered, and purposeful person into relationships with his family, friends, and others in his life. He says, "This mission has *everything* to do with adoption—what more can I say?"

HOW TO FIND DIRECTION

Which way do we go? Where do we find our life direction? How do we invest the time and talents God has given us? What do we love doing? What doors are opening for us? What are we passionate about? Look for where God is at work, step up, and ask what you can do to help.

A mentor once taught me a principle that has been a tremendous help to me in discerning God's will. Whenever faced with a decision, she said to ask myself which activity I am the most uniquely qualified to do. What can you do that others can't? For example, at one point in my life, I had entered graduate school to work on a degree in counseling in the realm of adoption. I also had the dream of starting Jewel Among Jewels Adoption Network with fellow-adoptee friend Jody Moreen. When I applied the principle, I knew that anyone could become a counselor but not everyone could do what I felt Jody and I were being called to do—to start a newsletter for fellow adoptees with a biblical perspective. That's the direction I chose and have never looked back!

Look for Confirming Circumstances

God confirms his will through circumstances, through his Word, and through other Christians. Thus, using Jody's and my dream about an adoption network, it seemed impossible at first. How would we establish a network for distribution? Through attending adoption conventions we obtained 250 names that comprised our readership database. Then we pooled our financial resources to have brochures printed and distributed. The first thing we needed was a logo, and Vicky Rockwell, a graphic artist and owner of Cavu Ltd. in Indianapolis, designed one based on the words "jewel among jewels," conveying the message we desired: that every person touched by adoption can become a jewel among jewels. Vicky presented us with a gorgeous design that depicted a huge, sparkling, purple jewel in the midst of other jewels. When I asked Vicky for a bill, she said, "Sherrie, I can't take money for this. This is something so pure—I want to do this."

In 1994, we published the four-page premier issue of *Jewel Among Jewels Adoption News*. Our target audience at that time was specifically adoptees and our mission was to provide a "safe place" for them to talk about adoption through telling their stories.

In one of the first issues I wrote an article titled "Twenty Things Adopted Kids Wish Their Adoptive Parents Knew," which described the often unspoken thoughts and feelings that are common among adoptees. Much to my surprise the article was widely praised.

As a result, wheels started turning in my head. Maybe it was time to write a book—a book with the same title as the article. Maybe there was an unmet need among adoptive parents and adults who were adopted as children.

Researching the market, I discovered that most adoption books were clinical. What I envisioned instead was a handbook that would assist adoptive parents and anyone who loves an adoptee to learn what the often unspoken thoughts and feelings are and then provide practical ways to meet the needs.

I contacted Traci Mullins, president of Eclipse Editorial Services, who had suggested seven years earlier when I first approached her with a book idea that I needed to heal emotionally before publishing my story. This time she thought my book idea and personal readiness were in sync, and I hired her as my agent/editor. Within two weeks a door opened with Dell, a division of Random House, Inc.

Jewel Among Jewels continues to thrive, both through online resources for parents and kids and through writing and public speaking. Random House is now reviewing the sequel to their successful *Twenty Things Adopted Kids Wish Their Adoptive Parents Knew*. It was birthed from my heartfelt belief that our parents need an extra measure of encouragement. The working title is *Twenty Things Adoptive Parents Need to Succeed*. It is due to be released in November of 2009.

Step Outside Your Comfort Zone

I was thrilled when Random House bought my proposal. And absolutely panicked. I couldn't see how I could *possibly* write a chapter for each one of those twenty sentences from the original article! I almost sabotaged myself, being so afraid that I was going to fail.

Traci, being a unique combination of tenderness and toughness, said after every accomplishment, "I feel like a proud mama duck!"

One year later, in October of 1999, *Twenty Things Adopted Kids*

Wish Their Adoptive Parents Knew was published. How thrilled I was and continue to be that the book was meeting the needs of both parents and adult adoptees. It continues to, after ten years of publication. During the writing process, Traci sent me these treasured words:

> *My dear baby duck,*
> *I think back so many years ago to a tiny duck named Sherrie who approached me with an idea for a book about her painful experience of reuniting with her birth mother. I knew she needed to write, write, write . . . for her own sake. For a catharsis. For her healing. She needed a little more time in the "nest" where she could be safe before heading out into the big wide world where everyone would know her story. She needed time to mine for the jewels within her own soul before she could begin handing them out as gifts to others.*
>
> *And now . . . she has transformed from a tiny duck into a lovely swan, beautiful and confident and strong enough to help other tiny ducks learn to fly. She has metamorphosed from a fledgling writer with journal and pen to a brilliant, real author who's even mastering the computer! Most of all, she has become a whole woman of God who is impacting others in profound ways . . . which have only just begun. I am so proud of her.*
>
> *I love you, dear Sherrie!*
> *Mama Duck* [2]

Since the publication of the book, I have received many invitations to speak. Please be aware that when I first received invitations, I was terrified. "God, send me to some remote country, but don't ask me to do public speaking."

Well, you'll never guess what I'm doing a lot of these days. You guessed it—public speaking. And what's so amazing is that I absolutely love it.

One of my first engagements was to keynote to physicians,

psychologists, adoptive parents, and adoptees.

After the emcee announced my name, I began walking toward the podium and these words came clearly into my mind, "Sherrie, I made you for this."

In the meantime, our four-page newsletter doubled in size and the readership multiplied by 500 percent within two years, reaching almost every state as well as an international audience. The archives are now online at www.sherrieeldridge.com. Please come visit. What began as a local outreach specifically to adoptees has become an international multifaceted educational organization targeting *anyone* touched by adoption.

We offer many services. Archives of all past issues of the newsletter. Free adoption workbooks for individuals, counselors/clients, or support groups. Coloring projects for parents and children.

Check Your Joy Barometer

Living out the purpose I was created for is the result of identifying my passion and going through open doors. Was I scared at times? You bet. Was I ever doubtful that I was on the right path? You bet. But the result has been incredible joy!

THE EVERLASTING ARMS

When Moses was 120 years old and facing death, he had accomplished all he was born for. God told him that even though he led the Israelites out of Egypt, he wouldn't be able to enter the Promised Land—he would see it only from a distance. I'll bet his life was passing before his eyes as he stood with his people on the banks of the Jordan.

Moses probably believed for years that he had irreparably derailed his life purpose by killing an Egyptian earlier in life, but look at what he became: one of the greatest leaders of all time. In his final message to the Israelites before they passed into the land God had promised them were these poignant, powerful words: "The eternal God is your refuge, and underneath are the everlasting arms."[3]

As we look back at our footprints over the sands of time, we will see that at times they zigzagged, turned circles, or stopped. But if we look closely enough, we will discover another, larger set of footprints right next to ours—and notice that our footprints were *inside* the larger footprints for a time, safely enclosed.[4] We gradually will come to realize that during the time when we felt adoption loss the most, we were securely held and lovingly led, even though we didn't realize it.

OUR REAL LIFE PURPOSE

Far greater and deeper a purpose is beckoning us, however. Remember the Ecclesiastes verse we read in earlier chapters about how God has set eternity in our hearts? That means that we were created to know and love him. That is our *true* life purpose. To enjoy him forever. That "eternity" in our hearts is a hole, left because of our sin against God. We can try to fill it with many things that don't bring peace. True peace comes when we realize that we are sinners and need a Savior. We need Someone to pay the penalty for our sin. That is what Jesus Christ did when he went to the cross for you and me. Jesus, who is God, became a baby. He took on human flesh, but he never sinned. When he was nailed to the cross, it was your sins and mine that nailed him there. It was *his choice* to remain on the cross. It was *his choice* to die, to enter death and hell. It was by *his power* that he rose from the dead and proved our sins are forgiven. Because of *his choice* to die for us, he's given us the privilege to choose to believe in him. It is by giving our lives to him, living in fellowship with him daily by reading the Bible and being with other Christians, that we experience true peace, no matter how painful or mysterious our past.

In light of the fact that we were created to walk a unique path with him long before

Our Choice

We need to choose to trust God with our past and find true peace from trusting in and enjoying his finished work for us on the cross.

the world began, what life-giving choice do we need to make?

How well I remember the births of four of my grandchildren, three of whom were rescued from death while still in the womb. As I watch them play, I wonder what is in store for them, for God went to great lengths to save their lives and I am certain he must have something exciting planned for their futures. I know there are good things ahead for you as well. We need only begin to open our eyes and our hearts.

DISCUSSION QUESTIONS FOR SUPPORT GROUPS OR PERSONAL REFLECTION

1. Do you believe that God created you to belong to him? What is your reaction to this statement?
2. Do you believe that your sins nailed Jesus to the cross?
3. Do you believe that he died in your place?
4. Have you received his free gift of forgiveness?

DIGGING DEEPER FOR ANSWERS TO OUR ADOPTION QUESTIONS

1. What does Psalm 119:2 say about those who seek God with all their hearts?
2. What does God do for those who earnestly seek him? See Hebrews 11:6.
3. Read Matthew 7:7. What are the three key words in this verse that explain how to earnestly seek God?
4. If you are earnestly seeking God, tonight before bed, or right now, get on your knees and apply those steps. You might pray a prayer something like this: Lord Jesus, I know that I'm a sinner. I've not honored, let alone loved you every moment of every day. I don't understand it all yet, but I believe as best I can that through your work on the cross, your shed blood provided forgiveness for my

sins. By faith, I give you my sin-filled heart and make the great exchange, taking your righteous heart as my own. Teach me to walk in your ways, to love your Word, and to enjoy our relationship. In Jesus' name, Amen.

The next and final chapter brings us full circle in our discussion about the adoption experience. What a blessing it is to discover that we can be "wounded healers"—those who can come alongside others who are hurting and give the kind of comfort we have already received from Jesus.

CHAPTER TWENTY-TWO

WHY DO WE FEEL PASSIONATE ABOUT LIVING OUT OUR LIFE PURPOSE?

A shared pain is no longer paralyzing but mobilizing, when understood as a way to liberation.

— HENRI J. M. NOUWEN

Having a heart for others who are hurting is strong evidence that salvation and your relationship with Jesus has occurred. If we attend support groups, we now do so not only to find healing for ourselves, but also to come alongside others who are struggling. If we give seminars and workshops, we do so not to build our egos and find a sense of identity, but to point out the road of restoration to those who have yet to find it. We long to reach out and help others discover the riches that we have found in Christ. The very pain we spent so long running from becomes our ticket into the fellowship of wounded healers.

I love Henri Nouwen's concept of the "wounded healer" because that is what I believe we can become after working through our own pain. Wounded healers are uniquely equipped to listen to and even enter into the pain of others without discomfort or fear.[1]

I remember my therapist saying, "I can go to the mat with you." What she meant is that she could go into the pain with me and not abandon me out of fear because she had numbed her own emotions so that she'd be frightened of mine. When I got in touch with my anger, she said, "Scream, Sherrie. Just scream!" Well, I was too self-conscious to do so, so *she* started and I joined in! Up until then I had been alone in my anger. I soon realized that I had a friend in the fire with me. Jesus was there, too, but my faith was too weak to realize his presence. What comfort! Susan is definitely a wounded healer.

Nouwen explains that we can offer hurting people a special kind of "hospitality" by giving them a safe, friendly, empty space where they can be whatever they want to be and find their souls.[2]

BLESSINGS OF WOUNDED HEALERS

From the lives of wounded healers flow blessings desperately needed by those who are still suffering.

An Ability to Empathize with Others

The primary task of a wounded healer, Nouwen explains, is not to take away pain but to deepen it to a level where it can be shared. When someone comes to a wounded healer with his loneliness, he can only expect that his loneliness will be understood and felt, so that he no longer has to run away from it but accept it as an expression of his basic human condition.[3]

The wounded healer isn't one who has his or her act together, but rather one who is willing to share the burden of personal pain with others. Because of Frieda Moore's experiences, she can empathize with others and listen with an unguarded and loving heart. She knows full well what it's like to not belong, to be rejected, and to wander in life. Because she has learned that she is not the only one to suffer such experiences, she feels free to share her life with others and to be the kind of "safe" person we all need.

Dawn Saphir doesn't mind sharing her pain, joys, failures, and triumphs because as an adoptee from South Korea her life has so often been an open book whether or not she wanted it to be. Because she has often been the subject of curiosity, she has learned to share her story over and over again. Today she participates in panel discussions and talks to prospective adoptive parents about some of her experiences growing up. As she tries to offer them insight into what their experiences might be with their adoptive children, it is a blessing for her and for them.

Cheri Manternach's adoption experience has helped her be supportive of girls who relinquished their babies for adoption when they weren't sure what they should do. It's also helped her be supportive of friends who have adopted.

Because Sheila Rounds has been willing to talk about her adoption experience, others have realized they are not alone. "When talking to people I refer to Mom as my birth mom. That alone attracts attention. I deal very well with people who feel loneliness or shame or are shy, because as an adoptee I have felt all of these things."

Karen says she has become the kind of person people come to for an ear, or for a friend. Being adopted has created within her an almost uncanny understanding of people and their feelings, of how things aren't always what they appear to be. She doesn't think she could do that without the experiences adoption has brought her.

Sandy Garrett says she has actually become eager to talk to folks about adoption . . . and reunion. She has a better understanding of birth mothers and all the emotional issues associated with their decisions to relinquish their children for adoption. She finds herself able to talk to all members of the adoption triad—adoptive parents, adoptees, and birth mothers—whether to give advice or just a shoulder. To Sandy, that is a true blessing. She says she would never be able to understand anyone in the triad if she had not been through all the ups and downs of adoption.

Jody Moreen says, "A passion began to grow within me to be available to encourage others in their adoption journeys. I have been involved in two adoption newsletter publications, have facilitated adoption support groups, and recently began leading an adoption Bible study for the adoption triad. I find it fascinating that my adoptee status has led me to help others touched by adoption. It is wonderful to find that even your most painful life experience can equip you to reach out to others!"

God Enlarges Our Capacity to Inspire Others

"I believe I can present people with a positive example of how well adoption can work out," says Rick Ennis. "Despite difficulties physically and emotionally that would make many parents shy away from accepting a child like me for adoption at age three, I am a poster child/adult of the power of nurture versus nature."

Thanks to Rick's many blessings, he feels motivated to speak to groups touched by adoption and to share with them that all of their hard work is worth it. He's stumbled into doing adoption presentations, originally intending to share professional knowledge. But along the way he noticed that his story was inspiring people in the audience not because of his knowledge but because of the many obstacles he's been able to overcome. "While it is not my intention to inspire by 'tooting my horn,'" Rick says, "it is a blessing to have a special story to share, and it is a pleasure to share that I am now proud to have been adopted. After all, I've been twice loved and doubly blessed!"

Bob Blanchard, one of the list owners of the Adoptees Internet Mailing List (AIML), the largest adoptee support group on the Internet, says, "I've had the privilege of helping thousands of adoptees through the many issues adoption brings into our lives. I've also helped countless others with their searches for their birth families. Many have resulted in life-changing reunions."

We Have a Heart for Serving God

Ron Hilliard says, "I am who I am today because of being relinquished and adopted. I believe that God was involved in the process and I am where I am, and who I am, as a result. If I had not been relinquished and adopted I would be a very different person, and while I might be serving God, it wouldn't be in the place where I am today."

The life accounts of these, my fellow adoptees, reminds me of a story about two men who were climbing different trails high in the mountains. After a while, they came to a place where their paths met. It was such a narrow ledge that only one person could get past. Their dilemma seemed impossible to resolve—there was no way both of them could make it.

It was then that one climber lay down and let the other walk over him. The other climber could subsequently go on to new heights. Neither man was left behind.[4]

That is what we are accomplishing when we serve as wounded healers. The painful repercussions of adoption loss won't completely dissipate for any of us, but they can become welcoming invitations for others to deal with their own issues and find fellowship and friendship. And so, what is our concluding choice?

Our Choice

To lay down our lives for others through transparently sharing our stories.

From all that has been shared by fellow adoptees in this book, it is clear that a painful beginning can be transformed into something of beauty. Broken wings can mend and learn to fly.

DISCUSSION QUESTIONS FOR SUPPORT GROUPS OR PERSONAL REFLECTION

1. Do you believe you're at a place in your life where you are willing to reach out to others who are hurting? A writing mentor once said to a beginning writer who was tired of feeling "green"

(unqualified), "If you want to be mightily used by God in the lives of others, get used to feeling green. You always will."

2. Would you consider starting a support group for fellow adoptees? There is a free workbook to help you at www.sherrieeldridge.com. Put an ad in the newspaper or church bulletin. You know how much we need one another!

DIGGING DEEPER FOR ANSWERS TO OUR ADOPTION QUESTIONS

1. Remember when Moses looked back on his life and saw the arms of his birth mother, the arms of his adoptive mother, and then the arms of God underneath them all? What would you write about each set of arms? Can you write a poem or a piece of writing about it? It may help someone else!
2. Reread Psalm 139 and put your name into it. Make it personal. If you really want a wonderful challenge, put it into your own words. Be sure to date it, for it will be a keeper.

In closing, I wish for you hearts that marvel at the incredible lessons that adoption can teach. Wherever you are in your process is where you're supposed to be. Search out safe people. Embrace the pain. Listen to the echoes of loss, and turn over every stone in coming to peace with your past. Start enjoying friendships with fellow adoptees, if you haven't already, and realize that in God's eyes, you are a jewel among jewels. And as you do all of this, know that I am your number one cheerleader, urging you to find your true life purpose through a relationship with Jesus Christ. Only in him can we find true peace. If I can help you in any way in learning more about Jesus, please contact me at mail@sherrieeldridge.com.

WHAT THE BIBLE SAYS
ABOUT ADOPTION

- God knows your feelings of rejection and abandonment and calls you forth to life as a jewel among jewels. (Ezekiel 16:4-7, TLB)
- Our lives began not at conception, not at birth, not on adoption day, but in eternity past—in the very heart of God the Father. (Jeremiah 1:5; Ephesians 1:4-6)
- God created our lives—our lives are not a mistake. (John 1:3)
- God planned our biological and adoptive families. (Psalm 139:16)
- God will never forget us—he has our names inscribed on the palms of his hands as proof. (Isaiah 49:15-16)
- Adoptees have a right to know their biological heritage—Jesus did. (Matthew 1:1,17)
- Jesus understands how it feels to be rejected by our birth family—he came to his own and they didn't want him. (John 1:11)
- We can trust God with our unanswered questions about adoption. It would be nothing for him to reveal answers if he knew we needed them. Until he does, he holds the answers in his loving hands. (Deuteronomy 29:29)
- We have an awesome legacy as an adoptee—God himself becomes our Father. (Psalm 68:5)

- God promises to hear even our faintest cry. (Exodus 22:22-24)
- God has a unique plan for the orphan in history. (Esther 2:15)

NOTES

CHAPTER ONE
1. 1 Corinthians 2:9, NIV.
2. Isaiah 49:15-16, NIV.

CHAPTER TWO
1. Exodus 3:12, NIV.
2. Judith Viorst, *Imperfect Control: Our Lifelong Struggles with Power and Surrender* (New York: Simon & Schuster, 1998), 16.
3. Rosamund Stone Zander and Benjamin Zander, *The Art of Possibility: Transforming Professional and Personal Life* (Boston: Harvard Business School Press, 2000), 9–10.
4. Spencer Johnson, MD, *One Minute for Yourself: A Simple Strategy for a Better Life* (New York: Quill-William Morrow, 1991), 26.

CHAPTER THREE
1. John Bowlby, as quoted by Bob Mullan in *Are Mothers Really Necessary?* (New York: Weidenfield and Nicholson, 1987), 71.
2. Peter Nathananielsz, MD, PhD, *The Prenatal Prescription* (New York: HarperCollins, 2001), 3.
3. Thomas Verny, MD, *The Secret Life of the Unborn Child* (New York: Dell, 1981), 78.
4. Judith Viorst, *Necessary Losses* (New York: Simon & Schuster, 1986), 22–23.

5. Dr. Arthur Janov, *The New Primal Scream* (Wilmington, DE: Enterprise Publishing Inc., 1991), 26–27.

6. Psalm 139:13-18, NIV.

7. Mary Watkins and Susan Fisher, *Talking with Young Children about Adoption* (New Haven and London: Yale University Press), 226.

8. Louise Kaplan, as quoted by Daniel A. Hughes, PhD, in *Facilitating Developmental Attachment* (North Bergen, N.J., London: Jason Aronson Inc., 1997), 14–15, 20.

9. Penny Callan Partridge, *Pandora's Hope* (Amherst, MA: Self-published, 1997). Used with permission.

10. Deuteronomy 33:27, NIV.

CHAPTER FOUR

1. Exodus 2:6, NIV.

2. *New American Exhaustive Concordance of the Bible*, 1948.

3. Gregory C. Keck, PhD, as quoted in an interview by Sherrie Eldridge, 2001.

4. J. I. Rodale, *The Synonym Finder* (Emmaus, PA: Rodale Press, 1978), 1319.

5. Nancy Verrier, *The Primal Wound* (Baltimore: Gateway Press, 1994), 77.

6. John and Paula Sanford, *Healing the Wounded Spirit* (South Plainfield, NJ: Bridge Publishing, Inc., 1985), 30.

7. Selma Fraiberg, *Every Child's Birthright: In Defense of Mothering* (New York: Bantam Books, 1997), 72.

8. Gregory C. Keck, PhD, as quoted in an interview by Sherrie Eldridge, 2001.

9. David M. Brodzinsky and Marshall D. Schechter, *The Psychology of Adoption* (New York, Oxford: Oxford University Press, 1990), 45–46.

10. From *Ghost at Heart's Edge*, edited by Susan Ito and Tina Cervin ©1999. Published by North Atlantic Books. Reprinted by

permission of the publisher.

11. Corrine Chilstrom, *Andrew, You Died Too Soon* (Minneapolis: Augsburg Fortress, 1993), 17.

CHAPTER SIX

1. David M. Brodzinsky and Marshall D. Schechter, *The Psychology of Adoption* (New York, Oxford: Oxford University Press, 1990), 85.

2. J. I. Rodale, *The Synonym Finder* (Emmaus, PA: Rodale Press, 1978), 740.

3. Marilyn Schoettle, MA, *The WISE-UP˚ Powerbook* (Silver Spring, MD: The Center for Adoption Support and Education, Inc., 2000), 16–19. Contact C.A.S.E. (11120 New Hampshire Ave., Suite 205, Silver Spring, MD 20904) at their Web site: www. adoptionsupport.org. Used by permission.

4. Eleanor Doan, *Speaker's Sourcebook* (Grand Rapids, MI: Zondervan, 1960).

CHAPTER SEVEN

1. John 3:17, MSG.

2. David M. Brodzinsky and Marshall D. Schechter, *The Psychology of Adoption* (New York, Oxford: Oxford University Press, 1990), 26.

3. http://syncorva.cortland.edu/~ANDERSMD/ERIK/ WELCOME.HTML, February 28, 2002.

4. Malcolm L. West and Adrienne E. Sheldon-Keller, *Patterns of Relating: An Adult Attachment Perspective* (New York, London: The Guilford Press, 1994), 83.

5. Robert J. Morgan, *Nelson's Complete Book of Stories, Illustrations, and Quotes* (Nashville: Thomas Nelson, 2000), 15–16.

6. Lillian Glass, PhD, *Toxic People: 10 Ways of Dealing with People Who Make Your Life Miserable* (New York: St. Martin's Griffin, 1997), 55.

7. David Augsburger, *Caring Enough to Hear and Be Heard* (Ventura, CA: Regal, 1982), 72. Used by permission.

8. Augsburger, 83. Used by permission.

CHAPTER EIGHT

1. Ephesians 4:26, NASB.

2. Ephesians 4:26, MSG.

3. Carol Komissaroff, *Quest: The Newsletter of KinQuest, Inc.*, Vol. IV, No. 2, Issue #14, Autumn, 1992.

4. Romans 12:19, MSG.

5. 1 Peter 2:20, NIV.

CHAPTER NINE

1. See 2 Corinthians 12:1-10.

2. See Exodus 33:11.

3. Psalm 17:15, NIV.

4. Institute in Basic Life Conflicts, Inc., *Character Sketches — Volume One* (Chicago: Rand McNally and Co., 1979), 179–180. Used by permission of Institute in Basic Life Conflicts, Inc.

CHAPTER TEN

1. Patrick Thomas Malone, MD, and Thomas Patrick Malone, MD, *The Art of Intimacy* (New York: Simon & Schuster, 1992), 19.

2. N. Bohman and A. L. von Knorring, "Psychiatric Illness Among Adults Adopted As Infants," *Acta Paediatrica Scandinavica* 60, 106–112.

CHAPTER ELEVEN

1. Ezekiel 16:5-7, TLB.

2. See Exodus 3–4.

3. Isobel Kuhn, *Stones of Fire* (Republic of Singapore: OMF, 1989), Prelude.

Chapter Twelve

1. Joyce Maguire Pavao, as quoted by Sherrie Eldridge in *Jewel Among Jewels Adoption News* (Indianapolis: Jewel Among Jewels Adoption Network, Inc., Summer 1997), 7.
2. Ibid.

Chapter Thirteen

1. David M. Brodzinsky and Marshall D. Schechter, *The Psychology of Adoption* (New York: Oxford University Press, 1990), 87.
2. David M. Brodzinsky, Marshall D. Schechter, and Robin Marantz Henig, *Being Adopted: The Lifelong Search for Self* (New York: Doubleday, 1992), 79.
3. *The Random House College Dictionary*, Revised Edition (New York: Random House, 1975), 360.
4. www.pastor2youth.com/Illustration/G/guiltfalse.html, July 5, 2002.
5. John 1:3, NIV.
6. 1 John 1:8-9, MSG.
7. Exodus 4:14, NIV.
8. John 8:32, NIV.

Chapter Fourteen

1. J. I. Rodale, *The Synonym Finder* (Emmaus, PA: Rodale Press, 1978), 685.
2. 1 Corinthians 13:6-7, MSG.
3. 1 Corinthians 13:11-12, MSG.

Chapter Fifteen

1. Isaiah 30:21, NIV.

CHAPTER SIXTEEN

1. Jayne Askin, *Search* (Phoenix: Oryx Press, 1998), 12.
2. Corrie ten Boom, *Tramp for the Lord* (Old Tappan, NJ: Revell, 1974), 53–54.

CHAPTER SEVENTEEN

1. Jayne Askin, *Search* (Phoenix: Oryx Press, 1998), 1–2.
2. Eleanor Doan, *Speaker's Sourcebook* (Grand Rapids, MI: Zondervan, 1960).
3. Dr. Paul Brand with Philip Yancey, *The Gift Nobody Wants* (New York: HarperCollins, 1993), 83–84.

CHAPTER EIGHTEEN

1. *The Random House College Dictionary*, Revised Edition (New York: Random House, 1975), 1113.
2. Ron Nydam, "Doing Rejection" (Indianapolis: Jewel Among Jewels Adoption News, Winter 1999), 4.
3. See 1 Samuel 22:1-2; 23:1-4.
4. See Jeremiah 49:11.
5. See Isaiah 1:17.
6. See Exodus 22:22-24.
7. See Psalm 68:5.
8. See Job 29:12.
9. See Hosea 14:3-4.
10. See Deuteronomy 14:29.
11. See Esther 4:14.
12. See Malachi 3:5.
13. *Our Daily Bread*, as quoted by Robert J. Morgan in *Nelson's Complete Book of Stories, Illustrations, and Quotes* (Nashville: Thomas Nelson, 2000), 298.
14. J. I. Rodale, *The Synonym Finder* (Emmaus, PA: Rodale Press, 1978), 999.

Chapter Twenty

1. See Genesis 21:1-14.
2. Eleanor Doan, *Speaker's Sourcebook* (Grand Rapids, MI: Zondervan, 1960).
3. Beth Moore, *Living Beyond Yourself* (Nashville: LifeWay Press, 1998), 120.
4. David Augsburger, *The Freedom of Forgiveness* (Chicago: Moody, 1988), 46.
5. Corrie ten Boom, *Tramp for the Lord* (Old Tappan, NJ: Revell, 1974).
6. www.pastor2youth.com/Illustrations/L/lust.html, July 5, 2002.

Chapter Twenty-One

1. Psalm 139:13-14, NIV.
2. Traci Mullins, personal letter to author, 1999. Used with permission.
3. Deuteronomy 33:27, NIV.
4. www.wowzone.com/prints2.htm, February 26, 2002.

Chapter Twenty-Two

1. Henri J. M. Nouwen, *The Wounded Healer* (New York, London, Toronto, Sydney, Auckland: Image Books-Doubleday, 1990), 92–93.
2. Nouwen, 92–93.
3. Nouwen, 92.
4. Eleanor Doan, *Speaker's Sourcebook* (Grand Rapids, MI: Zondervan, 1960).

ABOUT THE AUTHOR

SHERRIE ELDRIDGE, an adoption expert and internationally known speaker and author of the best-selling *Twenty Things Adopted Kids Wish Their Adoptive Parents Knew* (Bantam Dell, 1999), is celebrating ten years of publication, with more than 130,000 copies in print.

Sherrie is a ClubMom Adoption Expert and has been featured on WebMD.com, Seventeen.com, CBN Asia, and Moody Radio. Articles about her have appeared in the *Wall Street Journal,* the *Indianapolis Star,* and *Indianapolis Woman Magazine.*

Other books include *Forever Fingerprints: An Amazing Discovery for Adopted Children* and an upcoming sequel to *Twenty Things* for adoptive parents *Twenty Things Adoptive Parents Need to Succeed* (Random House, 2009). Visit her website at www .sherrieeldridge.com for free resources.

Sherrie earned her BA degree from Indiana University. She has been married to her husband, Bob, for forty-three years. They live in Fishers, Indiana, and have two married daughters and six grandchildren, one who joined their family through adoption.

More adoption resources available from NavPress!

The Whole Life Adoption Book [revised and updated]
Jayne E. Schooler and Thomas C. Atwood
978-1-60006-165-3

With the most current information, research, and parenting strategies, this book is a practical resource every adoptive family should own. And it's now recommended reading by the National Council For Adoption (NCFA). You'll understand the impact of adoption on birth children and learn about links to other resources for the journey ahead.

Adopting the Hurt Child
Gregory C. Keck, PhD, and Regina M. Kupecky, LSW
978-1-57683-094-9

Discover the real hope that hurting children can be healed through adoptive and foster parents, social workers, and others who care. Includes information on foreign adoptions.

Parenting the Hurt Child
Gregory C. Keck, PhD, and Regina M. Kupecky, LSW
978-1-57683-314-8

Using insights gathered through years of working with adopted kids who have experienced early trauma, Gregory C. Keck and Regina M. Kupecky explain how to manage a hurting child with loving wisdom and resolve. If you've adopted a child, whatever the circumstances, you'll find hope and healing on these pages—for you, your family, and especially your adopted child.

To order copies, call NavPress at 1-800-366-7788
or log on to www.navpress.com.

Here's a resource to help you pray with more

Power, *Passion* & Purpose

Every issue of *Pray!* brings you:

- **Special Themes** that deal with specific, often groundbreaking topics of interest that will help you grow in your passion and effectiveness in prayer
- **Features** on important and intriguing aspects of prayer, both personal and corporate
- **Ideas** to stimulate creativity in your prayer life and in the prayer life of your church
- **Empowered**: a special section written by church prayer leaders, for church prayer leaders
- **Prayer News** from around the world, to get you up-to-date with what God is doing through prayer all over the globe

- **Prayer Journeys**: a guest-authored column sharing how God moved him or her closer to Jesus through prayer
- **Intercession Ignited**: providing encouragement, inspiration, and insight for people called to the ministry of intercession
- **Classics**: featuring time-tested writings about prayer from men and women of God through the centuries
- **Inspiring Art** from a publication that has been recognized nationally for its innovative approach to design
- And much, much more!

No Christian who wants to connect more deeply with God should be without *Pray!*

Six issues of *Pray!* are only $21.97*

Canadian and international subscriptions are only $29.97 (Includes Canadian GST).

Subscribe now at www.praymag.com or call **1-800-691-PRAY** (or 1-515-242-0297) and mention code H7PRBK when you place your order.